Math Diagnosis and Intervention System 2.0

BOOKLET G: OPERATIONS WITH WHOLE NUMBERS, GRADES 4–6

Teacher's Pages
Intervention Lessons

PEARSON

Glenview, Illinois • Boston, Massachusetts • Chandler, Arizona • Hoboken, New Jersey

PEARSON

ISBN-13: 978-0-328-86285-6
ISBN-10:   0-328-86285-1

4 17

CONTENTS

MDIS 2.0

CONTENTS (continued)

MDIS 2.0

ADDITION PROPERTIES

Addition Properties

Materials 4 half sheets of paper, 24 color tiles (8 each of 3 colors) per pair

1. Show 2 + 5 and 5 + 2 by placing the tiles on the paper.

2. Add. 2 + 5 = __7__ and 5 + 2 = __7__

3. The Commutative Property says that you can change the order of the addends and the sum will be the same.

So, 2 + 5 = 5 + __2__.

4. Use the tiles to show (4 + 3) + 1. Use 3 different colors of tiles.

5. Add. Remember the parentheses show which numbers to add first.

(4 + 3) + 1 = __7__ + 1 = __8__

6. Move the paper with 3 tiles closer to the paper with 1 tile to show 4 + (3 + 1).

7. Add. 4 + (3 + 1) = 4 + __4__ = __8__

8. The Associative Property says that you can group addends in any way and the sum will be the same.

So, (4 + 3) + 1 = 4 + (__3__ + __1__).

G1 (student p. 1)   MDIS 2.0

Addition Properties (continued)

9. Use tiles to show 3 + 0.

10. Add: 3 + 0 = __3__.

11. The Identity Property says that the sum of any number and 0 is that number.

So, 3 + 0 = __3__.

Find each sum.

12. (4 + 6) + 2 = __10__ + 2 = __12__   13. (7 + 1) + 2 = __8__ + 2 = __10__

    4 + (6 + 2) = 4 + __8__ = __12__   7 + (1 + 2) = 7 + __3__ = __10__

14. 9 + 3 = __12__   15. 5 + 8 = __13__   16. 6 + 9 = __15__

    3 + 9 = __12__   8 + 5 = __13__   9 + 6 = __15__

17. 7 + 0 = __7__   18. 0 + 13 = __13__   19. 5 + 0 = __5__

Write each missing number.

20. 4 + 6 = 6 + __4__   21. 7 + 4 = __4__ + 7   22. 6 + 9 = 9 + __6__

23. 4 + __0__ = 4   24. 0 + __8__ = 8   25. 7 + __0__ = 7

26. (7 + 8) + 2 = 7 + (8 + __2__)   27. 9 + (1 + 8) = (9 + 1) + __8__

28. **Reasoning** Carla ate 2 bananas and 10 raisins. The next day she ate 10 raisins and 2 bananas. Did Carla eat the same number of pieces of fruit each day? Explain.
Yes; 2 + 10 = 10 + 2. Carla ate 12 pieces of fruit the first day and 12 pieces of fruit the next day.

G1 (student p. 2)   MDIS 2.0

Objective Students will use the Commutative, Associative, and Identity Properties to add two and three numbers.

Vocabulary Commutative Property, Associate Property, Identity Property, sum, addend

Materials 4 half-sheets of paper, 24 color tiles (8 each of 3 colors) per pair of students

❶ Conceptual Development
Use with Exercises 1–11.

In this lesson, you will learn about certain addition relationships that are always true.

Have students work in pairs. Distribute the paper and color tiles to each pair. For Exercise 1, have one partner show 2 + 5 and the other partner show 5 + 2 by placing the tiles on the paper. *What is 2 + 5? 7 What is 5 + 2? 7 The Commutative Property says that you can change the order of the addends and the sum will be the same.* For Exercises 4–8, have students use 4 sheets of paper to model the Associative Property.

❷ Practice Use with Exercises 12–28.

Remind students that they can choose which order to add the numbers. For Exercises 12 and 13, make sure students add the numbers in parentheses first.

Error Intervention If students have trouble finding the sums, review addition strategies such as doubles, near doubles, counting on, and making 10 to add.

If You Have More Time Give students three index cards and have them write their own examples for each of the addition properties, two per property.

❸ Assessment

In this lesson, students used addition properties to add. Use the **Quick Check** problem to assess students' understanding.

Quick Check   **Formative Assessment**

Write the missing number. 5 + (5 + 7) = (5 + 5) + ___. 7 Which property is this? Associative Property

---

Name _____

Intervention
Lesson **G2**

Relating Addition and Subtraction

Materials 16 counters per student

1. Use counters to show each number sentence in the table. Find the missing number. Draw the counters you used in the table.

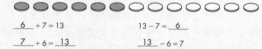

Addition	Subtraction
$3 + \underline{5} = 8$	$8 - 5 = \underline{3}$
Addition	**Subtraction**
$\underline{5} + 3 = 8$	$\underline{8} - 3 = 5$

2. Related addition and subtraction facts have the same numbers. These same numbers are called a fact family. What three numbers were used in the fact family above? _3, 5, and 8_

3. Fill in the blanks to complete the fact family.

$\underline{6} + 7 = 13$ $13 - 7 = \underline{6}$

$\underline{7} + 6 = \underline{13}$ $\underline{13} - 6 = 7$

4. What three numbers were used in the fact family in Question 3? _6, 7, and 13_

Name _____

Intervention
Lesson **G2**

Relating Addition and Subtraction (continued)

Complete the related addition and subtraction facts.

5.

$3 + 7 = \underline{10}$ $7 + 3 = \underline{10}$

$10 - 3 = \underline{7}$ $10 - 7 = \underline{3}$

6.

$\underline{5} + 7 = 12$ $7 + \underline{5} = 12$

$12 - 7 = \underline{5}$ $12 - \underline{5} = 7$

Complete each fact family. You may use counters to help.

7. $4 + 8 = \underline{12}$ $12 - \underline{4} = 8$ 8. $5 + 9 = \underline{14}$ $\underline{14} - 5 = 9$

$\underline{8} + 4 = 12$ $\underline{12} - 8 = 4$ $9 + \underline{5} = 14$ $14 - \underline{9} = 5$

9. $8 + 3 = \underline{11}$ $11 - 8 = \underline{3}$ 10. $6 + \underline{7} = 13$ $13 - \underline{6} = 7$

$3 + \underline{8} = 11$ $\underline{11} - 3 = 8$ $7 + \underline{6} = 13$ $\underline{13} - 7 = 6$

11. **Reasoning** John has 14 pencils. He gives some to Sonja. He has 8 left. How many pencils did John give to Sonja?   _6 pencils_

12. Write two facts that are related to the subtraction fact $14 - 8 = 6$.
Possible answers: $6 + 8 = 14$; $8 + 6 = 14$; $14 - 6 = 8$

Objective Students will write related addition and subtraction facts to make fact families.
Vocabulary Fact family
Materials Two-color counters, 16 per student

① Conceptual Development
Use with Exercises 1–4.

In this lesson, you will review how addition and subtraction sentences are related.

Have students work in pairs. Distribute counters to each pair. Tell them to use the picture to complete the first addition sentence and the first subtraction sentence in Exercise 1. Then, have students model the other two sentences using the counters. *What do you notice about all the numbers in these equations?* They are the same three numbers every time. *These numbers make up a fact family. What three numbers are used in the fact family?* 3, 5, and 8 Have students complete Exercises 3 and 4.

② Practice **Use with Exercises 5–12.**

Encourage students to use the counters to model the problems in Exercises 7–10.

Error Intervention If students have trouble finding a missing number, remind them that a fact family uses the same three numbers. The facts must be an arrangement of only those three numbers.

If You Have More Time Have students work in pairs. Write 4, 7, and ___ on the board. Have each pair write two fact families for these numbers by first finding the sum of 4 and 7 and then finding the difference.

③ Assessment

In this lesson, students wrote fact families. Use the **Quick Check** problem to assess students' understanding.

Quick Check **Formative** Assessment

Write three number sentences to complete the fact family that includes the addition sentence $5 + 10 = 15$.
$10 + 5 = 15$, $15 - 5 = 10$, and $15 - 10 = 5$

Name _____

Intervention
Lesson **G3**

Using Mental Math to Add

Materials place-value blocks: 6 tens and 12 ones per pair

Find the sum of 26 and 42 by breaking apart each addend.

1. Show 26 with place value blocks.

   2 tens = __20__ 6 ones = __6__

2. Show 42 with place value blocks.

   4 tens = __40__ 2 ones = __2__

3. Add the tens. 20 + __40__ = __60__

   Add the ones. 6 + __2__ = __8__

4. Add the tens and the ones together. __60__ + 8 = __68__

   So, 26 + 42 = __68__.

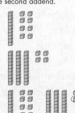

Find the sum of 18 and 34 by breaking apart the second addend.

5. Show 18 with place value blocks.

   1 ten = __10__ 8 ones = __8__

6. Show 34 with place value blocks.

   3 tens = __30__ 4 ones = __4__

7. Take 2 ones from the 34 and add them to 18. What sum do you have now?

   18 + 34 = __20__ + __32__

8. Add. 20 + 32 = __52__

   So, 18 + 34 = __52__.

G3 (student p. 1) MDIS 2.0

Name _____

Intervention
Lesson **G3**

Using Mental Math to Add (continued)

Find each sum using mental math.

9. 22 + 56 = __78__   10. 37 + 24 = __61__   11. 43 + 36 = __79__

12. 55 + 32 = __87__   13. 23 + 21 = __44__   14. 43 + 44 = __87__

15. 44 + 34 = __78__   16. 52 + 32 = __84__   17. 45 + 4 = __49__

18. 45 + 34 = __79__   19. 37 + 51 = __88__   20. 23 + 46 = __69__

21. 64 + 23 = __87__   22. 26 + 73 = __99__   23. 35 + 63 = __98__

24. 88 + 26 = __114__   25. 39 + 45 = __84__   26. 57 + 16 = __73__

Fill in the blanks to show how to add mentally.

27. 35 + 12 = 40 + __7__ = __47__   28. 83 + 46 = __120__ + 9 = __129__

29. 49 + 16 = 50 + __15__ = __65__   30. 78 + 24 = 80 + __22__ = __102__

31. Reggie has 25 crayons. Brett gives him 14 more. How many crayons does he have now?   __39__

32. Darla bought 32 stickers on Monday. Two days later she bought 46 more. How many stickers does she have altogether?   __78__

33. Rafael has 41 rocks in his rock collection. His friend gave him 18 more rocks. How many rocks does he have now?   __59__

34. **Reasoning** To add 59 and 16, Juan took one from the 16 to make the 59 a 60. What number should he add to 60?   __15__

35. **Reasoning** To add 24 and 52, Ashley first added 24 and 50. What numbers should she add next?   __74 + 2__

G3 (student p. 2) MDIS 2.0

Objective Students will use mental math to add.
Vocabulary Addend, sum
Materials Place-value blocks

① Conceptual Development
Use with Exercises 1–8.

In this lesson, you will learn to use mental math to add.

Have students work in pairs. Distribute 6 tens rods and 12 ones cubes to each pair. Guide students through Exercises 1–4. *The sum is the answer to an addition problem. Find the sum of 26 and 42. First, you break apart the addends. Show 26 with place-value blocks. How much is 2 tens?* 20 *How many ones?* 6 *Now, show 42 with place-value blocks. How much is 4 tens?* 40 *How many ones?* 2 *Add the tens. What is 20 plus 40?* 60 *Add the ones. What is 6 + 2?* 8 *Now, add the tens and ones together. What is 60 plus 8?* 68 *So, 26 + 42 is 68.* Have students complete Exercises 5–8.

② Practice Use with Exercises 9–35.

Point out the strategy used in Exercises 34–35. Tell students that making multiples of ten can make mental math easier, since adding 0 is easier than adding digits 1–9.

Error Intervention
If students have trouble remembering what they broke each addend into, encourage them to write the addition problem above each addend. For example, in 23 + 45, have students write 20 + 3 above the 23 and 40 + 5 above the 45.

If You Have More Time
Label items in the room with two-digit prices written on index cards. Have students "shop" for two items. Tell them to use mental math to find the cost of the two items.

③ Assessment

In this lesson, students learned to use mental math to add. Use the **Quick Check** problem to assess students' understanding.

Quick Check  **Formative** Assessment

How would you break apart 42 + 36? 42 = 4 tens and 2 ones; 36 = 3 tens and 6 ones *What numbers do you add now?* 40 + 30 and 2 + 6 *What is the sum?* 78

USING MENTAL MATH TO SUBTRACT

Name _____

Using Mental Math to Subtract

```
20 21 22 23 24 25 26 27 28 29 30 31 32 33 34 35 36 37 38 39 40 41 42 43 44 45 46 47 48 49 50
```

Find the difference of 46 − 27 one way, by doing the following.

1. Round the number being subtracted.

   27 rounded to the nearest ten is __30__

2. Solve the new problem.

   46 − 30 = __16__

3. Since you rounded 27 to 30, did you subtract too much or too little from 46?   __too much__

4. How much more is 30 than 27? __3__

5. Since 30 is **3 more than** 27, you subtracted too much. You must now add 3 to the difference in Question 2.

   16 + 3 = __19__

6. So, 46 − 27 = __19__

Find the difference of 46 − 27 another way, by doing the following.

7. How much needs to be added to the 27 so that it forms a ten?   27 + __3__ = 30

8. Since you added 3 to 27, you need to add 3 to 46.   46 + 3 = __49__

9. Solve the new problem.   49 − 30 = __19__

10. So, 46 − 27 = __19__

11. How can you change 52 − 18 to make it easier to subtract mentally?

    52 − 18 = __54__ − 20 = __34__

G4 (student p. 1)   MDIS 2.0

Name _____

Using Mental Math to Subtract (continued)

Find each difference using mental math.

12. 57 − 38 = __19__   13. 32 − 17 = __15__   14. 61 − 26 = __35__

15. 85 − 29 = __56__   16. 43 − 28 = __15__   17. 67 − 42 = __25__

18. 32 − 18 = __14__   19. 52 − 46 = __6__   20. 41 − 18 = __23__

21. 28 − 16 = __12__   22. 55 − 33 = __22__   23. 86 − 23 = __63__

24. 39 − 26 = __13__   25. 57 − 28 = __29__   26. 93 − 34 = __59__

27. 62 − 47 = __15__   28. 33 − 16 = __17__   29. 84 − 35 = __49__

30. **Reasoning** To find 56 − 48, add the same amount to both numbers to make it easier to subtract. Explain what you did to solve the problem.

    56 − 48
    Add 2 to both numbers: 56 + 2 = 58; 48 + 2 = 50.
    58 − 50 = 8; So, 56 − 48 = 8.

31. Lupe has $32. She buys a present for her mother and gets $9 in change. How much money did she spend on the present? $23

32. **Reasoning** Becca subtracts 73 − 26 mentally by thinking: "73 − 30 = 43, and 43 − 4 = 39. The answer is 39." What did she do wrong? Explain.
    Sample answer: Becca added 4 to the 26 to get 30. Since she subtracted 4 too much, she should have added 4 to the difference. The answer should be 43 + 4 = 47.

G4 (student p. 2)   MDIS 2.0

Objective Students will use mental math to subtract.
Vocabulary Difference, round
Materials Index cards

① Conceptual Development
Use with Exercises 1–11.

In this lesson, you will use mental math to subtract.

Have students work in pairs. *One way to find the difference of 46 − 27 is to round the number being subtracted. When you round to the nearest ten, you find the ten that is closest to the number. Find 27 on the number line. What is 27 rounded to the nearest ten?* 30 *So, what is 46 − 30?* 16 *Did we subtract too much or too little from 46?* Too much *Since 30 is 3 more than 27, add 3 to the difference you just found. What is 16 + 3?* 19 *So, what is 46 − 27?* 19 Guide students through Exercises 7–10 using mental math. Have students complete Exercise 11 on their own.

② Practice Use with Exercises 12–32.

Remind students that they can use either of the methods described on the previous page.

Error Intervention If students forget to add the extra to the number being subtracted from, encourage them to say, "What I do to one, I have to do to the other." Then, have them put the number being added above the original numbers. For example, in 23 − 17, the student would write "+3" above both the 23 and the 17.

If You Have More Time Write the following on the board: *Cara bought a box of 45 crayons. She gave 18 away. How many crayons are left?* 27 Tell students to solve the problem using mental math. Have them write their answer on an index card and hold it up. Ask volunteers to share their methods.

③ Assessment

In this lesson, students learned to use mental math to subtract. Use the **Quick Check** problem to assess students' understanding.

Quick Check **Formative** Assessment

When solving 38 − 23, which number would you round to the nearest ten? 23 *Why?* It's easier to subtract 20 from a number than it is to subtract a number from 40.

ESTIMATING SUMS

Name _____

Estimating Sums

When Joseppi added 43 and 28, he got a sum of 71. To check that this answer is reasonable, use estimation.

1. Round each addend to the nearest ten.

43 rounded to the nearest ten is __40__.

28 rounded to the nearest ten is __30__.

2. Add the rounded numbers.

40 + 30 = __70__

Since 71 is close to 70, the answer is reasonable.

When Ling added 187 and 242, she got a sum of 429. To check that this answer is reasonable, use estimation.

3. Round each addend to the nearest hundred.

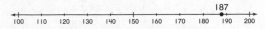

187 rounded to the nearest hundred is __200__.

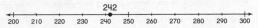

242 rounded to the nearest hundred is __200__.

4. Add the rounded numbers.

200 + 200 = __400__

Since 429 is close to 400, the answer is reasonable.

G5 (student p. 1)   MDIS 2.0

Name _____

Estimating Sums (continued)

Estimate by rounding to the nearest ten.

5. 71 + 36   6. 24 + 81   7. 43 + 91   8. 54 + 66
    110   100   130   120

9. 68 + 27   10. 19 + 93   11. 89 + 75   12. 54 + 33
    100   110   170   80

Estimate by rounding to the nearest hundred.

13. 367   14. 791   15. 506   16. 458
   + 141   + 632   + 249   + 891
    500   1,400   700   1,400

17. 940 + 190   18. 675 + 460   19. 531 + 776
    1,100   1,200   1,300

20. 369 + 481   21. 151 + 260   22. 705 + 936
    900   500   1,600

23. **Reasoning** Jaime was a member of the school chorus for 3 years. Todd was a member of the school band for 2 years. The chorus has 43 members and the band has 85 members. About how many members do the two groups have together?   __130__

24. Luis sold 328 sport bottles and Jorge sold 411. About how many total sport bottles did the two boys sell?   __700__

25. **Reasoning** What is the largest number that can be added to 46 so that the sum is 70 when both numbers are rounded to the nearest ten? Explain.
24; Since 46 rounds to 50, and 20 + 50 = 70, you need the largest number that rounds to 20, which is 24.

G5 (student p. 2)   MDIS 2.0

Objective Students will estimate sums.
Vocabulary Addends, estimate, reasonable, round, sum

① Conceptual Development
Use with Exercises 1–4.

In this lesson, you will learn to estimate sums.

Have students work in small groups. *When you estimate, you find a number that is close to the exact number. You can estimate by rounding. Rounding means you change an addend to its nearest ten or hundred. Addends are numbers that are added together. Look at the number line in Exercise 1. Is 43 closer to 40 or to 50? 40 So, 43 rounded to the nearest 10 is 40. Is 28 closer to 20 or to 30? 30 So, 28 rounded to the nearest 10 is 30. Now you will find the sum, or answer. What is the sum of 40 plus 30? 70 Since 70 is close to 71, the answer is reasonable. A reasonable answer is one that makes sense.* Monitor students to be sure they complete Exercises 1–2 correctly. Have students complete Exercises 3–4.

② Practice Use with Exercises 5–25.

Remind students that they are not to find exact answers but to estimate. Their estimates will be multiples of 10.

Error Intervention
If students have trouble rounding to the nearest ten or hundred, have them use erasable number lines. Draw number lines on lengths of sentence strips and mark ten equally spaced vertical lines. Students can lightly fill in the numbers with pencil. They can erase the numbers when they need to draw a new number line.

If You Have More Time
Write *548 + 221* on the board. Have students estimate to find a reasonable answer.

③ Assessment

In this lesson, students learned to estimate sums. Use the **Quick Check** problem to assess students' understanding.

Quick Check **Formative Assessment**

When estimating 124 plus 138, which would give a closer estimate, rounding to the nearest ten or to the nearest hundred? Rounding to the nearest ten.

Name _____

Estimating Differences

Intervention Lesson **G6**

When Jarvis subtracted 41 − 29, he got a difference of 12.
To check that this answer is reasonable, use estimation.

1. Round each number to the nearest ten.

41 rounded to the nearest ten is __40__.

29 rounded to the nearest ten is __30__.

2. Subtract the rounded numbers.

40 − 30 = __10__

Since 12 is close to 10, the answer is reasonable.

DaNitra subtracted 685 − 279 and got a difference of 406.
To check that this answer is reasonable, use estimation.

3. Round each number to the nearest hundred.

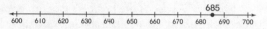

685 rounded to the nearest hundred is __700__.

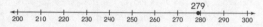

279 rounded to the nearest hundred is __300__.

4. Subtract the rounded numbers.

700 − 300 = __400__

Since 406 is close to 400, the answer is reasonable.

G6 (student p. 1)   MDIS 2.0

Name _____

Estimating Differences (continued)

Intervention Lesson **G6**

Estimate by rounding to the nearest ten.

5.	47 − 19 30	6.	82 − 34 50	7. 67 − 51 20	8. 94 − 48 40
9.	71 − 12 60	10.	65 − 49 20	11. 89 − 24 70	12. 51 − 38 10
13.	93 − 45 40	14.	88 − 32 60	15. 57 − 18 40	16. 28 − 17 10

Estimate by rounding to the nearest hundred.

17.	586 − 195 400	18.	941 − 362 500	19. 442 − 181 200	20. 861 − 298 600
21.	418 − 125 300	22.	546 − 234 300	23. 945 − 119 800	24. 681 − 132 600
25.	935 − 464 400	26.	322 − 176 100	27. 709 − 649 100	28. 550 − 214 400

29. **Reasoning** Marlee has collected baseball cards for 3 years. Kin has collected baseball cards for 2 years. Marlee has 845 baseball cards and Kin has 612 baseball cards. About how many more baseball cards does Marlee have than Kin? __200__

30. **Reasoning** What is the smallest number that can be subtracted from 723 so that the difference is 200 when both numbers are rounded to the nearest hundred? Explain.
Sample answer: 450. Since 723 will round to 700, 500 would need to be taken away from it. The smallest number that rounds to 500 when rounded to the nearest hundred is 450.

G6 (student p. 2)   MDIS 2.0

Objective Students will estimate differences.
Vocabulary Difference, estimate, reasonable, round

① Conceptual Development
Use with Exercises 1–4.

In this lesson, you will learn to estimate differences.

Have students work in small groups. Read the word problem to the students. *You can estimate differences by rounding before you subtract. Round 41 and 29 to the nearest ten. Is 41 closer to 40 or to 50 on the number line? 40 Is 29 closer to 20 or to 30? 30 Now subtract 30 from 40 to find the difference, or answer. 10 Since 12 is close to 10, the answer is reasonable. A reasonable answer is one that makes sense.* Monitor students to be sure they complete Exercises 1–2 correctly. Then have students complete Exercises 3–4.

② Practice Use with Exercises 5–30.

Remind students that each estimate should be a multiple of ten. If it is not, then their answer is not correct.

Error Intervention If students have trouble identifying the closest ten in exercises for which number lines are not provided, encourage them to use counting back to count back to the ten before and counting on to count up to the next ten. The ten that requires the fewest counts is the closest ten.

If You Have More Time Have students work with a partner. Each student should write a three-digit number. Then students can estimate the difference of the two numbers by rounding to the nearest hundred.

③ Assessment

In this lesson, students learned to estimate differences. Use the **Quick Check** problem to assess students' understanding.

Quick Check   **Formative** Assessment

How can you estimate the difference of 412 minus 399? Subtract 400 minus 400 to get zero. *Does this estimate make sense?* Yes, because the difference is closer to zero than 100

ADDING TWO-DIGIT NUMBERS

Name _____

Adding Two-Digit Numbers

Materials place-value blocks: 6 tens and 13 ones per pair

There are 25 boys and 38 girls at the library. How many students total?

1. Show 25 using place-value blocks.

2. Show 38 using place-value blocks.

3. Add 25 + 38 to find the total students.

   Add the ones. 5 + 8 = ___13___

4. Do you have more then 10 ones? ___yes___

	Tens	Ones
	1	
	2	5
+	3	8
	6	3

5. Since you have 13 ones, regroup them into tens and ones

   13 ones = ___1___ ten and ___3___ ones

6. Record the 3 ones at the bottom of the ones column of the Tens and Ones chart. Record the 1 ten at the top of the tens column.

7. Add the tens. Add the 1 ten that you regrouped, the 2 tens from the 25, and the 3 tens from the 38.

   1 ten + 2 tens + 3 tens = ___6___ tens

8. Record the tens at the bottom of the tens column of the Tens and Ones chart.

9. So, 25 + 38 = ___63___

   How many students are at the library? ___63___

	Tens	Ones
	1	
	4	6
+	2	9
	7	5

10. Use place value-blocks and the Tens and Ones chart to add 46 + 29.

G7 (student p. 1)   MDIS 2.0

Name _____

Adding Two-Digit Numbers (continued)

Add.

11.

	Tens	Ones
	1	
	1	3
+	2	8
	4	1

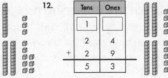

12.

	Tens	Ones
	1	
	2	4
+	2	9
	5	3

Add. Use a tens and ones chart if you like.

13. 58
   + 17
   75

14. 56
   + 11
   67

15. 18
   + 19
   37

16. 20
   + 28
   48

17. 46
   + 45
   91

18. 36
   + 17
   53

19. 17
   + 49
   66

20. 45
   + 14
   59

21. 32
   + 66
   98

22. 26
   + 37
   63

23. 22
   + 65
   87

24. 33
   + 33
   66

25. 21
   + 39
   60

26. 17
   + 29
   46

27. 36
   + 16
   52

28. 64
   + 27
   91

29. A puppy weighs 15 pounds. His mother weighs 65 pounds. How much do the puppy and his mother weigh together? ___80 pounds___

30. **Reasoning** What number do you add to 19 to get 30? ___11___

G7 (student p. 2)   MDIS 2.0

Objective Students will add two-digit numbers.
Vocabulary Regroup
Materials Place-value blocks

1 Conceptual Development
Use with Exercises 1–10.

In this lesson, you will learn to add two-digit numbers.

Have students work in pairs. Distribute place-value blocks: 6 tens and 13 ones to each pair. *You will use place-value blocks and a tens and ones chart to add two-digit numbers. Sometimes you may need to regroup. When you regroup, you make a ten from 10 ones.* Guide students through Exercises 1–9 by reading aloud each step. Have students fill in the blanks as you read each exercise. *How much is 5 + 8?* 13 *Regroup 13 into tens and ones. How many tens do you have?* 1 *How many ones?* 3 For Exercise 6, have students write 3 in the ones column. Read Exercise 7. *How many tens are there in all?* 6 *So, what is 25 + 38?* 63 Have students complete Exercise 10.

2 Practice Use with Exercises 11–30.

Remind students to use place-value blocks and a tens and ones chart if needed to solve the problems.

Error Intervention If students have trouble adding three tens after regrouping, have them first find the sum of two numbers. Then, have them count on the third number to find the sum of the three numbers.

If You Have More Time Have students create a how-to pamphlet describing how to add two-digit numbers. Tell them their audience is younger students who need to learn this skill. Encourage them to illustrate their pamphlet with models of the problems.

3 Assessment

In this lesson, students learned to add two-digit numbers. Use the **Quick Check** problem to assess students' understanding.

Quick Check **Formative** Assessment

Solve 47 + 27. 74 *Without working the problem, how do you know you will have to regroup?* Because there are more than 9 ones

---

Name _____

Subtracting Two-Digit Numbers

Materials place-value blocks: 3 tens and 20 ones per pair

There are 34 kittens and 16 puppies. How many
more kittens than puppies are there?

1. Show 34 with place-value blocks.

2. Do you have enough ones to take away
   6 ones? ___no___

3. Regroup 1 ten into 10 ones. Show this with
   your place-value blocks.

   3 tens and 4 ones = __2__ tens and 14 ones

4. Cross out the 3 tens in the Tens and Ones chart
   and write 2 above it. Cross out the 4 ones and
   write 14 above it.

5. Now, take away 6 ones and write the difference
   at the bottom of the ones column.

   14 ones − 6 ones = __8__ ones

6. Subtract the tens and write the difference at the
   bottom of the tens column.

   2 tens − 1 ten = __1__ ten

Tens	Ones
2	14
3̶	4̶
− 1	6
1	8

7. So, 34 − 16 = __18__ .

   How many more kittens than puppies
   are there? ___18___

8. Use place-value blocks and the Tens and Ones
   chart to subtract 56 − 27.

Tens	Ones
4	16
5̶	6̶
− 2	7
2	9

G8 (student p. 1) MDIS 2.0

Name _____

Subtracting Two-Digit Numbers (continued)

Subtract.

9.
Tens	Ones
3	12
4̶	2̶
− 1	9
2	3

10.
Tens	Ones
4	10
5̶	0̶
− 2	4
2	6

Subtract. Use a Tens and Ones chart if you like.

11. 2 15
     3̶5̶
   − 17
     18

12. 7 10
     8̶0̶
   − 38
     42

13. 3 15
     4̶5̶
   − 39
      6

14. 5 11
     6̶1̶
   − 13
     48

15. 6 14
     7̶4̶
   − 45
     29

16. 1 12
     2̶2̶
   − 18
      4

17. 4 10
     5̶0̶
   − 32
     18

18. 48
   − 20
     28

19. 8 15
     9̶5̶
   − 69
     26

20. 2 14
     3̶4̶
   − 7
     27

21. 5 11
     6̶1̶
   − 26
     35

22. 8 10
     9̶0̶
   − 74
     16

23. Thompson has 32 flowers. If he plants 18 flowers in
    the front yard, how many will he have left? ___14___

24. **Reasoning** In which problem do you need to regroup to
    subtract, 53 − 28 or 58 − 23? Explain.

    53 − 28; There are not enough ones in 53 to take away the 8 ones
    in 28. However, there are enough ones in 58 to take away the 3
    ones in 23.

G8 (student p. 2) MDIS 2.0

Objective Students will subtract two-digit numbers.
Vocabulary Regroup
Materials Place-value blocks

1 Conceptual Development
Use with Exercises 1–8.

*In this lesson, you will learn to subtract two-digit
numbers.*

Have students work in small groups. Distribute place-
value blocks: 3 tens and 20 ones for each group.
Read the problem together as a class. *When you want
to know how many more, do you add or subtract?*
Subtract *Sometimes when you subtract, you need to
regroup. When you regroup, you break a ten into
10 ones.* Tell students to show 34 with place-value
blocks. *How many ones do you have? 4 Do you have
enough ones to take away 6 ones?* No *You need to
regroup. How many ones do you have now?* 14 *How
many tens are left?* 2 Guide students through Exercises
4–7. Have them work in groups to complete Exercise 8.

2 Practice Use with Exercises 9–24.

Remind students that if they forget a basic subtraction
fact, they can think of a related addition fact. For
example, if they do not know 12 − 8, they can ask
themselves, "What plus 8 equals 12?"

Error Intervention If students do not recognize
the need to regroup and simply subtract the smaller
ones value from the larger ones value, then encourage
students to circle the greater ones value. If the circled
number is on the bottom, then they need to regroup.

If You Have More Time Have students write
a subtraction word problem requiring regrouping.
Then, have them exchange problems with a partner
and illustrate the solution to the problem. Have the
partners check each other's work.

3 Assessment

In this lesson, students learned to subtract two-digit
numbers. Use the **Quick Check** problem to assess
students' understanding.

Quick Check **Formative
Assessment**

Solve 34 − 18. 16 *Without working the problem, how
do you know you will need to regroup?* Because 4 is
less than 8

MENTAL MATH STRATEGIES

Name _____

Mental Math Strategies

You can add or subtract mentally by breaking apart numbers.

Find the difference of 647 − 235.

1. Break apart each number into its expanded form.

   647 = 600 + __40__ + __7__   235 = __200__ + 30 + __5__

2. Subtract the hundreds in both numbers.   600 − 200 = __400__

3. Subtract the tens in both numbers.   40 − __30__ = __10__

4. Subtract the ones in both numbers.   __7__ − 5 = __2__

5. Add the differences of the hundreds, tens, and ones.

   400 + 10 + 2 + = __412__

6. So, 647 − 235 = __412__.

You can also add or subtract mentally by using compensation.

Find the sum of 235 + 197.

7. Find the number closest to a multiple of 100 and round.

   197 rounded to the nearest hundred is __200__.

8. Solve the new problem.   235 + 200 = __435__

9. Since you rounded 197 to 200, did you add too much or too little to 235?   __too much__

10. How much more is 200? __3__

11. Since 200 is 3 more than 197, you added too much. You now must subtract 3 from the sum to compensate for adding 3.   435 − 3 = __432__

12. So, 235 + 197 = __432__.

G9 (student p. 1)   MDIS 2.0

Name _____

Mental Math Strategies (continued)

Add or subtract mentally. Use breaking apart.

13. 313 + 216	14. 842 + 115	15. 283 + 114	16. 254 + 621
529	957	397	875

17. 365 + 423	18. 457 + 222	19. 947 − 516	20. 786 − 314
788	679	431	472

21. 466 − 325	22. 579 − 256	23. 688 − 232	24. 875 − 231
141	323	456	644

Add or subtract mentally. Use compensation.

25. 462 + 399	26. 618 + 296	27. 256 + 195	28. 326 + 295
861	914	451	621

29. 145 + 197	30. 328 + 598	31. 540 − 298	32. 742 − 394
342	926	242	348

33. 916 − 497	34. 732 − 296	35. 867 − 395	36. 683 − 499
419	436	472	184

37. On vacation, the Gonzales family traveled 595 miles in one day. Their destination is 949 miles from their home. How much farther do they need to travel to get there?   __354 miles__

38. **Reasoning** To subtract 767 − 496, Wang first found 767 − 500 = 267. Now should he add 4 to 267 or subtract 4 from 267?   __add 4__

G9 (student p. 2)   MDIS 2.0

Objective Students will use mental math to add and subtract.

Vocabulary Compensation, expanded form

❶ Conceptual Development
Use with Exercises 1–12.

In this lesson, you will learn to use mental math to add and subtract.

Have the class work together. *You can add or subtract mentally by writing numbers in expanded form. Expanded form is a way of writing a number to show the value of each place. What is the expanded form of 647?* 600 + 40 + 7 *What is the expanded form of 235?* 200 + 30 + 5 Have students complete Exercise 1. Guide students through Exercises 2–6. *Another strategy you can use for mental math is compensation. In compensation, you round one number to the nearest hundred and you change the other number to keep the number sentence balanced. Find the number closest to a multiple of 100 and round. What is 197 rounded to the nearest hundred?* 200 *Is this more or less than 197?* More *How much more is 200 than 197?* 3 Read and complete Exercises 8–12 together as a class.

❷ Practice Use with Exercises 13–38.

For subtraction Exercises 31–36, tell students to round the second number to the nearest hundred.

Error Intervention If students have trouble keeping the number sentence balanced in the compensation strategy, have them write the number being added above the original numbers.

If You Have More Time Have students use the compensation strategy for Exercises 13 to 24 and check their answers against their previous work.

❸ Assessment

In this lesson, students learned to use mental math to add and subtract. Use the **Quick Check** problem to assess students' understanding.

Quick Check **Formative Assessment**

When finding 495 minus 297 with mental math, why wouldn't you round the 495 to 500 and then subtract 5 more? Sample answer: It is much easier to round 297 to 300 and then subtract 300 from 500.

ADDING THREE-DIGIT NUMBERS

Name _____

Adding Three-Digit Numbers

Materials place-value blocks: 4 hundreds, 12 tens,
15 ones per pair or group

There are 176 trucks and 249 cars. How many vehicles total?

1. Show 176 using place-value blocks.

2. Show 249 using place-value blocks.

3. Add 176 + 249 to find the total vehicles.

   Add the ones. 6 + 9 = ___15___

4. Do you have more then 9 ones? __yes__

5. Regroup the 15 ones into tens and ones.

   15 ones = ___1___ ten and ___5___ ones

6. Record the 5 ones at the bottom of the
   ones column of the Hundreds, Tens, and
   Ones chart. Record the 1 ten at the top
   of the tens column.

Hundreds	Tens	Ones
1	1	
1	7	6
+ 2	4	9
4	2	5

7. Add the tens.

   1 ten + 7 tens + 4 tens = ___12___ tens

8. Regroup the 12 tens into hundreds and tens.

   12 tens = ___1___ hundred and ___2___ tens

9. Record the 2 tens in the tens column of the chart. Record the 1 hundred at the top
   of the hundreds column.

10. Add the hundreds.

    1 hundred + 1 hundred + 2 hundreds = ___4___ hundreds

11. Record the 4 hundreds in the hundreds column of the chart.

12. How many total vehicles are there? __425__

G10 (student p. 1) MDIS 2.0

Name _____

Adding Three-Digit Numbers (continued)

Add.

13.
Hundreds	Tens	Ones
1	1	
3	4	8
+ 1	8	4
5	3	2

Add. Use place-value blocks if you like.

14.
```
  11
 135
+168
 303
```

15.
```
   1
 149
+370
 519
```

16.
```
  11
  23
+388
 411
```

17.
```
   1
 136
+215
 351
```

18.
```
   1
 217
+548
 765
```

19.
```
   1
 353
+274
 627
```

20.
```
  11
 731
+ 85
 816
```

21.
```
   1
 636
+271
 907
```

22.
```
   1
 407
+175
 582
```

23.
```
   1
 540
+370
 910
```

24.
```
   1
  84
+555
 639
```

25.
```
   1
 811
+109
 920
```

26. Kelvin has 526 pennies in one jar and 378 pennies
    in another jar. How many pennies does he have total? ___904___

27. LaTasha picked 281 cherries from a tree. Liz picked
    237 cherries. How many cherries did they pick together? ___518___

28. **Reasoning** How many times do you need to regroup to
    add 347 to 276? Explain.

    Two times. The 7 ones and 6 ones is more than
    9 ones. The 4 tens and 7 tens is more than 9 tens.

G10 (student p. 2) MDIS 2.0

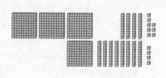

Objective Students will add three-digit numbers.
Vocabulary Regroup, sum
Materials Place-value blocks

❶ Conceptual Development
Use with Exercises 1–12.

*In this lesson, you will learn to add three-digit
numbers.*

Have students work in small groups. Distribute place-
value blocks: 4 hundreds, 12 tens, and 15 ones for
each group. Read the problem to the class. *To find the
total, or sum, you will add.* Have students model the
problem with place-value blocks. Then have students
add the ones. *You have more than 9 ones, so you
must regroup. When you regroup, you make a ten
from 10 ones. How many tens in 15?* 1 *How many
ones?* 5 *Record your answer on the Hundreds, Tens,
Ones chart.* Have students work in their groups to
complete Exercises 7–12.

❷ Practice Use with Exercises 13–28.

Tell students that the order of the numbers in an
addition problem does not matter. They can change
the order of the numbers in Exercises 16 and 24, if
they prefer the greater number on top.

Error Intervention If students have difficulty
keeping digits aligned in correct place value, then
have them write the problem in a Hundreds, Tens,
Ones chart.

If You Have More Time Have students cut
out 10 squares and write one digit, 0 through 9,
on the squares. Have one partner pick 3 squares
and write a three-digit number with the digits in the
order they were picked. Have the second partner
pick 3 squares and do the same. Have the pair work
together to find the sum of the three-digit numbers.

❸ Assessment

In this lesson, students learned to add three-digit
numbers. Use the **Quick Check** problem to assess
students' understanding.

Quick Check 🌸 **Formative** Assessment

Solve 458 plus 295. 753 *Which places did you have
to regroup?* Ones and tens *Why?* They had more than 9.

G10 MDIS 2.0

Left page (student worksheet)

Name _____

Intervention
Lesson **G11**

Subtracting Three-Digit Numbers

Materials place-value blocks: 3 hundreds, 14 tens, 13 ones per pair or group

There are 353 students at lunch. After 165 students went back to class, how many are still at lunch?

1. Subtract 353 − 165 to find how many students are still at lunch

   Show 353 using place-value blocks.

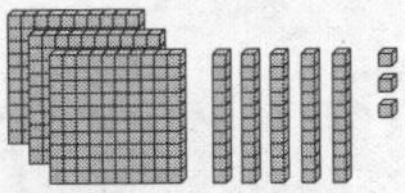

2. You have 3 ones. Do you have enough ones to take away 5 ones? ___no___

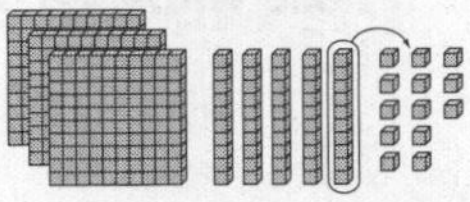

3. Regroup 1 ten as 10 ones. Show this with your place-value blocks.

   5 tens and 3 ones = 4 tens and __13__ ones

4. Cross out the 5 tens in the Hundreds, Tens, and Ones chart and write 4 above it. Cross out the 3 ones and write 13 above it.

Hundreds	Tens	Ones
2	14	13
3̶	5̶	3̶
− 1	6	5
1	8	8

5. Now, take away 5 ones and write the difference at the bottom of the ones column.

   13 ones − 5 ones = __8__ ones

6. You now have 4 tens. Is this enough tens to take away 6 tens? __no__

7. Regroup 1 hundred into 10 tens. Show this with your place-value blocks.

   3 hundreds and 4 tens = __2__ hundreds and 14 tens.

8. Record the regrouping in the chart. Cross out the 3 hundreds and write 2 above it. Make the 4 tens, 14 tens.

9. Subtract the tens and write the difference in the chart.

   14 tens − 6 tens = __8__ tens

G11 (student p. 1)   MDIS 2.0

Name _____

Intervention
Lesson **G11**

Subtracting Three-Digit Numbers (continued)

10. You now have 2 hundreds. Is this enough hundreds to take away 1 hundred? ___yes___

11. Subtract the hundreds and write the difference in the chart.

    2 hundreds − 1 hundred = __1__ hundred

12. So, 353 − 165 = __188__.

    How many students are still at lunch? __188__.

Subtract.

13. 436
    − 167
    ──────
    269

14. 564
    − 285
    ──────
    279

15. 826
    − 593
    ──────
    233

16. 332
    − 151
    ──────
    181

17. 731
    − 256
    ──────
    475

18. 443
    − 175
    ──────
    268

19. 561
    − 299
    ──────
    262

20. 253
    − 167
    ──────
    86

21. 438 − 244 = __194__

22. 826 − 539 = __287__

23. 165 − 146 = __19__

24. 336 − 277 = __59__

25. **Reasoning** The school has 646 students. On Tuesday, 177 students left the school to go to an art museum. How many students remained in school that day?
    469 students

26. **Number Sense** How many times do you need to regroup to subtract 316 from 624? Explain.
    One time. Four ones is less than 6 ones, but 2 tens is more than 1 ten.

G11 (student p. 2)   MDIS 2.0

Right page (teacher notes)

Objective Students will subtract three-digit numbers.
Vocabulary Regroup
Materials Place-value blocks

1 Conceptual Development
Use with Exercises 1–12.

In this lesson, you will learn to subtract three-digit numbers.

Have students work in small groups. Distribute place-value blocks: 3 hundreds, 14 tens, and 13 ones for each group. Read aloud the problem at the top of the page. Have students model the problem as shown in Exercises 1–3. *When you regroup in subtraction, you break apart a ten to make 10 ones. Do you have enough ones to take away 5 ones?* No Have students complete Exercises 3–5. *Now you have 4 tens. Do you need to regroup again?* Yes Have students complete Exercises 6–9 as a group.

2 Practice Use with Exercises 13–26.

Have students complete Exercises 10–12 in their groups. Tell them to work independently on the remaining problems, but refer them to Page 1 if they need reminders about how to solve the problems.

Error Intervention If students do not recognize the need to regroup and subtract the smaller one or ten from the larger of the same place value, then encourage students to circle the greater digit for each place value. If the circled number is on the bottom, then they need to regroup.

If You Have More Time Have students make up 5 problems that need only 1 regrouping and 5 problems that need 2 regroupings. Have them exchange problems with a classmate and solve.

3 Assessment

In this lesson, students learned to subtract three-digit numbers. Use the **Quick Check** problem to assess students' understanding.

Quick Check **Formative** Assessment

Solve 716 − 483. 233 *Which place did you regroup?* The tens place.

Name _____

Intervention
Lesson **G12**

Adding and Subtracting Money

To find $2.67 + $3.25, add as you would with whole numbers.

1. Add the pennies.

2. Since you have 12 pennies, regroup them into dimes and pennies.

12 pennies = __1__ dime

and __2__ pennies

	Dollars	Dimes	Pennies
		1	
	$2	. 6	7
+	3	. 2	5
	$5	. 9	2

3. Record the 2 pennies at the bottom of the pennies column of the chart. Record the 1 dime at the top of the dimes column.

4. Add the dimes. 1 + 6 + 2 = __9__ dimes
Record this value at the bottom of the dimes column.

5. Add the dollars. 2 + 3 = __5__ dollars
Record this value at the bottom of the dollars column.

6. Write the answer in dollars and cents by placing the dollar sign and decimal point.

So, $2.67 + $3.25 = __$5.92__.

To find $5.73 − $1.91, subtract as you would with whole numbers.

7. Subtract the pennies. 3 − 1 = __2__
Record the value at the bottom of the pennies column.

	Dollars	Dimes	Pennies
	4	17	
	$5	. 7	3
−	1	. 9	1
	$3	. 8	2

8. Since you cannot subtract 9 dimes from 7 dimes, regroup 1 dollar into 10 dimes.

5 dollars and 7 dimes = 4 dollars

and __17__ dimes

9. Record this regrouping in the chart. Cross out the 5 dollars and write 4 above it. Change the 7 dimes to 17 dimes.

G12 (student p. 1)   MDIS 2.0

Name _____

Intervention
Lesson **G12**

Adding and Subtracting Money (continued)

10. Subtract the dimes. 17 − 9 = __8__ dimes
Record this value at the bottom of the dimes column.

11. Subtract the dollars. 4 − 1 = __3__ dollars
Record this value at the bottom of the dollars column.

12. Write the answer in dollars and cents by placing the dollar sign and decimal point.

So, $5.73 − $1.91 = __$3.82__.

Add or subtract.

13.
$2.92
+ 0.74
$3.66

14.
$2.78
+ 0.94
$3.72

15.
$0.99
+ 2.49
$3.48

16.
$5.70
− 1.35
$4.35

17.
$2.30
+ 1.95
$4.25

18.
$7.15
− 5.09
$2.06

19.
$4.84
− 1.36
$3.48

20.
$6.65
+ 3.25
$9.90

21.
$8.42
− 2.08
$6.34

22.
$9.11
+ 0.09
$9.20

23.
$5.03
+ 3.58
$8.61

24.
$6.45
− 1.26
$5.19

25.
$3.58
+ 0.29
$3.87

26.
$7.40
− 1.26
$6.14

27.
$5.68
+ 0.90
$6.58

28.
$4.41
− 4.17
$0.24

29. Reasoning Which is easier for you to subtract, $3.87 − $1.63 or $4.15 − $2.89? Explain.

$3.87 − $1.63 is easier to subtract because it does not need regrouping. $4.15 − $2.89 needs to be regrouped two times.

G12 (student p. 2)   MDIS 2.0

Objective Students will add and subtract money.
Vocabulary Regroup

① Conceptual Development
Use with Exercises 1–12.

In this lesson you will learn to add and subtract money.

Review the relative values of a penny, dime, and dollar. Have students complete Exercise 1. Discuss how to *regroup* 10 pennies as 1 dime. *How many pennies equal 1 dime?* 10 *How can you rewrite 12 pennies?* 1 dime and 2 pennies Have students complete Exercises 2–3. Remind students to add numbers in the same place value. Then have them complete Exercises 4–6. Explain that subtracting money is like subtracting whole numbers. *What happens if you cannot subtract the bottom number from the top number?* Regroup from the next place value *When working with money, what must the answer have?* A decimal point and a dollar sign Have students complete Exercises 7–12.

② Practice Use with Exercises 13–29.

Remind students that the order of the numbers matters in subtraction. If the number being subtracted is greater than the number it is being subtracted from, they must regroup.

Error Intervention If students have difficulty adding money, have them model the addition using play money.

If You Have More Time Have students use an advertisement to find the price of a product. Then have them determine how much change they would get if they paid with $20. If the item costs more than $20, have students find how much more money they need to buy it. Check students' work.

③ Assessment

In this lesson students learned to add and subtract money. Use the **Quick Check** problem to assess students' understanding.

Quick Check **Formative** Assessment

Solve: $8.64 − $2.98 $5.66

Estimating Sums and Differences of Greater Numbers

Name _____

When Juanita added 4,287 and 4,683, she got a sum of 8,970.
To check that this answer is reasonable, use estimation.

1. Round each addend to the nearest thousand.

4,287   4,683
◄┼──┼──┼──●─┼──┼──┼──●─┼──┼──┼►
4,000 4,100 4,200 4,300 4,400 4,500 4,600 4,700 4,800 4,900 5,000

4,287 rounded to the nearest thousand is __4,000__.

4,683 rounded to the nearest thousand is __5,000__.

2. Add the rounded numbers.

4,000 + 5,000 = __9,000__

Since 8,970 is close to 9,000, the answer is reasonable.

Martin subtracted 8,319 − 3,910 and got a difference of 4,409.
To check that this answer is reasonable, use estimation.

3. Round each number to the nearest thousand.

8,319
◄┼──●─┼──┼──┼──┼──┼──┼──┼──┼►
8,000 8,100 8,200 8,300 8,400 8,500 8,600 8,700 8,800 8,900 9,000

8,319 rounded to the nearest thousand is __8,000__.

3,910
◄┼──┼──┼──┼──┼──┼──┼──┼──┼●─┼►
3,000 3,100 3,200 3,300 3,400 3,500 3,600 3,700 3,800 3,900 4,000

3,910 rounded to the nearest thousand is __4,000__.

4. Subtract the rounded numbers.

8,000 − 4,000 = __4,000__

Since 4,409 is close to 4,000, the answer is reasonable.

Name _____

Estimating Sums and Differences of Greater Numbers (continued)

Estimate each sum by rounding to the nearest thousand.

5. 6,729   **6.** 4,919   **7.** 2,886 + 2,341   **8.** 5,098 + 3,921
     + 2,490   + 1,834
     ───────   ───────   __5,000__   __9,000__
      9,000   7,000

9.   972   **10.** 3,326   **11.** 8,229 + 1,304   **12.** 1,101 + 1,010
     + 6,127   + 4,812
     ───────   ───────   __9,000__   __2,000__
      7,000   8,000

13. 7,825   **14.** 4,444   **15.** 5,907 + 1,856   **16.** 2,298 + 6,371
      + 2,481   + 3,333
      ────────   ───────   __8,000__   __8,000__
       10,000   7,000

Estimate each difference by rounding to the nearest thousand.

17. 5,986   **18.** 9,341   **19.** 4,142 − 1,981   **20.** 8,761 − 2,985
      − 1,595   − 3,662
      ───────   ───────   __2,000__   __6,000__
       4,000   5,000

21. 4,018   **22.** 5,746   **23.** 9,945 − 1,119   **24.** 6,881 − 1,732
      − 1,825   − 2,734
      ───────   ───────   __9,000__   __5,000__
       2,000   3,000

25. 8,935   **26.** 3,222   **27.** 7,009 − 6,049   **28.** 5,850 − 2,314
      − 4,164   − 1,076
      ───────   ───────   __1,000__   __4,000__
       5,000   2,000

29. **Reasoning** The theater sold 7,893 tickets on Friday
night. There were 5,123 tickets sold on Saturday
night. About how many more tickets were sold on   __3,000__
Friday night than Saturday night?

30. **Reasoning** What is the smallest number that can be added
to 2,791 so that the sum is 7,000 when both numbers are
rounded to the nearest thousand? Explain.
Sample answer: 3,500. Since 2,791 rounds to 3,000, and
3,000 + 4,000 = 7,000, the second number needs to round to 4,000.
The smallest number that rounds to 4,000 to the nearest thousand is 3,500.

Objective Students will estimate sums and differences
of greater numbers.
Vocabulary Estimate, sum, difference
Materials 4 number cubes

❶ Conceptual Development
Use with Exercises 1–4.

*In this lesson you will learn to estimate sums and
differences of greater numbers.*

Explain that estimation can help you check to be
sure an answer is reasonable. To *estimate*, you will
round the numbers. *What is the greatest place value
for these numbers?* Thousands *What place value will
you look at to round them?* Hundreds Have students
complete Exercises 1–2. *How do you know Juanita's
sum was reasonable?* Her answer is close to 9,000,
the estimate. Explain that students will use a similar
process to estimate a *difference*. Have students
complete Exercises 3–4.

❷ Practice Use with Exercises 5–30.

Caution students not to add or subtract and then
round. They should round each number and then
add or subtract.

Error Intervention If students have difficulty
estimating, have them underline the digit they are
rounding and circle the digit to its right. Explain that
if the circled digit is 5 or greater, the highlighted digit
will increase by 1.

If You Have More Time Have students roll
four number cubes to make a four-digit number and
then repeat so that they have two four-digit numbers.
Then have them estimate the sum and the difference of
the two numbers. Check students work.

❸ Assessment

In this lesson students learned to estimate sums and
differences of greater numbers. Use the **Quick
Check** problem to assess students' understanding.

Quick Check **Formative**
Assessment

Estimate the sum by rounding to the nearest thousand:
2,499 + 3,502 6,000

ADDING THREE NUMBERS

Name _____

Adding Three Numbers

Intervention
Lesson **G14**

Materials place-value blocks: 2 hundreds, 6 tens, and 14 ones per pair or group

How many total pieces of fruit are in a box containing
45 apples, 107 oranges, and 112 bananas?

1. Show 45, 107, and 112 using place-value blocks.

2. Add 45 + 107 + 112 to find the total pieces of
   fruit in the box.

3. Do you have more then 10 ones? _yes_
   Add the ones.

   5 ones + 7 ones + 2 ones = _14_ ones

4. Since you have 14 ones, regroup them into
   tens and ones.

   14 ones = _1_ ten and _4_ ones

5. Record the 4 ones at the bottom of the
   ones column of the Hundreds, Tens,
   and Ones chart. Record the 1 ten at
   the top of the tens column.

Hundreds	Tens	Ones
	1	
	4	5
1	0	7
+ 1	1	2
2	6	4

6. Add the tens.

   1 ten + 4 tens + 1 ten = _6_ tens

7. Do you have more than 10 tens? _no_

8. Record the tens at the bottom of the tens column of the chart.

9. Add the hundreds and record the value at the bottom of the
   hundreds column.

   1 hundred + 1 hundred = _2_ hundreds

10. So, 45 + 107 + 112 = _264_

    How many total pieces of fruit are in the box? _264_

Name _____

Adding Three Numbers (continued)

Intervention
Lesson **G14**

Add.

11.
Hundreds	Tens	Ones
	1	
2	5	4
1	2	9
+	6	2
4	4	5

12.
Hundreds	Tens	Ones
	1	
1	1	7
1	0	6
+	7	4
2	9	7

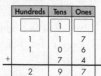 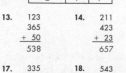

13.
```
  123
  365
+  50
  538
```

14.
```
  211
  423
+  23
  657
```

15.
```
   23
   45
+  14
   82
```

16.
```
  322
   43
+  16
  381
```

17.
```
  335
  125
+  32
  492
```

18.
```
  543
  144
+  46
  733
```

19.
```
  613
  205
+  64
  882
```

20.
```
  851
   32
+  40
  923
```

21. There were 234 books returned to the library on
    Monday, 109 books returned on Tuesday, and
    41 books returned on Wednesday. How many
    books were returned to the library in the three days? _384_

22. **Reasoning** Write the smallest 2-digit number that
    when added to 345 and 133 would require
    regrouping of both the ones and the tens. _22_

Objective Students will add three numbers.
Vocabulary Regroup, sum
Materials Place-value blocks

① Conceptual Development
Use with Exercises 1–10.

In this lesson, you will learn to add three numbers.

Distribute place-value blocks: 2 hundreds, 6 tens, and
14 ones for each student. Read the problem to the
class. *To find the total, or sum, you will add.* Have
students model the problem with place-value blocks.
Then have students add the ones. *You have more than
9 ones, so you must regroup. When you regroup,
you make a ten from 10 ones. How many tens in
14? 1 How many ones? 4 Record your answers on
the Hundreds, Tens, Ones chart.* Have the students
complete Exercises 6–10. Monitor the students to be
sure they complete the exercises correctly.

② Practice Use with Exercises 11–22.

Some students may have trouble working with
Exercises 13–20 in the space provided. Remind
them to use a Hundred, Tens, Ones chart to keep the
problems organized.

Error Intervention If students have trouble
adding three numbers, have them first find the sum
of two numbers. Then have them count on the third
number to find the sum of the three numbers.

If You Have More Time Have each student
write a two- or three-digit number on paper. Then
place students into groups of three and find the sum
of the three numbers. Continue to have students form
random groups three more times. Have each student
share with the class their highest and lowest sums.

③ Assessment

In this lesson, students learned to add three numbers.
Use the **Quick Check** problem to assess students'
understanding.

Quick Check **Formative** Assessment

Write *114 plus 489 plus 236* on the board. *How
many times would you need to regroup when solving
this problem? 2 How do you know?* There are more
than 9 ones and more than 9 tens.

Name _____

Intervention
Lesson **G15**

Subtracting Four-Digit Numbers

The Pacific Crest Trail is 2,655 miles long. The California Coastal Trail is 1,294 miles long. How much longer is the Pacific Coast Trail than the California Coastal Trail?

1. Write 2,655 − 1,294 in the chart.

Thousands	Hundreds	Tens	Ones
	5	15	
2	6	5	5
− 1	2	9	4
1	3	6	1

2. Look at the ones column. Do you have enough ones to subtract 4 ones? __yes__

3. Subtract the ones and record this value at the bottom of the ones column.

   5 ones − 4 ones = __1__ one

4. Look at the tens column. Do you have enough tens to subtract 9 tens? __no__

5. Regroup 1 hundred into 10 tens. Cross out the 6 hundreds and write 5 above it. Cross out the 5 tens and write 15 above it.

6. Subtract the tens. Record this value at the bottom of the tens column.

   15 tens − 9 tens = __6__ tens

7. Do you have enough hundreds to subtract 2 hundreds? __yes__

8. Subtract the hundreds. Record this value at the bottom of the hundreds column.
   5 hundreds − 2 hundred = __3__ hundreds

9. Subtract the thousands. Record this value at the bottom of the thousands column.
   2 thousands − 1 thousand = __1__ thousand

10. How much longer is the Pacific Crest Trail than the California Coast Trail? __1,361__ miles

---

Name _____

Intervention
Lesson **G15**

Subtracting Four-Digit Numbers (continued)

Subtract.

11.

Thousands	Hundreds	Tens	Ones
3	11	10	13
4	2	1	3
− 1	8	5	7
2	3	5	6

12. 8,156
    − 5,948
    2,208

13. 14,951
    − 8,965
    5,986

14. 7,811
    − 2,766
    5,045

15. 9,056
    − 4,128
    4,928

16. 7,510
    − 3,295
    4,215

17. 8,152
    − 965
    7,187

18. 5,874
    − 2,287
    3,587

19. 4,213
    − 1,464
    2,749

20. 6,182
    − 2,741
    3,441

21. 5,623
    − 1,278
    4,345

22. 2,132
    − 856
    1,276

23. 3,814
    − 1,735
    2,079

24. At its greatest depth, the Atlantic Ocean is 9,219 meters deep, the Indian Ocean is 7,455 meters deep, and the Caribbean Sea is 6,946 meters deep. How much deeper is the Indian Ocean than the Caribbean Sea? __509 meters__

25. **Reasoning** Explain how to find 1,500 − 499 using mental math.
    499 + 1 = 500; 1,500 is 1,000 more than 500. So, 1,500 − 499 = 1,001.

Objective Students will subtract four-digit numbers.
Vocabulary Digit

① Conceptual Development
Use with Exercises 1–10.

In this lesson you will learn to subtract four-digit numbers.

Read the problem aloud with students. *What operation will tell you how much longer one trail is than the other?* Subtraction *Which digits will you line up before you subtract?* 2 and 1, 6 and 2, 5 and 9, and 5 and 4 *Which place value do you start with when you subtract?* Ones Have students complete Exercises 1–3. *What happens when you cannot subtract 9 tens from 5 tens?* Regroup *How will you regroup?* Convert 1 hundred into 10 tens Have students complete Exercises 4–6. *Will you need to regroup before subtracting the hundreds?* No *How do you know?* 5 hundreds are greater than 2 hundreds. Have students complete Exercises 7–10.

② Practice Use with Exercises 11–25.

Review the difference between digits and numbers. Remind students that when subtracting, the first number must be greater than the second number. Sometimes the digit on top is less than the digit on the bottom, but the number on top is always greater than the number on the bottom.

Error Intervention If students have difficulty subtracting, help them identify when they need to regroup by highlighting when the top digit is less than the bottom digit.

If You Have More Time Have students look up the lengths of rivers or the heights of mountains and subtract to find the differences in lengths or heights. Check students' work.

③ Assessment

In this lesson students learned to subtract four-digit numbers. Use the **Quick Check** problem to assess students' understanding.

Quick Check   Formative Assessment

Subtract: 6,429 − 3,551 2,878

Name _____

Subtracting Across Zero

Materials place-value blocks: 6 hundreds; 10 tens and 10 ones for each group

There were 600 students at school. After lunch, 245 students went on a field trip. How many students were left at school?

1. Subtract 600 − 245 to find the number of students left at school. Show 600 using place-value blocks.

2. You have 0 ones. Do you have enough ones to take away 5 ones? __no__

3. Do you have tens to regroup? __no__

4. Go to the hundreds. Regroup 1 hundred into 10 tens. Show this with your place-value blocks.

   6 hundreds = 5 hundreds and __10__ tens

5. Record this in the Hundreds, Tens, Ones chart: Cross out the 6 hundreds and write 5 above it. Cross out the 0 tens and write 10 above it.

6. Now, regroup 1 ten into 10 ones. Show this with your place-value blocks.

   1 hundred = __9__ tens and 10 ones.

7. Record this in the chart: Cross out the 10 tens and write 9 above it. Cross out the 0 ones and write 10 above it.

8. Subtract. Write each difference in the bottom row of the chart.

   10 ones − 5 ones = __5__ ones   9 tens − 4 tens = __5__ tens

   5 hundreds − 2 hundreds = __3__ hundreds

9. How many students were left at school? __355__

Hundreds	Tens	Ones
	9	
5	10	10
6̸	0̸	0̸
− 2	4	5
3	5	5

G16 (student p. 1)   MDIS 2.0

Name _____

Subtracting Across Zero (continued)

Subtract

10. Use the place value chart to find 4,000 − 2,512.

Thousands	Hundreds	Tens	Ones
	9	9	
3	10	10	10
4	0	0	0
− 2	5	1	2
1	4	8	8

11. 802
    − 561
    241

12. 760
    − 395
    365

13. 400
    − 254
    146

14. 500
    − 298
    202

15. 7,800
    − 4,324
    3,476

16. 8,050
    − 6,045
    2,005

17. 6,000
    − 4,560
    1,440

18. 3,000
    − 1,875
    1,125

19. 6,000
    − 2,020
    3,980

20. 8,500
    − 1,362
    7,138

21. 700
    − 222
    478

22. 660
    − 387
    273

23. **Reasoning** What is the missing number?
    4,000 − ■ = 3,200   800

24. There are 500 students at an elementary school. Of those students, 229 are involved in sports. How many students are not involved in sports?   271 students

G16 (student p. 2)   MDIS 2.0

Objective Students will subtract across zeros.
Vocabulary Regroup
Materials Place-value blocks, grocery ads

1 Conceptual Development
Use with Exercises 1–9.

In this lesson, you will subtract across zeros.

Have students work in small groups. Distribute place-value blocks: 6 hundreds, 10 tens, and 10 ones for each group. Complete Exercises 1–5 as a class. Have students model the problem with place-value blocks. *You need to subtract 245 from 600. Do you have enough ones to take away 5 ones?* No *You need to regroup. When you regroup in subtraction, you break a larger number into a smaller number. Do you have tens to regroup?* No *Regroup 1 hundred into 10 tens.* Have students model regrouping. *How many hundreds do you have now?* 5 *How many tens do you have?* 10 Have students show the regrouping on the chart and work in groups to complete Exercises 6–9.

2 Practice Use with Exercises 10–24.

Point out to students that if they make a Hundreds, Tens, Ones chart for Exercises 11–24, they need to include two boxes.

Error Intervention If students struggle to complete the Hundreds, Tens, Ones chart, remind them that when they regroup, they add a multiple of 10 to a place value.

If You Have More Time Tell students they have $100 to spend at the grocery store. Give grocery store ads to students in small groups. Have students "buy" groceries. Then have students subtract their purchases from $100 to find out how much money they have left.

3 Assessment

In this lesson, students learned to subtract across zeros. Use the **Quick Check** problem to assess students' understanding.

Quick Check   **Formative** Assessment

Write *400 − 271* on the board. *Can you take away 1 from 0?* No *How many hundreds will you have after you have finished regrouping?* 3 *How many tens?* 9 *How many ones?* 10

ADDING FOUR-DIGIT NUMBERS

Adding 4-Digit Numbers

Name _____

On Friday, 2,931 people attended the school play. On Saturday, 3,246 people attended the school play. How many total people attended the school play?

	Thousands	Hundreds	Tens	Ones
	[1]	[ ]	[ ]	[ ]
	2	9	3	1
+	3	2	4	6
	6	1	7	7

1. Write 2,931 and 3,246 in the place value chart.

2. Add the ones and record the sum in the ones column.

   1 one + 6 ones = __7__ ones

3. Add the tens and record the value in the tens column.

   3 tens + 4 tens = __7__ tens

4. Add the hundreds and record the value in the hundreds column.

   9 hundreds + 2 hundreds = __11__ hundreds

5. Since you have 11 hundreds, regroup them.

   11 hundreds = __1__ thousand and 1 hundred

6. Record the hundred in the hundreds column and record the thousand at the top of the thousands column.

7. Add the thousands and record the value in the thousands column.

   1 thousand + 2 thousands + 3 thousands = __6__ thousands

8. So, 2,931 + 3,246 = __6,177__

9. How many total people attended the school play on Friday and Saturday?

   _____6,177 people_____

G17 (student p. 1)   MDIS 2.0

Name _____

Adding 4-Digit Numbers (continued)

Add

10.

	Thousands	Hundreds	Tens	Ones
	[1]	[ ]	[1]	[ ]
	4	8	2	9
+	3	5	6	7
	8	3	9	6

11. 4,687 + 3,250 7,937	12. 2,479 + 1,431 3,910	13. 6,354 + 2,125 8,479	14. 3,218 + 5,673 8,891
15. 5,927 + 3,073 9,000	16. 1,032 + 4,668 5,700	17. 3,640 + 5,270 8,910	18. 3,063 + 4,137 7,200
19. 9,135 + 681 9,816	20. 6,754 + 137 6,891	21. 2,136 4,021 + 1,345 7,502	22. 3,275 1,342 + 5,123 9,740

23. 2,124 + 4,205   24. 7,126 + 2,574   25. 3,025 + 1,975
    6,329   9,700   5,000

26. A truck driver traveled 2,175 miles in June and 1,745 miles in July. How many total miles did the truck driver travel?

    _____3,920_____ miles

27. **Reasoning** Sara wrote 5,236 + 2,673 = 7,809. What mistake did Sara make? Write the correct sum.

    Sara did not add the regrouped tens.

    The correct answer is 7,909.

G17 (student p. 2)   MDIS 2.0

Objective Students will add four-digit numbers.
Vocabulary Digit

① Conceptual Development
Use with Exercises 1–9.

In this lesson you will learn to add four-digit numbers.

Read the problem aloud with students. Revisit the term *digit* if needed. *What operation will you use to find the total number of people who attended the play?* Addition *How will the place-value chart help you solve this problem?* It will help align the digits correctly. *Which place value do you start with when you add?* Ones Have students complete Exercises 1–3. *What happens when the sum of the digits in a column is greater than 10?* You have to regroup. *How will you regroup 11 hundreds?* Make 1 thousand and 1 hundred Have students complete Exercises 4–6. *How do you add three digits?* Add two and then add the third digit to the sum Have students complete Exercises 7–9.

② Practice Use with Exercises 10–27.

Explain to students that it is easier to add numbers when they are stacked vertically. Remind students that digits in like place values should be aligned.

Error Intervention If students have difficulty aligning digits vertically, have them write the problem on grid paper, with one digit in each square.

If You Have More Time Have students work in groups of four. Each person should name a digit. Repeat so that there are two 4-digit numbers. Students should each add the numbers and compare their sums to those of the other members in their group.

③ Assessment

In this lesson students learned to add four-digit numbers. Use the **Quick Check** problem to assess students' understanding.

Quick Check ❧ **Formative** Assessment

Add: 4,548 + 2,735 7,283

ADDING GREATER NUMBERS

Name _____

Adding Greater Numbers

On Monday, 26,833 tickets sold for a concert. On Tuesday, 35,106 tickets were sold.
What is the total number of tickets sold?

1. Write 26,833 and
   35,106 in the
   place value chart.

2. Add the ones and
   record the sum in
   the ones column.

   3 ones + 6 ones

   = __9__ ones

Ten Thousands	Thousands	Hundreds	Tens	Ones
1				
2	6	8	3	3
+ 3	5	1	0	6
6	1	9	3	9

3. Add the tens and record the value in the tens column.

   3 tens + 0 tens = __3__ tens

4. Add the hundreds and record the value in the hundreds column.

   8 hundreds + 1 hundred = __9__ hundreds

5. Add the thousands.

   6 thousands + 5 thousands = __11__ thousands

6. Since you have 11 thousands, regroup them.

   11 thousands = __1__ ten thousand and 1 thousand

7. Record the thousand in the thousands column and record the ten thousands
   at the top of the ten thousands column.

8. Add the ten thousands and record the value.
   1 ten thousand + 2 ten thousands + 3 ten thousands

   = __6__ ten thousands

9. So, 26,833 + 35,106 = __61,939__
   How many total concert tickets were sold on Monday and
   Tuesday?   61,939

G18 (student p. 1)   MDIS 2.0

Name _____

Adding Greater Numbers (continued)

Add

10.

Ten Thousands	Thousands	Hundreds	Tens	Ones
1			1	
5	4	3	2	7
+ 1	7	5	4	8
7	1	8	7	5

11. 7,169
   + 1,943
     9,112

12. 4,275
   + 2,786
     7,061

13. 5,184
   + 2,936
     8,120

14. 2,943
   + 178
     3,121

15. $38.64
   + 19.98
    $58.62

16. $475.98
   + 269.23
    $745.21

17. 12,975
   + 8,166
     21,141

18. 42,973
   + 17,127
     60,100

19. $245.89
     174.03
   + 108.25
    $528.17

20. 71,043
      9,481
   + 6,055
     86,579

21. 4,379
   + 2,851
     7,230

22. 5,612
   + 3,399
     9,011

23. 1,102 + 6,931 =
    8,033

24. 11,070 + 982 =
    12,052

25. 62,800 + 3,225 =
    66,025

26. Louisiana has an area of 49,651 square miles.
    Mississippi has an area of 48,286 square miles.
    What is their combined area?   __97,937__ square miles

27. **Reasoning** Alex wrote 33,123 + 56,879 = 80,002.
    What mistake did Alex make? Write the correct sum.
    Alex did not add the regrouped thousands.
    The correct answer is 90,002.

G18 (student p. 2)   MDIS 2.0

Objective Students will add greater numbers.
Vocabulary Digit

❶ Conceptual Development
Use with Exercises 1–9.

In this lesson you will learn to add greater numbers.

Read the problem aloud with students. *What
operation will tell you the total number of tickets sold?*
Addition *How many digits are in each number?* 5
When you add, what digits do you start with? Ones
Have students complete Exercises 1–3. *What happens
when the sum of the digits in a column is greater
than 10?* You have to regroup. Have them look at the
place-value chart and predict when they think they
will need to regroup. *In which column will you need
to regroup first?* Thousands *How do you know?* The
digits add to more than 10. Have students complete
Exercises 4–9.

❷ Practice Use with Exercises 10–27.

Explain to students that adding greater numbers
involves the same steps as adding lesser numbers.
Encourage them to carefully add the digits in each
place value, starting with the ones, and regroup if
necessary.

Error Intervention If students have difficulty
regrouping, have them draw a picture for the sum in
that place value, showing a group of 10 when the
sum is 10 or greater.

If You Have More Time Have students
make up a multi-digit addition problem and solve it.
Then have them trade with a partner. Each person
should then solve the other person's problem. Check
students' work.

❸ Assessment

In this lesson students learned to add greater numbers.
Use the **Quick Check** problem to assess students'
understanding.

Quick Check Formative Assessment

Add: 13,297 + 28,765 42,062

SUBTRACTING GREATER NUMBERS

Student Page 1

Name _____

Subtracting Greater Numbers

The local grocery made $341,272 profit this year and $298,432 last year. How much more profit did they make this year than last year?

1. Subtract $341,272 − $298,432 to find the difference in profit. The numbers are shown in the place-value chart below.

Hundred Thousands	Ten Thousands	Thousands	Hundreds	Tens	Ones
2	13	10	12		
3	4	1	2	7	2
− 2	9	8	4	3	2
	4	2	8	4	0

2. Subtract the ones and record the value in the place-value chart.

   2 ones − 2 ones = ___0___ ones

3. Subtract the tens and record the value in the chart.

   7 tens − 3 tens = ___4___ tens

4. Since you only have 2 hundreds, regroup one thousand as 10 hundreds.

   How many thousands do you now have? ___0___

   How many hundreds? ___12___ Record this value in the chart.

5. Subtract the hundreds and record the value in the chart.

   12 hundreds − 4 hundreds = ___8___ hundreds

6. Since you have 0 thousands, regroup one ten thousand as 10 thousands.

   How many ten thousands do you now have? ___3___

   How many thousands? ___10___

7. Subtract the thousands and record the value in the chart.

   10 thousands − 8 thousands = ___2___ thousands

Student Page 2

Name _____

Subtracting Greater Numbers (continued)

8. Since you only have 3 ten thousands, regroup one hundred thousand for 10 ten thousands.

   How many hundred thousands do you now have? ___2___

   How many ten thousands? ___13___
   Record this value in the chart.

9. Subtract the ten thousands and record the value in the chart.

   13 ten thousands − 9 ten thousands = ___4___ ten thousands

10. Subtract the hundred thousands.

    2 hundred thousands − 2 hundred thousands = ___0___ hundred thousands

11. How much more profit did the grocery make this year than last year? ___$42,840___

Subtract.

12. 25,049
    − 12,651
    12,398

13. 30,675
    − 21,599
    9,076

14. $261.05
    − 95.14
    $165.91

15. $745.16
    − 394.29
    $350.87

16. $809.47
    − 152.68
    $656.79

17. 68,714
    − 59,856
    8,858

18. 220,915
    − 114,876
    106,039

19. 172,560
    − 143,695
    28,865

20. Gretta has $250 to spend on supplies for a dance. If the table decorations cost $188.65, how much money will she have left to spend on balloons? ___$61.35___

21. **Reasoning** Explain how to regroup in order to subtract 22,000 − 10,452.
    Trade 2 thousands for 1 thousand, 9 hundreds, 9 tens, and 10 ones.

Objective Students will subtract greater numbers.
Vocabulary Profit

1 Conceptual Development
Use with Exercises 1–11.

In this lesson you will learn to subtract greater numbers.

Read the problem aloud with students. *What is profit?* How much money you make minus your expenses Remind students that sometimes they need to regroup when subtracting numbers. Have them look at the place-value chart and predict where they think they will have to regroup. *When do need to regroup?* When the second digit is greater than the first Have students complete Exercises 1–3. *In which column will you need to regroup first?* The hundreds column *How do you regroup?* You regroup 1 from the place value to the left and add 10 to the place value you are subtracting. Have students complete Exercises 4–11.

2 Practice Use with Exercises 12–21.

Review place value to the hundred thousands. Remind students that, when subtracting, they must subtract digits of the same place value.

Error Intervention If students have difficulty regrouping, have them rewrite a subtraction problem on another piece of paper so that they will have more room to work. Then have them draw a box above each column of numbers, as shown in Exercise 1, and use the boxes to show regrouping.

If You Have More Time Have students make up multi-digit subtraction problems about profit. Have them explain their solutions to a partner. Check students' problems and solutions.

3 Assessment

In this lesson students learned to subtract greater numbers. Use the **Quick Check** problem to assess students' understanding.

Quick Check   **Formative Assessment**

Subtract: 514,127 − 238,089 276,038

Name _____

Intervention
Lesson **G20**

Multiplication as Repeated Addition

Materials 24 counters and 4 half-sheets of paper per student
or pair

Freyja has 4 plates. Each plate has 5 cherries. Answer 1 to 6 to
find how many cherries she has in all.

You can use multiplication to find how many in all when you
have equal groups.

1. Show 4 plates with 5 cherries on each using counters.

2. Use addition to find how many cherries Freyja has.

   $\underline{5} + \underline{5} + \underline{5} + \underline{5} = 20$

3. How many plates? $\underline{4}$

4. How many cherries on each plate? $\underline{5}$

5. Use multiplication to find how many cherries Freyja
   has in all.

   $\underline{\quad 4 \quad} \times \underline{\quad 5 \quad} = 20$
   Number   Number of
   of Plates   Cherries on
             Each Plate

6. How many cherries does Freyja have in all? $\underline{20}$

7. Use counters and repeated addition to find 3×8.

   $3 \times 8 = 8 + \underline{8} + \underline{8}$

   $= \underline{24}$

G20 (student p. 1)   MDIS 2.0

Name _____

Intervention
Lesson **G20**

Multiplication as Repeated Addition (continued)

Add. Then multiply. Use counters if you like.

8. ♡♡♡ ♡♡♡

   $3 + 3 = \underline{6}$

   $2 \times 3 = \underline{6}$

9. (balloons)

   $2 + 2 + 2 + 2 = \underline{8}$

   $4 \times 2 = \underline{8}$

Use the pictures to fill in the blanks.

10. (shells: 4 rows of 3)

    3 groups of $\underline{4}$

    $4 + \underline{4} + \underline{4} = \underline{12}$

    $3 \times \underline{4} = \underline{12}$

11. (stars: 3 rows of 6)

    3 groups of $\underline{6}$

    $6 + \underline{6} + \underline{6} = \underline{18}$

    $3 \times \underline{6} = \underline{18}$

Fill in the blanks to make each number sentence true.

12. $\underline{8} + \underline{8} + \underline{8} + \underline{8} + \underline{8} + \underline{8} = 6 \times 8$

13. $9 + 9 + \underline{9} + \underline{9} = \underline{4} \times 9$

14. **Reasoning** Melissa says that $5 + 5 + 5 + 3$ is the same
    thing as 4×5. Explain why Melissa is wrong.

    The only way an addition problem can be written as a multiplication
    problem is if there are equal groups. There are three 5s and one 3,
    so there are not equal groups.

G20 (student p. 2)   MDIS 2.0

Objective Students will write multiplication
sentences.
Vocabulary Multiplication, factors, product
Materials 24 counters and 4 half-sheets of paper
per student

① Conceptual Development
Use with Exercises 1–7.

*In this lesson, you will learn how multiplication is like
repeated addition and how to use multiplication to
solve problems.*

Have students work in small groups. Ask a volunteer
to read the story problem at the top of the page.
Then, have students use counters to show four plates
with five cherries on each. *What addition sentence
does this show?* $5 + 5 + 5 + 5 = 20$ Have students
complete Exercises 2–4. *You can use multiplication to
find how many in all when you have equal groups.
We have four equal groups of five cherries. Write
4×5 on the board. The numbers that are being
multiplied, 4 and 5, are called factors.* Have students
write 4 and 5 in the correct blanks for Exercise
5. *How many cherries in all?* 20 *The answer to a
multiplication problem is called the product.* Do
Exercise 7 similarly.

② Practice Use with Exercises 8–14.

Remind students that the answers to both number
sentences in each problem should be the same.

Error Intervention If students have trouble
finding the sums, review how to skip count.

If You Have More Time Have students work
in pairs and take turns naming something that comes
in packages of two to nine items. One partner writes
a number sentence for how much would be in three
packages, and the other partner does the same for
four packages.

③ Assessment

In this lesson, students wrote repeated addition as
multiplication. Use the **Quick Check** problem to
assess students' understanding.

Quick Check 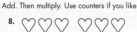 **Formative**
Assessment

Fill in the blank: $7 + 7 + 7 + 7 = \underline{\quad} \times 7.$ 4

Name _____

Arrays and Multiplication

Intervention
Lesson **G21**

Materials 16 counters per student

1. Show an array of 4 rows with 2 counters in each row.

2. Write a multiplication sentence for the array.

   <u> 4 </u> × <u> 2 </u> = <u> 8 </u>

   Number   Number of   Total
   of Rows   Counters in   Number of
      Each Row   Counters

3. How many counters are in the array? <u> 8 </u>

4. Show an array of 2 rows with 4 counters in each row.

5. Write a multiplication sentence for this array.

   <u> 2 </u> × <u> 4 </u> = <u> 8 </u>

   Number   Number of   Total
   of Rows   Counters in   Number of
      Each Row   Counters

6. How many counters are in this array? <u> 8 </u>

7. Both arrays have 8 counters.

   So, 4 × 2 = 2 × <u> 4 </u>.

8. Since both arrays have 8 counters then you can say,

   4 × 2 = 8, and 2 × 4 = <u> 8 </u>.

Knowing one multiplication fact means you know another.

9. If you know 3 × 8 = 24, then you know 8 × 3 = <u> 24 </u>

G21 (student p. 1)   MDIS 2.0

Name _____

Arrays and Multiplication (continued)

Intervention
Lesson **G21**

Write a multiplication sentence for each array.

10.
11.

     6 × 5 = 30   5 × 7 = 35

Draw an array to find each multiplication fact. Write the product.

12. 3 × 5 = <u> 15 </u>
    The array should show 3 rows of 5.

13. 2 × 6 = <u> 12 </u>
    The array should show 2 rows of 6.

Fill in the blanks.

14. 4 × 8 = 32, so 8 × 4 = <u> 32 </u>

15. 9 × 2 = 18, so <u> 2 </u> × 9 = 18

16. 5 × 7 = 35, so 7 × <u> 5 </u> = 35

17. 3 × 6 = 18, so <u> 6 </u> × 3 = 18

18. 2 × 4 = 8, so 4 × <u> 2 </u> = 8

19. 1 × 6 = 6, so 6 × 1 = <u> 6 </u>

20. **Reasoning** How does an array show equal groups?
    Each row has the same number of objects.

G21 (student p. 2)   MDIS 2.0

Intervention
Lesson **G21**

Objective Students will write multiplication sentences for arrays and use arrays to find products.

Vocabulary Array, multiplication sentence

Materials Counters, 16 per pair

① Conceptual Development
Use with Exercises 1–9.

In this lesson, you will use a model, called an array, to help you multiply.

Have students work in pairs. Distribute counters to students. *An array shows objects in equal rows.* Have students show an array of four rows with two counters in each row. *There are 4 rows of 2. What multiplication sentence does this array show?* 4 × 2 = 8 *So how many are in the array?* 8 Have students show an array of two rows with four counters in each row. *There are 2 rows of 4. What multiplication sentence does this array show?* 2 × 4 = 8 Have students complete Exercise 6. Then, work with students to complete Exercises 7–9.

② Practice Use with Exercises 10–20.

Remind students that when using an array to write a multiplication sentence, the number of rows is the first factor and the number in each row is the second factor.

Error Intervention
If students have trouble drawing the arrays in Exercises 12 and 13, have them read the multiplication facts as "3 rows of 5" instead of "3 times 5" and "2 rows of 6" instead of "2 times 6."

If You Have More Time
Have students work in pairs. One partner makes an array with counters and writes the multiplication sentence. The other partner makes an array for the corresponding fact, like 5 × 7 for 7 × 5, and writes the multiplication sentence for it.

③ Assessment

In this lesson, students wrote and used arrays to multiply. Use the **Quick Check** problem to assess students' understanding.

Quick Check **Formative Assessment**

What multiplication sentence does an array with 6 rows of 2 model? 6 × 2 = 12

Name _____

Intervention
Lesson **G22**

Using Multiplication to Compare

Materials 12 counters per student

Alicia has 2 stickers. Pedro has 3 times as many stickers as Alicia. How many stickers does Pedro have?

1. Show Alicia's stickers with counters. ◯ ◯

2. Show Pedro's stickers with counters. ◯ ◯ ◯ ◯ ◯ ◯

3. Write a multiplication sentence.

3	times	as many as Alicia has	equals	number Pedro has
↓	↓	↓	↓	↓
3	×	2	=	6

4. How many stickers does Pedro have? __6__

Mia has 4 yo-yos. Flo has twice as many as Mia. How many yo-yos does Flo have?

The word **twice** in a word problem means 2 times as many.

5. Show Mia's yo-yos with counters. ◯ ◯ ◯ ◯

6. Show Flo's yo-yos with counters. ◯ ◯ ◯ ◯ ◯ ◯ ◯ ◯

7. Write a multiplication sentence.

2	times	as many as Mia has	equals	number Flo has
↓	↓	↓	↓	↓
2	×	4	=	8

8. How many yo-yos does Flo have? __8__

G22 (student p. 1)   MDIS 2.0

Name _____

Intervention
Lesson **G22**

Using Multiplication to Compare (continued)

Solve. You may use drawings or counters to help.

9. Janos has 3 stickers. Lucy has twice as many stickers as Janos. How many stickers does Lucy have?
   _____ 6 stickers _____

10. Rob has 4 model airplanes. Julio has 3 times as many model airplanes as Rob. How many model airplanes does Julio have?
   _____ 12 model airplanes _____

11. Mr. King has 5 apples left in his store. Ruth needs twice as many apples to bake apple pies. How many apples does Ruth need?
   _____ 10 apples _____

Use the recipe to answer Exercises 12–15.

12. The recipe serves 5 people. Joan wants to make the recipe for 15 people. How many times more is this?
   _____ 3 times more _____

   Fruit Smoothie

   3 large bananas
   2 cups strawberries
   1 cup orange juice
   1 cup cranberry juice
   1 cup ice cubes

   Blend until smooth.
   Makes 5 servings.

13. How many bananas will Joan need to make the recipe for 15 people?
   _____ $3 \times 3 = 9$ bananas _____

14. How many cups of strawberries will Joan need to make the recipe for 15 people?
   _____ 6 cups _____

15. **Reasoning** If Joan wants to make twice as much as the recipe in the chart, what will she need to do to all of the ingredients?
   double them

G22 (student p. 2)   MDIS 2.0

Objective Students will use multiplication to compare amounts and solve problems.
Vocabulary Twice
Materials Counters, 12 per student

① Conceptual Development
Use with Exercises 1–8.

In this lesson, you will compare amounts and solve problems using multiplication.

Distribute counters to students and have a volunteer read the story problem at the top of the page. Have students use counters to show Alicia's stickers. Have students show Pedro's stickers. *If Pedro has three times as many, how many groups of two counters should you show?* 3 Have students do Exercises 3 and 4. Then, have another volunteer read the next story problem. *The word twice means "two times as many."* So, Flo has two times as many yo-yos as Mia. Have students show Mia's and Flo's yo-yos with counters and then do Exercises 7 and 8.

② Practice Use with Exercises 9–15.

Have students use counters to model the problems.

Error Intervention If students have trouble with Exercises 12–14, make sure they are referring to the right ingredient in the recipe to solve the problem.

If You Have More Time Have students work in pairs. Have one partner make up a story problem that involves twice as many of an object. The other partner writes a multiplication sentence to solve the problem.

③ Assessment

In this lesson, students found two and three times as many as a given number to solve problems. Use the **Quick Check** problem to assess students' understanding.

Quick Check **Formative** Assessment

Joe caught four fish. Mina caught twice as many fish as Joe. How many fish did Mina catch? 8

WRITING MULTIPLICATION STORIES

Name _____

Writing Multiplication Stories

Follow 1 to 5 below to write a multiplication story for 5 × 4 that is about hamburgers and pickle slices.

1. 5 × 4 means __5__ groups of __4__.

2. So, 5 × 4 might mean __5__ hamburgers with __4__ pickle slices each.

3. Write a story about 5 hamburgers with 4 pickle slices each.

   Mrs. __any last name__ went through a drive thru and

   bought __5__ hamburgers. Each hamburger had __4__

   pickle slices. How many __pickle slices__ were there in all?

4. Draw a picture to find how many   Drawing should
   pickle slices there were in all.   show 5 groups of 4.

   5 × 4 = __20__

5. How many pickle slices were there in all? __20__

6. Write a multiplication story for 6 × 3 about nests and eggs.

   Mr. __any last name__ found __6__ nests. Each nest had

   __3__ eggs. How many ____eggs____ did he find in all?

7. Draw a picture to find how many   Drawing should
   eggs he found in all.   show 6 groups of 3.

   6 × 3 = __18__

8. How many eggs did he find in all? __18__

G23 (student p. 1)   MDIS 2.0

Name _____

Writing Multiplication Stories (continued)

Write a multiplication story. Then find the product.

9.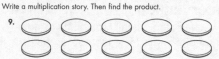

   2 × 5 = __10__

   Check students' stories.

Write a multiplication story for Exercises 10 and 11. Draw a picture to find each product.

10. 6 × 6 = __36__

    Check students' stories and pictures.

11. 4 × 5 = __20__

    Check students' stories and pictures.

12. There are 4 houses on Oak Street. Four people live in each house. How many people live on Oak Street?
    4 × 4 = 16 people

G23 (student p. 2)   MDIS 2.0

Objective Students will write math stories for given multiplication facts.
Vocabulary Multiplication

1 Conceptual Development
Use with Exercises 1–8.

In this lesson, you will write math stories for multiplication facts and draw pictures to solve them.

Have students work in pairs. *What does 5 × 4 mean?* 5 groups of 4. *With the hamburgers and pickle slices, what might 5 × 4 mean?* Sample answer: 5 hamburgers with 4 pickle slices each Have students complete the story in Exercise 3. Have students draw a picture to find the number of pickle slices there were. *How many pickle slices were there on the hamburgers?* 20 *When you write a multiplication story, how do you know what numbers to use in the story?* You use the factors in the multiplication fact. Have students read the last sentence in Exercise 3 again. *What should always be the last part of your story?* A question to be solved about how many in all Have students work with a partner to complete Exercises 6–8.

2 Practice Use with Exercises 9–12.

Have students work in pairs for these Exercises.

Error Intervention If students have trouble writing math stories, remind them that multiplication facts are usually about equal groups or arrays.

If You Have More Time Have students work in pairs. Give each pair two number cubes. Each partner rolls a number cube, and together they write a math story using the multiplication fact for the two numbers rolled.

3 Assessment

In this lesson, students wrote and solved math stories for given multiplication facts. Use the **Quick Check** problem to assess students' understanding.

Quick Check **Formative** Assessment

There are three birds' nests in a tree. Each nest has seven eggs in it. How many eggs in all? 21

Name _____

Intervention
Lesson **G24**

Multiplying by 2 and 5

1. Continue skip counting by 2s on the number line below.

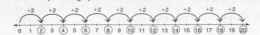

2. Each number that a hop lands on is a **multiple** of two. Circle each multiple of 2 on the number line. Then list them in the blanks below.

   2 4 6 8 10 12 14 16 18 20

3. To find 6×2, count by 2s until you have said 6 numbers.

   2, 4, __6__, __8__, 10, __12__,

   So, $6 \times 2 =$ __12__.

2s Facts

$0 \times 2 = 0$	$5 \times 2 =$ __10__
$1 \times 2 =$ __2__	$6 \times 2 = 12$
$2 \times 2 =$ __4__	$7 \times 2 =$ __14__
$3 \times 2 =$ __6__	$8 \times 2 =$ __16__
$4 \times 2 =$ __8__	$9 \times 2 =$ __18__

4. Repeat 3 above for each of the 2s facts in the table. Complete the table.

5. **Reasoning** What is the pattern in the products of the 2s facts?

   All of the multiples of 2 end in 0, 2, __4__, __6__, or __8__.

6. Continue skip counting by 5s on the number line below. Circle each multiple of 5 on the number line.

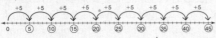

G24 (student p. 1) MDIS 2.0

Name _____

Intervention
Lesson **G24**

Multiplying by 2 and 5 (continued)

7. Circle each multiple of 5 on the number line. Then list them in the blanks below.

   5 10 15 20 25 30 35 40 45

8. To find 7×5, count by 5s until you have said 7 numbers.

   5, 10, 15, __20__, __25__,

   __30__, __35__

   So, $7 \times 5 =$ __35__.

5s Facts

$0 \times 5 = 0$	$5 \times 5 =$ __25__
$1 \times 5 =$ __5__	$6 \times 5 =$ __30__
$2 \times 5 =$ __10__	$7 \times 5 = 35$
$3 \times 5 =$ __15__	$8 \times 5 =$ __40__
$4 \times 5 =$ __20__	$9 \times 5 =$ __45__

9. Repeat 8 above for each of the 5s facts in the table.

10. **Reasoning** What is the pattern in the products of the 5s facts?

    All of the multiples of 5 end in __0__ or __5__.

Complete each multiplication problem.

11. $\begin{array}{r} 2 \\ \times 3 \\ \hline 6 \end{array}$
12. $\begin{array}{r} 2 \\ \times 6 \\ \hline 12 \end{array}$
13. $\begin{array}{r} 2 \\ \times 2 \\ \hline 4 \end{array}$
14. $\begin{array}{r} 2 \\ \times 1 \\ \hline 2 \end{array}$

15. $\begin{array}{r} 7 \\ \times 2 \\ \hline 14 \end{array}$
16. $\begin{array}{r} 7 \\ \times 5 \\ \hline 35 \end{array}$
17. $\begin{array}{r} 5 \\ \times 3 \\ \hline 15 \end{array}$
18. $\begin{array}{r} 8 \\ \times 5 \\ \hline 40 \end{array}$

19. $\begin{array}{r} 5 \\ \times 4 \\ \hline 20 \end{array}$
20. $\begin{array}{r} 1 \\ \times 5 \\ \hline 5 \end{array}$
21. $\begin{array}{r} 2 \\ \times 4 \\ \hline 8 \end{array}$
22. $\begin{array}{r} 5 \\ \times 2 \\ \hline 10 \end{array}$

23. **Reasoning** Movie tickets are on sale for $5 each. Ross, Emily, and John want to see the movie. Is $18 enough for all of their tickets? Explain.
    Yes; $3 \times 5 = 15$ and $\$15 < \$18$.

G24 (student p. 2) MDIS 2.0

Objective Students will use skip-counting patterns to multiply with 2 and 5 as factors.
Vocabulary Multiples, skip count

1 Conceptual Development
Use with Exercises 1–5.

In this lesson, you will learn how to use skip-counting patterns to complete multiplication tables.

Have students work in pairs. Have them skip count by 2s using the number line. *When you skip count by 2s, each number that you land on is a multiple of 2. A multiple is a product of a number and another whole number.* Have students circle the multiples of 2 on the number line and then list them in the blanks. *To find 6 times 2, start at 0 and count by 2s until you have said six numbers.* Have students count by 2s to 12. *What is 6 times 2?* 12 Have students count by 2s to find each multiple of 2 and complete the table in Exercise 4. Then, have students circle the ones digit for each product in the table and to complete Exercise 5.

2 Practice Use with Exercises 6–23.

Encourage students to use skip counting to answer the multiplication problems. Point out that if one of the factors is 2, they can also think about doubles.

Error Intervention If students have trouble knowing when to stop when skip counting, have them hold up one finger for each hop as they say the numbers.

If You Have More Time Ask a volunteer to explain why all multiples of 2 are even numbers. Have students count by 2s and list all the even numbers to 50.

3 Assessment

In this lesson, students used skip counting to multiply by 2 and 5. Use the **Quick Check** problem to assess students' understanding.

Quick Check 🌿 **Formative** Assessment

What is 9 times 2? 18 *What is 9 times 5?* 45

Multiplying by 9

Name _____

Intervention
Lesson **G25**

Learn how to multiply by 9 by answering 1 to 5.

1. Complete the table.

Fact	Product	Two Digits in the Product	Sum of the Two Digits in the Product
0 × 9 =	0	0 and 0	0 + 0 = 0
1 × 9 =	9	0 and 9	0 + 9 = 9
2 × 9 =	18	1 and 8	1 + 8 = 9
3 × 9 =	27	2 and 7	2 + 7 = 9
4 × 9 =	36	3 and 6	3 + 6 = 9
5 × 9 =	45	4 and 5	4 + 5 = 9
6 × 9 =	54	5 and 4	5 + 4 = 9
7 × 9 =	63	6 and 3	6 + 3 = 9
8 × 9 =	72	7 and 2	7 + 2 = 9
9 × 9 =	81	8 and 1	8 + 1 = 9

2. Reasoning Besides the product of 0 × 9, what pattern do you see in the sums of the digits of each product?
The sum of the digits is always 9.

3. Look at the number being multiplied by 9 in each product and the tens digit of that product.

When 3 is multiplied by 9, what is the tens digit of the product? __2__.

When 6 is multiplied by 9, what is the tens digit of the product? __5__.

G25 (student p. 1)   MDIS 2.0

Name _____

Intervention
Lesson **G25**

Multiplying by 9 (continued)

4. Reasoning Complete to describe the pattern you see in the tens digits of the products when a factor is multiplied by 9.

The tens digit of the product is __1__ less than the other factor.

5. Complete the following to find 7 × 9.

The tens digit is 7 − 1 = __6__.

The ones digit is 9 − 6 = __3__.

So, 7 × 9 = __63__ and 9 × 7 = __63__.

Find each product.

6.	1	7.	9	8.	9	9.	9
	× 9		× 2		× 4		× 0
	9		18		36		0

10.	6	11.	9	12.	8	13.	5
	× 9		× 9		× 9		× 9
	54		81		72		45

14.	9	15.	3	16.	2	17.	9
	× 7		× 9		× 9		× 6
	63		27		18		54

18. Reasoning Joshua and his sister have each saved $9. They wish to buy a new game that costs $20. If they put their savings together, do they have enough money to buy the game?
No, they only have $18; they are $2 short.

19. Reasoning Jane said that 7 × 9 = 62. Explain how you know this is incorrect.
The sum of the digits in the product does not equal 9.

G25 (student p. 2)   MDIS 2.0

Objective Students will use patterns to multiply with 9 as a factor.
Vocabulary Product, factor

❶ Conceptual Development
Use with Exercises 1–5.

In this lesson, you will use patterns to find the nines facts.

Have students examine the table in Exercise 1. Point out that all the products have been given. *Besides 0 times 9, what do you notice about the tens digit in each of the products, compared to the factors?* It is always one less than the factor that isn't 9. Work through the table together with students and then have them complete Exercises 2–4. Summarize the results. *When multiplying by 9, the tens digit in the product is always one less than the "other" factor being multiplied, and the sum of the digits of the product is always 9.* Have students complete Exercise 5.

❷ Practice Use with Exercises 6–19.

Encourage students to use the method presented in the lesson to find the products.

Error Intervention If students have trouble using the method described in the lesson, show them how to use their fingers to multiply by 9. Put both hands on your desk, palms down. Mentally number your fingers and thumbs from left to right, starting with 1. To find 3 × 9, bend down finger number 3. The number of fingers to the left of the bent finger shows the number in the tens place of the product, 2. The number of fingers to the right of the bent finger shows the number of ones in the product, 7. So, 3 × 9 = 27.

If You Have More Time Have pairs play *I'm Thinking of a Number*. One partner writes down a number from 0 to 9, such as 7, and says: I'm thinking of a number. When it is multiplied by 9, the product is 63. What is the number? The other partner says the number. Then, students change roles and repeat.

❸ Assessment

In this lesson, students used patterns to multiply by 9. Use the **Quick Check** problem to assess students' understanding.

Quick Check **Formative Assessment**

What is 4 times 9? 36 What is 7 times 9? 63

G25   MDIS 2.0

Student Page 1

Name _____

Intervention
Lesson **G26**

Multiplying by 1 or 0

Materials 9 counters and 9 half sheets of paper per student

Complete 1 to 6 to discover that when you multiply any number by 1, the product is the other number.

Use the paper to show groups and the counters to show the number in each.

1. Show 5 × 1.

2. How many counters in all? __5__   5 × 1 = __5__

3. Show 4 × 1.

4. How many counters in all? __4__   4 × 1 = __4__

1s Facts

5. Use the paper and counters to complete the table on the right.

6. **Reasoning** What pattern do you see in the table?
Sample answer: The product is the same as the number being multiplied by 1.

0 × 1 = 0	5 × 1 = 5
1 × 1 = _1_	6 × 1 = _6_
2 × 1 = _2_	7 × 1 = _7_
3 × 1 = _3_	8 × 1 = _8_
4 × 1 = 4	9 × 1 = _9_

Complete 7 to 12 to discover that when you multiply any number by 0, the product is 0.

7. Show 3 × 0. ☐ ☐ ☐

8. How many counters in all? __0__

9. Show 6 × 0. ☐ ☐ ☐ ☐ ☐ ☐

10. How many counters in all? __0__

Copyright © Pearson Education, Inc., or its affiliates. All Rights Reserved.   **G26** (student p. 1)   MDIS 2.0

Student Page 2

Name _____

Intervention
Lesson **G26**

Multiplying by 1 or 0 (continued)

0s Facts

11. Use the paper and counters to complete the table on the right.

12. **Reasoning** What pattern do you see in the table?
Sample answer: The product is always 0.

0 × 0 = 0	5 × 0 = _0_
1 × 0 = _0_	6 × 0 = 0
2 × 0 = _0_	7 × 0 = _0_
3 × 0 = 0	8 × 0 = _0_
4 × 0 = _0_	9 × 0 = _0_

Find each product.

13. 2 × 1 = _2_   14. 4 × 0 = _0_   15. 6 × 1 = _6_

16. 1 × 9 = _9_   17. 1 × 2 = _2_   18. 4 × 1 = _4_

19.	20.	21.	22.	23.
3	0	8	1	9
×0	×9	×1	×8	×1
0	0	8	8	9

24.	25.	26.	27.	28.
5	5	1	1	7
×1	×0	×1	×0	×1
5	0	1	0	7

29. **Reasoning** Explain why 1 × 0 = 0.
Possible Answer: Because when you multiply any number by zero, the answer is always zero. Also, when you multiply any number by one, the answer is always the other number.

Copyright © Pearson Education, Inc., or its affiliates. All Rights Reserved.   **G26** (student p. 2)   MDIS 2.0

Teacher Column

Objective Students will use patterns and properties to multiply with 0 and 1 as factors.
Vocabulary Identity Property of Multiplication, Zero Property of Multiplication
Materials Counters, half-sheets of paper

1 Conceptual Development
Use with Exercises 1–12.

In this lesson, you will learn patterns and properties that will help you multiply when 0 and 1 are factors.

Have students work in pairs. Distribute 9 counters and 9 sheets of paper to each pair. Have students do Exercises 1–6, modeling the groups with the paper and counters. *Look at the completed table. What do you notice happens when you multiply by 1?* The product is the same as the other factor. *The Identity Property of Multiplication says that when you multiply a number and 1, the product is that number.* Have students do Exercises 7–12 similarly. *What pattern do you see in the products for the zeros facts?* The product is always 0. *The Zero Property of Multiplication says that when you multiply a number and zero, the product is zero.*

2 Practice Use with Exercises 13–29.

Remind students that, if one of the factors is 0, the product is 0. If one of the factors is 1, the product is the other factor.

Error Intervention If students have trouble finding the products, have them write the Identity and Zero Properties of Multiplication in their notebooks and refer to them as they complete the exercises.

If You Have More Time Have students write multiplication stories for 5 × 1 and 5 × 0.

3 Assessment

In this lesson, students used patterns and properties to multiply with factors of 0 and 1. Use the **Quick Check** problem to assess students' understanding.

Quick Check **Formative Assessment**

What is 625 times 1? 625 *How do you know?* I know because any number times 1 is that number.

Name _____

Multiplying by 3

Materials 18 counters, 6 inch piece of yarn per student

Use 1s facts and 2s facts to multiply by 3.

1. Show a 3 × 6 array.

2. Place the piece of yarn between the first and second row of the array. Fill in the blanks.

$1 \times \underline{6} = \underline{6}$

$\underline{2} \times 6 = \underline{12}$

3. So, 3 × 6 = 6 + 12 = __18__

4. Use 1s and 2s facts to find 3 × 7 by doing the following.

$1 \times 7 = \underline{7}$

$2 \times 7 = \underline{14}$

So, $3 \times 7 = \underline{7} + \underline{14} = \underline{21}$

5. Use 1s and 2s facts to find 3 × 8 by doing the following.

$1 \times 8 = \underline{8}$

$2 \times 8 = \underline{16}$

So, $3 \times 8 = \underline{8} + \underline{16} = \underline{24}$

G27 (student p. 1)   MDIS 2.0

Name _____

Multiplying by 3 (continued)

Find each product.

6. $2 \times 3 = \underline{6}$

7. $1 \times 3 = \underline{3}$

8. $7 \times 3 = \underline{21}$

9. $3 \times 4 = \underline{12}$

10. $3 \times 6 = \underline{18}$

11. $3 \times 7 = \underline{21}$

12. $\begin{array}{r} 5 \\ \times 3 \\ \hline 15 \end{array}$

13. $\begin{array}{r} 8 \\ \times 3 \\ \hline 24 \end{array}$

14. $\begin{array}{r} 3 \\ \times 8 \\ \hline 24 \end{array}$

15. $\begin{array}{r} 3 \\ \times 6 \\ \hline 18 \end{array}$

16. $\begin{array}{r} 3 \\ \times 1 \\ \hline 3 \end{array}$

17. $\begin{array}{r} 3 \\ \times 2 \\ \hline 6 \end{array}$

18. $\begin{array}{r} 3 \\ \times 3 \\ \hline 9 \end{array}$

19. $\begin{array}{r} 4 \\ \times 3 \\ \hline 12 \end{array}$

20. $\begin{array}{r} 3 \\ \times 5 \\ \hline 15 \end{array}$

21. $\begin{array}{r} 9 \\ \times 3 \\ \hline 27 \end{array}$

22. The weatherman says the temperature is rising 3 degrees every hour. How much hotter is it after 2 hours have passed?   6 degrees

23. Mrs. Hernandez's class is raising money by selling boxes of cookies for $3 each. Alex sold 4 boxes to her mother and 2 more to her neighbor. How much money did Alex raise? $18

24. **Reasoning** If 3 × 6 can be solved by separating an array into a 1 × 6 and a 2 × 6 array, explain how 4 × 6 can be separated so that it can be solved with known facts? Then find 4 × 6.
Sample answer: It can be separated into two 2 × 6 arrays. 2 × 6 = 12 and 2 × 6 = 12; 12 + 12 = 24, so 4 × 6 = 24. Sample answer: It can be separated into a 1 × 6 array and a 3 × 6 array. 1 × 6 = 6 and 3 × 6 = 18; 6 + 18 = 24, so 4 × 6 = 24.

G27 (student p. 2)   MDIS 2.0

Objective Students will use known facts to find products with 3 as a factor.

Vocabulary Array, multiplication

Materials 6-inch pieces of yarn, counters

1 Conceptual Development
Use with Exercises 1–5.

In this lesson, you will use multiplication facts you already know to help find new facts.

Have students work in pairs. Distribute 18 counters and one piece of yarn to each pair. Have students show an array with three rows of six counters. Remind them that arrays show multiplication. *What multiplication fact does this array show?* 3 × 6 Have students place the piece of yarn between the first and second row of the array. *By breaking the array into two parts, you can use 1s facts and 2s facts to multiply by 3.* Have students complete Exercise 2. *So, 3 × 6 is the same as 6 + 12. What is 3 × 6 ?* 18 Do Exercises 4 and 5 similarly, using the counters and yarn to model each problem.

2 Practice Use with Exercises 6–24.

Allow students to use their counters and yarn to find each product if needed.

Error Intervention If students have trouble with Exercise 23, have them draw four rectangles and then two more rectangles to show the boxes of cookies. Have them label each rectangle $3 and then write a multiplication fact to solve the problem.

If You Have More Time Have students complete a threes fact multiplication table by skip counting on a number line to find the multiples of 3 to 30.

3 Assessment

In this lesson, students learned to multiply with 3 as a factor by breaking 3 into 1 and 2. Use the **Quick Check** problem to assess students' understanding.

Quick Check   **Formative Assessment**

What multiplication fact can be found using 1 × 4 plus 2 × 4? 3 × 4

Student Page 1

Name _____

Multiplying by 4

Intervention
Lesson **G28**

Materials 24 counters, 6 inch piece of yarn per student

Use 2s facts to multiply by 4.

1. Show a 4 × 6 array.

2. Place the piece of yarn between the second and third row of the array. Fill in the blanks.

   <u>2</u> × 6 = <u>12</u>

   2 × <u>6</u> = <u>12</u>

3. So, 4 × 6 is double the product of 2 × 6.

   2 × 6 = <u>12</u>

   Double the product: 12 + 12 = <u>24</u>   So, 4 × 6 = <u>24</u>

4. Use 2s facts to find 4 × 7 by doing the following.

   Find the product of 2 × 7.   2 × 7 = <u>14</u>

   Double the product: 14 + 14 = <u>28</u>   So, 4 × 7 = <u>28</u>

5. Use 2s facts to find 4 × 4 by doing the following.

   Find the product of 2 × 4.   2 × 4 = <u>8</u>

   Double the product: 8 + 8 = <u>16</u>   So, 4 × 4 = <u>16</u>

G28 (student p. 1)   MDIS 2.0

Student Page 2

Name _____

Multiplying by 4 (continued)

Intervention
Lesson **G28**

Find each product.

6. 8 × 4 = <u>32</u>   7. 3 × 4 = <u>12</u>   8. 1 × 4 = <u>4</u>

9. 4 × 4 = 16   10. 4 × 8 = 32   11. 9 × 4 = 36   12. 7 × 4 = 28   13. 6 × 4 = 24

14. 4 × 6 = 24   15. 4 × 1 = 4   16. 4 × 2 = 8   17. 4 × 5 = 20

18. 5 × 4 = 20   19. 4 × 7 = 28   20. 2 × 4 = 8   21. 4 × 3 = 12

22. **Reasoning** If 9 × 4 = 36, then 4 × <u>9</u> = 36.

23. Helen is planting a garden. She buys 3 trays of tomato plants. Each tray has 4 plants and costs $2. How many tomato plants did Helen buy?   <u>12 plants</u>

24. Jean reads 5 pages in a book before bedtime each night. Bedtime is at 9:00 P.M. How many pages does Jean read in 4 nights?   <u>20 pages</u>

25. How can you find 4 × 8 without using two 4 × 4 arrays? Sample answer: You could use a 1 × 8 and a 3 × 8 array.

G28 (student p. 2)   MDIS 2.0

Intervention Lesson G28

Objective Students will use known facts and doubles to find products with 4 as a factor.
Vocabulary Array, doubles
Materials 6-inch piece of yarn, 24 counters per pair

① Conceptual Development
Use with Exercises 1–5.

In this lesson, you will use doubles and multiplication facts you already know to multiply by 4.

Have students work in pairs. Distribute counters and yarn to students. Have them show an array with four rows of six counters. *What multiplication fact does this show?* 4 × 6 Have students place the piece of yarn between the second and third row of the array. *By breaking the array into two equal parts, you can use 2s facts and doubles to multiply by 4. What multiplication fact does the counters that are above the yarn show?* 2 × 6 = 12 *How about below the yarn?* 2 × 6 = 12 *So 4 × 6 is double the product of 2 × 6, or 12 + 12. What is 4 × 6?* 24 Do Exercises 4 and 5 similarly, using the counters and yarn to model each problem.

② Practice Use with Exercises 6–25.

Allow students to use their counters and yarn to find each product if needed.

Error Intervention If students have trouble with Exercises 23 and 24, encourage them to draw pictures to represent the problems and then use doubles and 2s facts to find the product.

If You Have More Time Have students complete a 4s fact multiplication table by skip counting on a number line to find the multiples of 4 to 40.

③ Assessment

In this lesson, students learned to multiply with 4 as a factor using doubles and 2s facts. Use the **Quick Check** problem to assess students' understanding.

Quick Check **Formative** Assessment

What multiplication fact can be found using 18 + 18? 4 × 9

Name _____

Intervention
Lesson **G29**

Multiplying by 6 or 7

Materials 56 counters, 6 inch piece of yarn per student or pair

Use 1s facts and 5s facts to multiply by 6.

1. A 6×7 array is 6 rows of __7__ .

2. Draw a line to separate the 6×7 array into 1 row of 7 and 5 rows of 7.

   $1 \times 7 =$ __7__ $5 \times 7 =$ __35__

   So, $6 \times 7 = 7 +$ __35__ $=$ __42__ .

Use 2s facts and 5s facts to multiply by 7.

3. A 7×8 array is 7 rows of __8__ .

4. Draw a line to separate the 7×8 array into 2 rows of 8 and 5 rows of 8.

   $2 \times 8 =$ __16__ $5 \times 8 =$ __40__

   So, $7 \times 8 = 16 +$ __40__ $=$ __56__ .

5. $6 \times 8 = 8 +$ __40__ $=$ __48__

6. $7 \times 7 = 14 +$ __35__ $=$ __49__

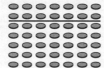

G29 (student p. 1)   MDIS 2.0

Name _____

Intervention
Lesson **G29**

Multiplying by 6 or 7 (continued)

Find each product.

7.   1
    $\times 7$
    ‾‾‾
    7

8.   6
    $\times 3$
    ‾‾‾
    18

9.   6
    $\times 8$
    ‾‾‾
    48

10.   9
    $\times 7$
    ‾‾‾
    63

11.   6
    $\times 9$
    ‾‾‾
    54

12.   7
    $\times 4$
    ‾‾‾
    28

13.   4
    $\times 6$
    ‾‾‾
    24

14.   3
    $\times 7$
    ‾‾‾
    21

15.   7
    $\times 7$
    ‾‾‾
    49

16.   2
    $\times 7$
    ‾‾‾
    14

17.   6
    $\times 6$
    ‾‾‾
    36

18.   6
    $\times 2$
    ‾‾‾
    12

19. $6 \times 1 =$ __6__   20. $7 \times 8 =$ __56__   21. $6 \times \$6 =$ __\$36__

22. **Reasoning** Complete the pattern. 6, 12, 18, __24__ , 30, __36__

23. Students in a classroom are in groups with 7 students in each group. There are 5 groups of students. How many students are there in the classroom?   __35 students__

24. A parking lot has 7 rows of parking spaces. There are six cars in each row. The charge to park in this lot is $2 each day. How many cars are in the parking lot?   __42 cars__

25. **Reasoning** How does knowing $3 \times 8 = 24$ help you find 6×8?
Sample answer: Two 3×8 arrays are the same as a 6×8 array, so you can double the product of 3×8 to find the product of 6×8.
$6 \times 8 = 24 + 24 = 48$

G29 (student p. 2)   MDIS 2.0

Objective Students will use known facts to multiply with 6 and 7 as factors.
Vocabulary Array, multiplication

① Conceptual Development
Use with Exercises 1–6.

In this lesson, you will learn how to use facts you know to find multiplication facts for 6 and 7.

Have students work in pairs. *Look at the array in Exercise 1. There are six rows of seven counters. What multiplication fact does this show?* 6×7 Have students draw a line between the first and second row of the array. *By breaking the array into these two parts, you can use 1s facts and 5s facts to multiply by 6. What multiplication fact does the top part of the array show?* 1×7 *What fact does the bottom part show?* 5×7 Have students complete Exercise 2. Do Exercises 3 and 4 using 2s and 5s facts. Have students complete Exercises 5 and 6.

② Practice Use with Exercises 7–25.

Encourage students to draw and break apart arrays to find each product if needed.

Error Intervention If students have trouble with the 6s facts, show them how to use doubles and 3s facts to multiply with 6 as a factor.

If You Have More Time Have groups of three students label three index cards with "6 or 7," "0 to 9," and "Product." Each student draws a card. The student who draws the "6 or 7" card says either 6 or 7. The student who draws the "0 to 9" card says a number from 0 to 9. The third student calculates the product of the numbers. Then students draw again.

③ Assessment

In this lesson, students learned to multiply with 6 and 7. Use the **Quick Check** problem to assess students' understanding.

Quick Check **Formative** Assessment

What is another way to find 7×8, besides 2×8 and 5×8? Sample answer: 3×8 and 4×8

Name _____

Intervention
Lesson **G30**

Multiplying by 8

Use 4s facts to multiply by 8.

1. An 8×7 array is __8__ rows of __7__ .

2. Draw a line to separate the 8×7 array into two arrays with 4 rows of 7.

3. Since the 8×7 array is the same thing as two 4×7 arrays, you can find the product of 4×7 and then double it.

   $4 \times 7 =$ __28__

   Double the product: 28
    +28
    56   So, $8 \times 7 =$ __56__

You can also use 3s facts and 5s facts to multiply by 8.

4. Draw a line to separate the 8×7 array into a 3×7 array and a 5×7.

   $3 \times 7 =$ __21__

   $5 \times 7 =$ __35__

5. Since the 8×7 array is the same thing as a 3×7 array plus a 5×7 array, add the products.

   $8 \times 7 = 21 +$ __35__

   $ = $ __56__   So, $8 \times 7 =$ __56__ .

6. **Reasoning** Explain two ways to find 8×6.

   $4 \times 6 = 24$ and $24 + 24 = 48$. So $8 \times 6 = 48$.
   $3 \times 6 = 18$, $5 \times 6 = 30$, and $18 + 30 = 48$.
   So $8 \times 6 = 48$.

G30 (student p. 1)   MDIS 2.0

Name _____

Intervention
Lesson **G30**

Multiplying by 8 (continued)

In Exercises 7–10, use 3s facts, 4s facts and 5s facts to fill in the blanks and find the product.

7. $8 \times 8 = 24 +$ __40__ $=$ __64__   8. $8 \times 8 = 32 +$ __32__ $=$ __64__

9. $8 \times 9 = 27 +$ __45__ $=$ __72__   10. $8 \times 9 = 36 +$ __36__ $=$ __72__

Find each product.

11. $8 \times 1 =$ __8__   12. $2 \times 8 =$ __16__   13. $6 \times 8 =$ __48__

14. $0 \times 8 =$ __0__   15. $8 \times 2 =$ __16__   16. $8 \times 4 =$ __32__

17. $\begin{array}{r} 1 \\ \times 8 \\ \hline 8 \end{array}$ 18. $\begin{array}{r} 8 \\ \times 3 \\ \hline 24 \end{array}$ 19. $\begin{array}{r} 8 \\ \times 6 \\ \hline 48 \end{array}$ 20. $\begin{array}{r} 9 \\ \times 8 \\ \hline 72 \end{array}$

21. $\begin{array}{r} 7 \\ \times 8 \\ \hline 56 \end{array}$ 22. $\begin{array}{r} 8 \\ \times 5 \\ \hline 40 \end{array}$ 23. $\begin{array}{r} 8 \\ \times 8 \\ \hline 64 \end{array}$ 24. $\begin{array}{r} 4 \\ \times 8 \\ \hline 32 \end{array}$

25. There are 8 ounces in each cup of water. A recipe calls for 3 cups of water. How many ounces of water are needed for the recipe?   __24 ounces__

26. Each chapter in a book has 8 pages and 3 pictures. There are 6 chapters in the book. How many pages are there in the book?   __48 pages__

27. **Reasoning** If $9 \times 8 = 72$, then $8 \times 9 =$ __72__ .

28. **Reasoning** Find 8×5. Tell how you found it.
    $8 \times 5 = 40$. Strategies will vary.

G30 (student p. 2)   MDIS 2.0

Objective Students will use known facts and doubles to find products with 8 as a factor.
Vocabulary Array, multiplication, doubles

❶ Conceptual Development
Use with Exercises 1–6.

In this lesson, you will use multiplication facts you already know and doubles to multiply by 8.

Have students work in groups. *Look at the array in Exercise 1. Fill in the number of rows and columns. What multiplication fact does this show?* 8×7 Have students draw a line to separate the array into two arrays with four rows of seven. *By breaking the array into two equal parts, you can use 4s facts and doubles to multiply by 8. What multiplication fact does each part of the array show?* $4 \times 7 = 28$ Have students complete Exercise 3. *So, what is 8×7?* 56 Do Exercises 4 and 5 similarly using 3s and 5s facts. Then have students do Exercise 6.

❷ Practice Use with Exercises 7–28.

Encourage students to use 4s facts and doubles to find each product and then check their answers by finding each product again using 3s facts and 5s facts.

Error Intervention If students cannot remember the 4s facts, remind them that they can use 2s facts and doubles to find the 4s facts.

If You Have More Time Have students work in pairs. Each pair numbers a cube 0 through 5 and another cube 0, 1, 2, 3, 3, and 4. One partner rolls both number cubes and then finds the sum. The other partner multiplies that sum by 8. Have students take turns rolling and computing.

❸ Assessment

In this lesson, students learned to multiply by 8. Use the **Quick Check** problem to assess students' understanding.

Quick Check **Formative** Assessment

What are four different ways you can find 8×8?
1×8, 7×8; 2×8, 6×8; 3×8, 5×8; 4×8, 4×8

Name _____

Intervention
Lesson **G31**

Multiplying by 10

Answer 1 to 5 to learn how to multiply by 10.

1. Continue skip counting by 10s on the number line below.

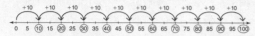

+10 +10 +10 +10 +10 +10 +10 +10 +10 +10

0 5 (10) 15 (20) 25 (30) 35 (40) 45 (50) 55 (60) 65 (70) 75 (80) 85 (90) 95 (100)

2. Each number a hop lands on is a **multiple** of ten. Circle each multiple of 10 on the number line. Then list them in the blanks below.

_10_ _20_ _30_ _40_ _50_ _60_ _70_ _80_ _90_ _100_

3. To find 6×10, count by 10s until you have said 6 numbers.

10, 20, _30_, _40_,

_50_, _60_

So, $6 \times 10 =$ _60_

4. Do this for each of the 10s facts. Complete the table.

5. **Reasoning** Complete to describe the patterns in the products of the 10s facts.

10s Facts	
$0 \times 10 = 0$	$6 \times 10 =$ _60_
$1 \times 10 =$ _10_	$7 \times 10 =$ _70_
$2 \times 10 =$ _20_	$8 \times 10 =$ _80_
$3 \times 10 =$ _30_	$9 \times 10 =$ _90_
$4 \times 10 =$ _40_	$10 \times 10 =$ _100_
$5 \times 10 =$ _50_	

All the multiplies of 10 end in what number? _0_

So, when you multiply a number by 10, you just write the number and a _0_.

6. **Reasoning** What is 10×7? Explain how you know.
$10 \times 7 = 7 \times 10$ and $7 \times 10 = 70$. So, $10 \times 7 = 70$.

G31 (student p. 1)   MDIS 2.0

Name _____

Intervention
Lesson **G31**

Multiplying by 10 (continued)

Find each product.

7. $2 \times 10 =$ _20_   **8.** $4 \times 10 =$ _40_   **9.** $6 \times 10 =$ _60_

10. $10 \times 6 =$ _60_   **11.** $10 \times 2 =$ _20_   **12.** $10 \times 5 =$ _50_

13.	14.	15.	16.	17.
3	10	8	10	9
× 10	× 9	× 10	× 8	× 10
30	90	80	80	90

18.	19.	20.	21.	22.
5	10	10	1	7
× 10	× 3	× 1	× 10	× 10
50	30	10	10	70

23. There are 8 markers in one box. How many markers are in 10 boxes?   _80 markers_

24. **Reasoning** Complete the pattern. 10, 20, _30_, _40_, 50, _60_, 70

25. **Reasoning** Seven friends get together to play a marble game. Sixty marbles are needed to play this game. Each friend brings ten marbles. Are there enough marbles to play the game?
Yes, they have 70 marbles and only 60 are needed.

26. **Reasoning** Jake said that 10×4 is 100. Is Jake correct? Explain.
No. 4×10 is 40.

G31 (student p. 2)   MDIS 2.0

Objective Students will use patterns to multiply with 10 as a factor.
Vocabulary Multiples, product, factor

1 Conceptual Development
Use with Exercises 1–6.

In this lesson, you will learn to multiply by 10.

Have students work individually and use the number line to skip count by tens to 100. Remind them that the numbers they land on are multiples of 10. Have them circle the multiples of 10. *What do you notice about each of the multiples of 10?* They all have a 0 in the ones place. Have students examine the table in Exercise 3. *All the products in the table should end in what number?* 0 To find 6×10, count by tens until you have said six numbers. Have students complete Exercises 3–6. Summarize the pattern for students. *When you multiply by 10, the number in the ones place should be 0, and the number in the tens place should match the factor you are multiplying by 10.*

2 Practice Use with Exercises 7–26.

Encourage students to refer to the table of tens facts to remind them of the pattern.

Error Intervention If students have trouble knowing when to stop when skip counting, have them hold up one finger for each hop as they say the numbers.

If You Have More Time Have students explain why counting the value of six dimes is the same as multiplying 6×10.

3 Assessment

In this lesson, students learned to multiply by 10. Use the **Quick Check** problem to assess students' understanding.

Quick Check **Formative** Assessment

How do you know that $10 \times 4 \neq 45$? I know the product is not 45, because when one of the factors is 10, the ones digit of the product must be 0.

MULTIPLYING THREE NUMBERS

Name _____

Intervention
Lesson **G32**

Multiplying Three Numbers

Does it matter how you multiply $5 \times 2 \times 3$? Answer 1–8 to find out.

To show the factors you are multiplying first, use parentheses as grouping symbols.

1. Group the first two factors together.   (_5_ × _2_) × 3

2. Multiply what is in the parentheses first. $5 \times 2 =$ _10_

3. Then, multiply the product of what is in parentheses by the third factor. $10 \times 3 =$ _30_

4. So, $(5 \times 2) \times 3 =$ _30_ .

5. Start again and group the last two factors together.   5 × (_2_ × _3_)

6. Multiply what is in the parentheses first. $2 \times 3 =$ _6_

7. Then, multiply 5 by the product of what is in parentheses. $5 \times 6 =$ _30_

8. So, $5 \times (2 \times 3) =$ _30_ .

It does not matter how the factors are grouped; the product will be the same.

9. $5 \times (2 \times 3) = (5 \times$ _2_ $) \times 3$

Find $3 \times 2 \times 4$ two different ways.

10. Do the 3×2 first.

   $3 \times 2 =$ _6_ $6 \times 4 =$ _24_   So, $(3 \times 2) \times 4 =$ _24_ .

11. Do the 2×4 first.

   $2 \times 4 =$ _8_ $3 \times 8 =$ _24_   So, $3 \times (2 \times 4) =$ _24_ .

G32 (student p. 1)   MDIS 2.0

Name _____

Intervention
Lesson **G32**

Multiplying Three Numbers (continued)

Find each product two different ways.

12. $(1 \times 3) \times 6 =$ _18_

   $1 \times (3 \times 6) =$ _18_

13. $(5 \times 2) \times 4 =$ _40_

   $5 \times (2 \times 4) =$ _40_

14. $(2 \times 4) \times 1 =$ _8_

   $2 \times (4 \times 1) =$ _8_

15. $(2 \times 2) \times 5 =$ _20_

   $2 \times (2 \times 5) =$ _20_

Find each product.

16. $2 \times 4 \times 3 =$ _24_   17. $7 \times 1 \times 3 =$ _21_   18. $3 \times 3 \times 2 =$ _18_

19. $3 \times 2 \times 6 =$ _36_   20. $(4 \times 2) \times 2 =$ _16_   21. $3 \times (0 \times 7) =$ _0_

22. $1 \times 7 \times 9 =$ _63_   23. $8 \times (2 \times 3) =$ _48_   24. $(2 \times 5) \times 6 =$ _60_

25. $9 \times 0 \times 3 =$ _0_   26. $4 \times 5 \times 1 =$ _20_   27. $(3 \times 6) \times 1 =$ _18_

28. **Reasoning** When multiplying three numbers, if one of the factors is zero, what will the answer be?   _Zero_

29. A classroom of students is getting ready to take a test. There are 5 rows of desks in the room and 4 students are in each row. Each student is required to have 2 pencils. How many pencils are needed?   _40 pencils_

G32 (student p. 2)   MDIS 2.0

Objective Students will multiply three numbers and use the Associative Property of Multiplication.

Vocabulary Associative Property of Multiplication

① Conceptual Development
Use with Exercises 1–9

In this lesson, you will use the Associative Property of Multiplication to multiply three numbers.

Have students work in small groups. *Let's multiply $5 \times 2 \times 3$. Put parentheses around the first two numbers. Multiply the numbers in the parentheses first.* Have students complete Exercises 1 and 2. *What is the answer when you multiply the product of the parentheses by the last factor?* 30 Have students complete Exercises 3 and 4. *Let's check our answer by multiplying in a different order. This time, group the last two factors by putting parentheses around them.* Have students complete Exercises 5–8. *Is the answer the same?* Yes *The Associative Property of Multiplication says that you can change the grouping of the factors and the product will be the same.* Have students complete Exercise 9.

② Practice Use with Exercises 10–29.

For Exercises 16–27, when there are no parentheses, encourage students to put them around the two numbers they plan to multiply first.

Error Intervention If students consistently find products that are too large, check that they understand that each factor is used only once.

If You Have More Time Have students work in pairs. Give each pair three number cubes. One partner rolls the number cubes and finds the product of the three numbers by grouping the first two factors. The other partner checks their answer by grouping the last two factors to find the product.

③ Assessment

In this lesson, students used the Associative Property to multiply three numbers. Use the **Quick Check** problem to assess students' understanding.

Quick Check  **Formative** Assessment

What are two ways to find $3 \times 4 \times 5$? $(3 \times 4) \times 5$ and $3 \times (4 \times 5)$

MEANINGS FOR DIVISION

Name _____

Meanings for Division

Materials 15 counters and 3 half sheets of paper, per pair

Martina has 15 dolls. She put them into 3 equal groups. Answer 1 to 3 to find how many dolls were in each group.

1. Count out 15 counters. Place the counters on the sheets of paper to form 3 equal groups.

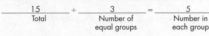

2. Write a number sentence to show division as sharing.

   $\underset{\text{Total}}{\underline{\quad 15 \quad}}$ ÷ $\underset{\substack{\text{Number of} \\ \text{equal groups}}}{\underline{\quad 3 \quad}}$ = $\underset{\substack{\text{Number in} \\ \text{each group}}}{\underline{\quad 5 \quad}}$

3. How many dolls were in each group?   5

Mrs. Gentry had only 6 tokens. As the students left her room, she gave each student 2 tokens. Answer 4 to 6 to find how many students got tokens.

4. Show 6 tokens.

5. Find the number of times 2 can be subtracted from 6 until nothing is left.

   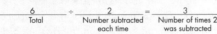

   $6 - 2 = 4$ 1 time
   $4 - 2 = 2$ 2 times
   $2 - 2 = 0$ 3 times

6. Write a number sentence to show division as repeated subtraction.

   $\underset{\text{Total}}{\underline{\quad 6 \quad}}$ ÷ $\underset{\substack{\text{Number subtracted} \\ \text{each time}}}{\underline{\quad 2 \quad}}$ = $\underset{\substack{\text{Number of times 2} \\ \text{was subtracted}}}{\underline{\quad 3 \quad}}$

7. How many students got tokens? ___3___

G33 (student p. 1)   MDIS 2.0

Name _____

Meanings for Division (continued)

Draw pictures to solve each problem. Check students' drawings.

8. Put 20 counters into 5 equal groups. How many counters are in each group?

   _____ 4 counters _____

9. Put 12 counters in a row. How many times can you subtract 4 counters?

   _____ 3 times _____

10. You put 24 cards into 4 equal piles. How many cards are in each pile?

    _____ 6 cards _____

11. You put 21 chairs into rows of 7. How many rows do you make?

    _____ 3 rows _____

12. You have 30 oranges. If you need 6 oranges to fill a bag, how many bags can you fill?

    _____ 5 bags _____

13. You put 10 marbles into equal groups of 5. How many groups are there?

    _____ 2 groups _____

14. Eight people went to the museum in two cars. The same number of people went in each car. How many people went in each car?

    _____ 4 people _____

15. **Reasoning** How can you use repeated subtraction to find 30 ÷ 5?

    Subtract 5 repeatedly from 30 until reaching zero, and then count the number of times 5 was subtracted, which is 6.

G33 (student p. 2)   MDIS 2.0

Objective Students will use models and write number sentences to solve division problems involving sharing.

Vocabulary Division, repeated subtraction

Materials Counters, half-sheets of paper

① Conceptual Development
Use with Exercises 1–7.

In this lesson, you will learn that when you want to share equally, you divide.

Have students work in pairs. Give students 15 counters and 3 half-sheets of paper. *Each half-sheet of paper represents a group.* Have a volunteer read the story problem at the top of the page. Have students place one counter at a time on each piece of paper until they run out. *How many counters are in each group? 5 So, 15 divided into 3 equal groups is 5. Division can be used to find how many equal groups or how many are in each group.* Have students complete Exercises 2 and 3. *You can also divide using repeated subtraction. For example, to find 6 ÷ 2, find the number of times you can subtract 2 from 6 until nothing is left.* Have students use counters to model and complete Exercises 4–7.

② Practice Use with Exercises 8–15.

Encourage students to use their counters or draw pictures to show groups. Remind them that each group should have an equal number of objects.

Error Intervention If students have trouble dividing by making groups, remind them that they can also use repeated subtraction.

If You Have More Time Have students explain which type of division they like best, division as sharing or division as repeated subtraction.

③ Assessment

In this lesson, students solved sharing problems using division. Use the **Quick Check** problem to assess students' understanding.

Quick Check **Formative Assessment**

You have 14 erasers. How can you share them equally between 7 friends? Each friend would get two erasers.

WRITING DIVISION STORIES

Name _____

Writing Division Stories

Materials counters, 18 per student or pair of students·

To write a division story for 18 ÷ 3 that is about 18 grapes and 3 sisters, fill in the blanks below.

1. Mrs. ___any last name___ put ___18___ grapes into

   a bowl. Mrs. ___any last name___'s daughters,

   ___any girl's name___, ___any girl's name___, and

   ___any girl's name___ shared the grapes equally. How

   many ___grapes___ did each sister get?

2. Use counters to show how many grapes there were in all.

3. Divide the 18 counters into 3 equal groups.

4. How many grapes did each sister get?   ___6___ grapes

5. Write a division story for 10 ÷ 5 about apples and bags.

   Mr. ___any last name___ bought ___10___ apples. He

   put ___5___ apples into each bag. How many ___bags___

   did he use?

6. Use counters to show how many apples he bought.

7. Divide the 10 counters into groups with 5 in each group.

8. How many bags did he use?   ___2___ bags

G34 (student p. 1)   MDIS 2.0

Name _____

Writing Division Stories (continued)

Write a division story for each number sentence below. Use the pictures to help. Then use counters or draw a picture to solve.

9. 15 ÷ 5 = ___3___

Check students' stories.

10. 12 ÷ 3 = ___4___

Write a division story. Then use counters or draw a picture to solve.

11. 14 ÷ 2 = ___7___   Check students' stories.

G34 (student p. 2)   MDIS 2.0

Objective Students will write and solve number stories involving division.

Vocabulary Division

Materials Counters, 18 per pair of students

❶ Conceptual Development
Use with Exercises 1–8.

In this lesson, you will learn to write and solve division stories.

Have students work in pairs and give each pair 18 counters. *To write a division story, you have to decide which number is being divided, and into how many groups.* Write 18 ÷ 3 on the board. *If we want to share 18 grapes equally among 3 people, which number is being divided?* 18 *How many groups are we going to make?* 3 Have students work together to do Exercise 1. *Use your counters to show how many grapes in all. Divide the counters into 3 groups that have the same number. How many grapes did each sister get?* 6 Have students complete Exercises 5–8.

❷ Practice Use with Exercises 9–11.

Allow students to work in pairs to complete the exercises.

Error Intervention If students have trouble writing a story problem for Exercise 11, have them draw a picture first, then write the story.

If You Have More Time Have students work in groups of three. Have each group number a cube 1, 2, 2, 2, 3, 3, and another cube 6, 6, 12, 12, 18, 18. Student A rolls the number cubes and writes a division problem using the two numbers. For example, if the numbers rolled are 3 and 12, Student A writes 12 ÷ 3. Student B tells a division story to match. Student C solves the division problem and finishes the story. Then students switch roles and repeat as time allows.

❸ Assessment

In this lesson, students wrote and solved story problems involving division. Use the **Quick Check** problem to assess students' understanding.

Quick Check **Formative Assessment**

Write and solve a division story for 16 ÷ 8. Check students' stories and solutions.

G34   MDIS 2.0

Name _____

Relating Multiplication and Division

Materials 36 color tiles per pair

1. Partner A show an array for 2×9, or 2 rows of 9.

2. Partner B show $18 \div 2$, by showing a total of 18 tiles in 2 rows.

3. What do you notice about the arrays each partner made?
They are exactly the same.

4. Partner A's tiles show:
$2 \times 9 = \underline{18}$

5. Partner B's tiles show:
$18 \div 2 = \underline{9}$

6. What do you notice about the numbers used in each number sentence?
Sample answer: They use the same numbers, but in a different order.

Multiplication and division are related to each other.
A **fact family** shows how they are related.

A fact family has two multiplication and two division number sentences written with the same 3 numbers.

Fact family for 2, 9, and 18

$2 \times 9 = 18$	$18 \div 2 = 9$
$9 \times 2 = 18$	$18 \div 9 = 2$

You can use multiplication to help you divide.

Find $30 \div 6$.

7. To find $30 \div 6$, think about the related multiplication problem.

6 times what number equals 30? $6 \times \underline{5} = 30$

8. Since you know $6 \times 5 = 30$, then you know $30 \div 6 = \underline{5}$.

G35 (student p. 1)   MDIS 2.0

Name _____

Relating Multiplication and Division (continued)

Use the array to complete each sentence.

9.

$4 \times \underline{5} = 20$

$20 \div 4 = \underline{5}$

10.

$3 \times \underline{6} = 18$

$18 \div 3 = \underline{6}$

11.

$3 \times \underline{3} = 9$

$9 \div 3 = \underline{3}$

12.

$6 \times \underline{2} = 12$

$12 \div 6 = \underline{2}$

Write a fact family for each product.

13. $3 \times 7 = 21$
$\underline{7 \times 3 = 21}$
$\underline{21 \div 3 = 7}$
$\underline{21 \div 7 = 3}$

14. $2 \times 4 = 8$
$\underline{4 \times 2 = 8}$
$\underline{8 \div 2 = 4}$
$\underline{8 \div 4 = 2}$

15. $3 \times 5 = 15$
$\underline{5 \times 3 = 15}$
$\underline{15 \div 3 = 5}$
$\underline{15 \div 5 = 3}$

16. **Reasoning** Why does the fact family for $3 \times 3 = 9$ only have 2 facts?
Sample answer: Because the factors are the same number. Both multiplication sentences are $3 \times 3 = 9$, and both division sentences are $9 \div 3 = 3$.

G35 (student p. 2)   MDIS 2.0

Objective Students will use arrays to write related multiplication and division facts.
Vocabulary Fact family
Materials Color tiles, 36 per pair of students

1 Conceptual Development
Use with Exercises 1–8.

In this lesson, you will use arrays to write fact families for multiplication and division facts.

Have students work in pairs and give each pair 36 color tiles. Have one partner show an array for 2×9 by making 2 rows of 9 tiles. The other partner should model $18 \div 2$ by showing a total of 18 tiles in 2 rows. *What do you notice about your arrays?* They are exactly the same. *What is 2×9?* 18 *What is $18 \div 2$?* 9 *What do you notice about these equations?* They use the same three numbers. *Multiplication and division are related to each other. A fact family shows how they are related. This means you can use multiplication to help you divide.* Have students complete Exercises 7 and 8.

2 Practice Use with Exercises 9–16.

Remind students that the equations in each exercise should use the same three numbers.

Error Intervention If students have trouble completing the multiplication and division sentences in Exercises 13–15, have them make or draw an array.

If You Have More Time Have students work in pairs. Give each pair 24 counters. Have them make an array and write the fact family for the array. Then, have them make a different array and write the fact family.

3 Assessment

In this lesson, students wrote related multiplication and division facts. Use the **Quick Check** problem to assess students' understanding.

Quick Check   Formative Assessment

What multiplication facts belong to the fact family for $10 \div 5 = 2$? $5 \times 2 = 10$ and $2 \times 5 = 10$

DIVIDING BY 2 THROUGH 5

Name _____

Dividing by 2 Through 5

Materials Have counters available for students to use.

You can use multiplication facts to help you divide.

Anna Maria has 24 leaves in her collection. She puts 4 leaves on each page in her scrap book. How many pages does she need for all her leaves?

Find 24 ÷ 4.

1. To find 24 ÷ 4, think about the related multiplication problem.

   4 times what number equals 24? $4 \times \underline{6} = 24$

2. Since you know $4 \times 6 = 24$, then you know $24 \div 4 = \underline{6}$.

3. How many pages does Anna Maria need for all her leaves? __6__

Find 45 ÷ 5.

4. 5 times what number equals 45? $5 \times \underline{9} = 45$

5. Since you know $5 \times 9 = 45$, then you know $45 \div 5 = \underline{9}$.

A division problem can be written two different ways.

   $30 \div 5 = 6$ $5\overline{)30}$ (with 6 above)

Both problems are read "30 divided by 5 equals 6."

6. Think: $3 \times \underline{5} = 15$ So, $3\overline{)15} = \underline{5}$.

7. Think: $4 \times \underline{4} = 16$ So $16 \div 4 = \underline{4}$.

8. Think: $2 \times \underline{9} = 18$ So $18 \div 2 = \underline{9}$.

G36 (student p. 1)   MDIS 2.0

Name _____

Dividing by 2 Through 5 (continued)

Use the multiplication fact to find each quotient.

9. $4 \times \underline{6} = 24$ 10. $6 \times \underline{5} = 30$ 11. $2 \times \underline{6} = 12$

   $24 \div 4 = \underline{6}$ $30 \div 6 = \underline{5}$ $12 \div 2 = \underline{6}$

12. $5 \times \underline{5} = 25$ 13. $3 \times \underline{9} = 27$ 14. $4 \times \underline{7} = 28$

   $25 \div 5 = \underline{5}$ $27 \div 3 = \underline{9}$ $28 \div 4 = \underline{7}$

Find each quotient.

15. $25 \div 5 = \underline{5}$ 16. $20 \div 4 = \underline{5}$ 17. $12 \div 3 = \underline{4}$

18. $5\overline{)35}$ (with 7)   19. $4\overline{)36}$ (with 9)   20. $3\overline{)21}$ (with 7)

21. Mario has 15 eggs. He wants to share them equally with 3 friends. How many eggs will each friend get?

   Think: $3 \times 5 = 15$. So, $15 \div 3 = 15 \div 3 = \underline{5}$ eggs.

22. Todd has 40 whistles. He wants to divide them evenly between his 5 friends. How many whistles will each friend get?   ___8 whistles___

23. **Reasoning** What multiplication fact can you use to find 27 ÷ 3? Explain how to find 27 ÷ 3.
   $3 \times 9 = 27$, so $27 \div 3 = 9$

24. If $4 \times 10 = 40$, then what is 40 ÷ 4? __10__

G36 (student p. 2)   MDIS 2.0

Objective Students will divide by 2, 3, 4, and 5.
Vocabulary Division
Materials Counters

① Conceptual Development
Use with Exercises 1–8.

In this lesson, you will use multiplication facts you already know to solve division problems, and you will learn a new symbol for division.

Have students work in small groups. Invite a volunteer to read the story problem at the top of the page. *To find 24 ÷ 4, think about a related multiplication fact. Four times what number equals 24?* 6 Have students complete Exercises 2 and 3. Do Exercise 4 and 5 similarly for 45 ÷ 5. *A division problem can be written in two ways.* Write $30 \div 5 = 6$ and $5\overline{)30}$ on the board. *Both problems are read "30 divided by 5 equals 6."* Have students complete Exercises 6–8.

② Practice Use with Exercises 9–24.

Remind students to think of a related multiplication fact to solve each division problem.

Error Intervention If students have trouble dividing using the vertical division notation, have them rewrite the problem using the ÷ symbol.

If You Have More Time Have students work in pairs. One partner writes a multiplication fact, and the other partner writes two related division facts using the vertical division notation. Then students switch roles and repeat as time allows.

③ Assessment

In this lesson, students used multiplication facts to divide by 2, 3, 4, and 5. Use the **Quick Check** problem to assess students' understanding.

Quick Check 🌸 **Formative Assessment**

What multiplication fact can help you find 18 ÷ 3? $3 \times 6 = 18$ *What is 18 ÷ 3?* 6

Name _____

Intervention
Lesson **G37**

Dividing by 6 and 7

Materials Have counters available for students to use.

You can use multiplication facts to help you divide.

Ahmed has 24 bugs to put on 6 boards. He wants the same number of bugs on each board. How many bugs should he put on each board?

Find 24 ÷ 6.

1. To find 24 ÷ 6, think about the related multiplication problem.

   6 times what number equals 24?   6 × __4__ = 24

2. Since you know 6 × 4 = 24, then you know 24 ÷ 6 = __4__.

3. How many bugs should Ahmed put on each board? __4__

Find 21 ÷ 7.

4. To find 21 ÷ 7, think about the related multiplication problem.

   7 times what number equals 21?   7 × __3__ = 21

5. Since you know 7 × 3 = 21, then you know 21 ÷ 7 = __3__.

6. Think: 6 × __5__ = 30   So, 6)30 = __5__.

7. Think: 7 × __7__ = 49   So 49 ÷ 7 = __7__.

8. Think: 6 × __8__ = 48   So 48 ÷ 6 = __8__.

9. **Reasoning** Explain how to find 63 ÷ 7.
   Think: 7 times what number equals 63. Since
   7 × 9 = 63, 63 ÷ 7 = 9.

G37 (student p. 1)   MDIS 2.0

Name _____

Intervention
Lesson **G37**

Dividing by 6 and 7 (continued)

Use the multiplication fact to find each quotient.

10. 6 × 5 = 30   11. 7 × 2 = 14   12. 6 × 1 = 6

    30 ÷ 6 = __5__   14 ÷ 7 = __2__   6 ÷ 6 = __1__

13. 7 × 5 = 35   14. 6 × __6__ = 36   15. 7 × __8__ = 56

    35 ÷ 7 = __5__   36 ÷ 6 = __6__   56 ÷ 7 = __8__

16. 6 × __4__ = 24   17. 6 × 9 = 54   18. 6 × 7 = 42

    24 ÷ 6 = __4__   54 ÷ 6 = __9__   42 ÷ 6 = __7__

Find each quotient.

19. 6)54 = 9   20. 7)42 = 6   21. 6)30 = 5

22. 7)7 = 1   23. 6)42 = 7   24. 7)70 = 10

25. 6)12 = 2   26. 7)14 = 2   27. 6)60 = 10

28. Mrs. Carpenter's class is dividing into groups
    for group work. There are 28 students in the
    class and 35 desks. How many students will
    be in each group if there are 7 groups?   __4 students__

29. **Reasoning** If you know that 6 × 12 = 72,
    then what is 72 ÷ 6.   __12__

G37 (student p. 2)   MDIS 2.0

Objective Students will divide by 6 and 7.
Vocabulary Division
Materials Counters

❶ Conceptual Development
Use with Exercises 1–9.

In this lesson, you will use multiplication facts you already know to divide by 6 and 7.

Have students work in pairs. Distribute counters for students to use if they need them. Invite a volunteer to read the division story problem at the top of the page to the class. *To find 24 ÷ 6, think about the related multiplication problem. 6 times what number equals 24?* 4 Have students do Exercises 1–3. *To find 21 ÷ 7, what multiplication problem should you think about?* 7 times what number equals 21? Have students do Exercises 4–8. For Exercise 9, invite a volunteer to tell how they would find 63 ÷ 7. Then, have students write the volunteer's answer in their own words.

❷ Practice Use with Exercises 10–29.

Allow students to use counters if needed. Remind them that they can make arrays to find related multiplication facts that will help them solve the division problems.

Error Intervention If students have trouble with Exercises 19–27, have them rewrite each problem using the ÷ symbol.

If You Have More Time Have students work in pairs. One partner writes a division story problem. The other partner solves the division problem and then writes a related multiplication story problem using numbers in the same fact family.

❸ Assessment

In this lesson, students used multiplication facts to divide by 6 and 7. Use the **Quick Check** problem to assess students' understanding.

Quick Check 🌸 **Formative** Assessment

What multiplication fact can help you find 48 ÷ 6?
6 × 8 = 48 *What is 48 ÷ 6?* 8

Name _____

Dividing by 8 and 9

Intervention
Lesson **G38**

Materials Have counters available for students to use.

You can use multiplication facts to help you divide.

At the museum, 32 students are divided into 8 equal groups.
How many students are in each group?

Find 32 ÷ 8.

1. To find 32 ÷ 8, think about the related multiplication problem.

   8 times what number equals 32?   8 × __4__ = 32

2. Since you know 8 × 4 = 32, then you know 32 ÷ 8 = __4__.

3. How many students are in each group at the museum? __4__ students

Find 36 ÷ 9.

4. To find 36 ÷ 9, think about the related multiplication problem.

   9 times what number equals 36?   9 × __4__ = 36

5. Since you know 9 × 4 = 36, then you know 36 ÷ 9 = __4__.

Find 8)‾80‾

6. To find 8)‾80‾, think about the related multiplication problem.

   8 times what number equals 80?   8 × __10__ = 80

7. Since you know 8 × 10 = 80, then you know 8)‾80‾ = __10__.

8. **Reasoning** Explain how to find 56 ÷ 8.
   Think: 8 times what number equals 56. Since
   8 × 7 = 56, 56 ÷ 8 = 7.

Name _____

Dividing by 8 and 9 (continued)

Intervention
Lesson **G38**

Use the multiplication fact to find each quotient.

9. 8 × 2 = 16

   16 ÷ 8 = __2__

10. 9 × 5 = 45

    45 ÷ 9 = __5__

11. 8 × 3 = 24

    24 ÷ 8 = __3__

12. 9 × 6 = 54

    54 ÷ 9 = __6__

13. 8 × __4__ = 32

    32 ÷ 8 = __4__

14. 8 × __6__ = 48

    48 ÷ 8 = __6__

15. 9 × __3__ = 27

    27 ÷ 9 = __3__

16. 9 × __10__ = 90

    90 ÷ 9 = __10__

17. 8 × __9__ = 72

    72 ÷ 8 = __9__

Find each quotient.

18. 9)‾63‾ (7)

19. 8)‾32‾ (4)

20. 9)‾36‾ (4)

21. 8)‾64‾ (8)

22. 9)‾81‾ (9)

23. 8)‾16‾ (2)

24. 9)‾45‾ (5)

25. 8)‾56‾ (7)

26. 8)‾40‾ (5)

27. **Reasoning** If you know that 8 × 12 = 96,
    then what is 96 ÷ 8?   ____12____

28. Nine friends go to lunch and split the $54
    ticket evenly. How much does each
    friend pay?   ____$6____

Objective Students will divide by 8 and 9.
Vocabulary Division, fact family
Materials Counters

➊ Conceptual Development
Use with Exercises 1–8.

*In this lesson, you will divide by 8 and 9 using
multiplication facts you already know.*

Have students work in pairs and distribute counters
for students to use if they need. Invite a volunteer to
read the division story problem at the top of the page.
*To find 32 ÷ 8, think about the related multiplication
problem. 8 times what number equals 32? 4* Have
students do Exercises 1–3. *To find 36 ÷ 9, what
multiplication problem should you think about?
9 times what number equals 36?* Have students do
Exercises 4–7 similarly. For Exercise 8, have students
write the fact family for the numbers 7, 8, and 56,
and then answer the question.

➋ Practice Use with Exercises 9–28.

Have students write multiplication tables for 8 and 9
before solving the division problems.

Error Intervention If students have trouble
remembering the nines facts, remind them how the
pattern works for finding multiples of 9.

If You Have More Time Have teams of
two or three make a game like Memory by writing
expressions on one card and quotients on another
card for the 8 and 9 division facts. Then, have them
shuffle all the cards and place them facedown in an
array. One student turns over two cards. If they match,
the student keeps the two cards and goes again.
When a match is not made, the cards are turned back
over, and it is another student's turn. The game is
finished when all cards are matched. The student with
the most matches wins.

➌ Assessment

In this lesson, students used multiplication facts to
divide by 8 and 9. Use the **Quick Check** problem to
assess students' understanding.

Quick Check **Formative**
Assessment

What two division facts can you write using 8 × 9?
72 ÷ 8 = 9 and 72 ÷ 9 = 8

0 AND 1 IN DIVISION

Name _____

0 and 1 in Division

Think about related multiplication facts to help you divide.

Find 5 ÷ 1.

1. Think: 1 times what number equals 5? $1 \times \underline{\ 5\ } = 5$

2. Since you know $1 \times 5 = 5$, then you know $5 \div 1 = \underline{\ 5\ }$.

3. If Karina had 5 oranges to put equally in 1 basket, how many oranges would go in each basket? _____ __5__ oranges

Find 9 ÷ 1.

4. $1 \times \underline{\ 9\ } = 9$ So, $9 \div 1 = \underline{\ 9\ }$

5. What is the result when any number is divided by 1? __The number__

Find 0 ÷ 7.

6. Think: 7 times what number equals 0? $7 \times \underline{\ 0\ } = 0$

7. Since you know $7 \times 0 = 0$, then you know $0 \div 7 = \underline{\ 0\ }$.

8. If Karina had 0 oranges to put equally in 7 baskets, how many oranges would go in each basket? __0__ oranges

Find 0 ÷ 2.

9. $2 \times \underline{\ 0\ } = 0$ So, $0 \div 2 = \underline{\ 0\ }$.

10. What is the result when zero is divided by any number (except 0)? __0__

Find 5 ÷ 0.

11. **Reasoning** If Karina had 5 oranges to put equally in 0 baskets, how many oranges would go in each basket? Explain. Karina can not put 5 oranges into 0 baskets.

You cannot divide a number by 0.

G39 (student p. 1)   MDIS 2.0

Name _____

0 and 1 in Division (continued)

Find 4 ÷ 4.

12. Think: 4 times what number equals 4? $4 \times \underline{\ 1\ } = 4$

13. Since you know $4 \times 1 = 4$, then you know $4 \div 4 = \underline{\ 1\ }$.

14. If Karina had 4 oranges to put equally in 4 baskets, how many oranges would go in each basket? __1__ orange

Find 8 ÷ 8.

15. $8 \times \underline{\ 1\ } = 8$ So, $8 \div 8 = \underline{\ 1\ }$.

16. What is the result when any number (except 0) is divided by itself? __1__

Find each quotient.

17. $4 \div 1 = \underline{\ 4\ }$ 18. $0 \div 5 = \underline{\ 0\ }$ 19. $6 \div 6 = \underline{\ 1\ }$

20. $3\overline{)0}$ **0**   21. $9\overline{)9}$ **1**   22. $5\overline{)5}$ **1**

23. $1\overline{)6}$ **6**   24. $1\overline{)1}$ **1**   25. $8\overline{)0}$ **0**

26. **Reasoning** Use the rule for division by 1 to find $247 \div 1$. Explain. A number divided by 1 equals the same number, so $247 \div 1 = 247$.

27. Larry has 3 friends who would like some cookies but he has no cookies to give them. How many cookies can Larry give each friend? Each friend gets zero cookies.

G39 (student p. 2)   MDIS 2.0

Objective Students will solve division problems that involve 0 and 1.
Vocabulary Division

1 Conceptual Development
Use with Exercises 1–11.

In this lesson, you will learn how to divide with 0 and 1.

Have students work in pairs. *To find 5 ÷ 1, think about the related multiplication problem. 1 times what number equals 5?* 5 Have students do Exercises 1–5. *To find 0 ÷ 7, what multiplication problem should you think about?* 7 times what number equals 0? Remind students that any number times 0 is 0. Have students do Exercises 6–10. Before students do Exercise 11, explain that division by 0 is not possible because when you put objects in equal groups, there cannot be 0 groups. Have students do Exercise 11.

2 Practice Use with Exercises 12–27.

Remind students that a number divided by 1 is that number. A number divided by itself is 1.

Error Intervention If students have trouble dividing 0 by a number, remind them that 0 objects divided into any number of groups is still 0 objects.

If You Have More Time Have students write a general rule and an example for each of the following division problems: a number divided by 1; a number divided by itself; a number divided by 0; and 0 divided by a number.

3 Assessment

In this lesson, students learned to divide with 0 and 1. Use the **Quick Check** problem to assess students' understanding.

Quick Check **Formative Assessment**

What is 0 ÷ 245? 0 *What is 245 ÷ 1?* 245

MDIS 2.0

MENTAL MATH: MULTIPLICATION PATTERNS

Name _____

Mental Math: Multiplication Patterns

Materials place-value blocks: 12 unit cubes, 12 tens rods, and 12 hundreds blocks for each group

There are 300 paint brushes in a box. The art teacher bought 4 boxes of brushes. How many paint brushes did he buy altogether? Answer 1 to 8.

Use basic facts and place-value blocks to find 4 × 300.

1. What basic fact can you use? _____4 × 3_____

2. Show 4 × 3 using unit cubes.

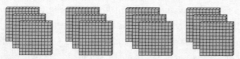

3. What is 4 × 3? ___12___

4. Show 4 × 30 using tens rods.

5. What is 4 × 30? ___120___

6. Show 4 × 300 using hundreds blocks.

7. What is 4 × 300? ___1,200___

8. How many paint brushes did the art teacher buy? ___1,200___

9. **Reasoning** How can you use 4 × 3 to find 4 × 300 using zeros instead of place-value blocks?
   Since 4 × 3 = 12, 4 × 300 is 12 with two more zeros.

G40 (student p. 1)   MDIS 2.0

Name _____

Mental Math: Multiplication Patterns (continued)

Find 5 × 200.

10. Think: 5 × 2 = ___10___

11. Think: 5 × 20 = ___100___

12. Think: 5 × 200 = ___1,000___

Use the basic facts and patterns to find each product.

13.	2 × 3 = ___6___	14.	3 × 7 = ___21___	15.	4 × 5 = ___20___
	2 × 30 = ___60___		3 × 70 = ___210___		4 × 50 = ___200___
	2 × 300 = ___600___		3 × 700 = ___2,100___		4 × 500 = ___2,000___
16.	7 × 6 = ___42___	17.	5 × 9 = ___45___	18.	3 × 6 = ___18___
	7 × 60 = ___420___		5 × 90 = ___450___		3 × 60 = ___180___
	7 × 600 = ___4,200___		5 × 900 = ___4,500___		3 × 600 = ___1,800___

Find each product.

19.	60	20.	700	21.	30	22.	800
	× 3		× 5		× 8		× 4
	180		3,500		240		3,200

23. Mark, Ryan, and Jenny are each collecting pennies for a school fundraiser. If each student collects 400 pennies, how many have they collected altogether? ___1,200 pennies___

24. **Reasoning** How can the basic fact 5 × 8 = 40 and zeros help you

    find the missing number in the problem 5 × ___?___ = 4,000?
    The missing number must be 8 with two zeros, so it is 800; 5 × 800 = 4,000.

G40 (student p. 2)   MDIS 2.0

Objective Students will use mental math to find multiplication patterns.
Vocabulary Product, fact
Materials Place-value blocks: 12 unit cubes, 12 tens rods, and 12 hundreds blocks for each group

❶ Conceptual Development
Use with Exercises 1–12.

In this lesson you will learn to use mental math to find multiplication patterns.

Review the terms *product* and *fact* as needed. Read the problem together. *If you cover up the zeros, what basic fact do you see in 4 × 300? 4 × 3 How did knowing the basic fact 4 × 3 help you find 4 × 300?* If you know that 4 × 3 = 12, then you can use hundreds blocks to show that 4 × 300 = 1,200. Have students complete Exercises 1–12.

❷ Practice Use with Exercises 13–24.

To help find the basic fact when multiplying larger numbers, encourage students to cover up the zeros in the problem.

Error Intervention If students have difficulty using mental math to find the multiplication patterns, allow them more time to use the place-value blocks.

If You Have More Time Have students solve the following problem and explain their methods: *Mary was unsure of how to solve 800 × 9. What basic fact can she start with, and how can she use the pattern to find the product?* She can go back to 8 × 9 = 72, and then 80 × 9 = 720, and finally 800 × 9 = 7,200.

❸ Assessment

In this lesson students learned to use mental math to find multiplication patterns. Use the **Quick Check** problem to assess students' understanding.

Quick Check   **Formative Assessment**

What happens to the product when a zero is added to the end of a single number in a multiplication problem? One zero is added to the product for every zero that is added to the end of a number in the problem.

Name _____

Mental Math: Division Patterns

Materials place-value blocks: 16 ones, 16 tens rods, and
16 hundreds blocks per group

Find 1,600 ÷ 8.

1. Use a basic fact and place-value blocks to find 1,600 ÷ 8.

2. Show 16 unit cubes. Divide them into 8 equal groups.

3. How many cubes are in each group? __2__

4. What is 16 ÷ 8? __2__

5. Show 16 ten rods. Divide them
   into 8 equal groups.

6. How many ten rods are in each group? __2__

7. So, 160 ÷ 8 = 16 tens ÷ 8 = __2__ tens = __20__

8. What is 160 ÷ 8? __20__

9. Show 16 hundred blocks. Divide them into 8 equal groups.

10. How many hundred blocks are in each group? __2__

11. So, 1,600 ÷ 8 = 16 hundreds ÷ 8 = __2__ hundreds = __200__

12. What is 1,600 ÷ 8? __200__

13. **Reasoning** How can you use 16 ÷ 8 to find 1,600 ÷ 8
    using zeros instead of place-value blocks?
    Since 16 ÷ 8 = 2, 1,600 ÷ 8 is 2 with two more zeros.

G41 (student p. 1)   MDIS 2.0

Name _____

Mental Math: Division Patterns (continued)

14. Find 1,500 ÷ 5.

    Think: 15 ÷ 5 = __3__

    Think: 150 ÷ 5 = __30__

    Think: 1,500 ÷ 5 = __300__

Use the basic facts and patterns to find each quotient.

15. 36 ÷ 6 = __6__   16. 28 ÷ 7 = __4__   17. 16 ÷ 2 = __8__

    360 ÷ 6 = __60__   280 ÷ 7 = __40__   160 ÷ 2 = __80__

    3,600 ÷ 6 = __600__   2,800 ÷ 7 = __400__   1,600 ÷ 2 = __800__

18. 45 ÷ 9 = __5__   19. 21 ÷ 7 = __3__   20. 64 ÷ 8 = __8__

    450 ÷ 9 = __50__   210 ÷ 7 = __30__   640 ÷ 8 = __80__

    4,500 ÷ 9 = __500__   2,100 ÷ 7 = __300__   6,400 ÷ 8 = __800__

Find each quotient.

21. 60 ÷ 2 = __30__   22. 150 ÷ 3 = __50__   23. 200 ÷ 5 = __40__

24. There are 60 books in a stack. The teacher wants
    to divide the books equally between 3 classes.
    There are 20 students in each class. How many
    books will each class receive?   __20 books__

25. **Reasoning** How are 1,200 ÷ 2 and 12 ÷ 2 alike and how
    are they different?
    The divisors are both 2 and the dividends both have
    the same first two digits, however, 1,200 has two more
    zeros than the 12.

26. How many zeros are in the quotient 7,200 ÷ 9? __2__

G41 (student p. 2)   MDIS 2.0

Objective Students will use mental math to find
division patterns.
Vocabulary Quotient
Materials Place-value blocks: 16 unit cubes,
16 tens rods, and 16 hundreds blocks for each group

① Conceptual Development
Use with Exercises 1–14.

*In this lesson you will learn to use mental math to find
division patterns.*

Review the term *quotient* as needed. Read the
problem together. *If you cover up the zeros, what
basic fact do you see in 1,600 ÷ 8?* 16 ÷ 8 *How
did knowing the basic fact 16 ÷ 8 help you find
1,600 ÷ 8?* If you know that 16 ÷ 8 = 2, then you can
use hundreds blocks to show that 1,600 ÷ 8 = 200.
Have students complete Exercises 1–14.

② Practice **Use with Exercises 15–26.**

Point out to students that as one zero is added to the
problem, one zero is added to the answer.

Error Intervention If students have difficulty
using mental math to find the quotients, allow them
more time to use the place-value blocks.

If You Have More Time Have students solve
the following problem and explain their methods:
Solve 900 ÷ 3. I can use the fact 9 ÷ 3 = 3, see that
90 ÷ 3 = 30, and finally 900 ÷ 3 = 300.

③ Assessment

In this lesson students learned to use mental math to
find division patterns. Use the **Quick Check** problem
to assess students' understanding.

Quick Check **Formative** Assessment

Divide: 2,400 ÷ 3 800

ESTIMATING PRODUCTS

Name _____

Estimating Products

During Field Day, the students at Sunrise Elementary were placed into 4 activity groups. Each group had 78 students. About how many students were in all 4 groups?

Estimate 4 × 78.

1. What is 78 rounded to the nearest ten? ___80___

2. What is 4 × 80? ___320___

3. What is a good estimate for 4 × 78? ___320___

4. About how many students were in all 4 groups during Field Day? ___320___ students

5. **Reasoning** How do the place-value blocks below show that 320 is a good estimate for 4 × 78?

Sample answer: The 4 groups of 78 have almost as many in all as the 4 groups of 80, which has 320 in all.

Estimate 6 × 345.

6. What is 345 rounded to the nearest hundred? ___300___

7. What is 6 × 300? ___1,800___

8. What is a good estimate for 6 × 345? ___1,800___

G42 (student p. 1) MDIS 2.0

Name _____

Estimating Products (continued)

Estimate each product.

9. 7 × 38
___280___

10. 8 × 34
___240___

11. 5 × 91
___450___

12. 4 × 57
___240___

13. 7 × 47
___350___

14. 3 × 72
___210___

15. 6 × 52
___300___

16. 2 × 75
___160___

17. 3 × 87
___270___

18. 2 × 623
___1,200___

19. 5 × 177
___1,000___

20. 4 × 532
___2,000___

21. 3 × 318
___900___

22. 4 × 863
___3,600___

23. 2 × 804
___1,600___

24. Each of the eight delivery trucks carried 94 packages. About how many packages were there altogether? ___720 packages___

25. There are 43 carrots in each of 7 bags of carrots. About how many carrots altogether? ___280 carrots___

26. **Reasoning** What is a good estimate for 6 × 26? Explain how you estimated.
180; 6 × 26 is about 6 × 30 = 180.

27. **Reasoning** Mark estimated the product of 4 × 54 to be about 280. Was his estimation reasonable? Explain your reasoning.
No, his estimate is too large. The best estimate is 4 × 50 = 200. Another reasonable estimate is 4 × 60 = 240.

G42 (student p. 2) MDIS 2.0

Objective Students will use rounding to estimate products.

Vocabulary Product, estimate

1 Conceptual Development
Use with Exercises 1–8.

In this lesson you will learn to use rounding to estimate products.

Have students read the first problem. Review the terms *product* and *estimate* as needed. *How do you round to the nearest ten?* If the ones digit is 4 or less, round down; if it is 5 or more, round up. Have students complete Exercises 1–5. *When you estimated the product, what was the first step?* We rounded 78 to 80. Have students complete Exercises 6–8.

2 Practice Use with Exercises 9–27.

Tell students that they need to round only the greater number in each exercise. They then multiply by the rounded number by the single-digit number.

Error Intervention If students have difficulty rounding, encourage them to use a number line to place each number they are rounding. They can then more easily see which number it is closer to.

If You Have More Time Have students solve the following problem and explain their methods: *Delaney collected canned goods from 32 people. Each person donated 4 cans. Delaney said she collected about 160 canned goods. Is she correct? Why or why not?* No; 32 rounds down to 30, not up to 40, so she collected about 120 canned goods.

3 Assessment

In this lesson students learned to use rounding to estimate products. Use the **Quick Check** problem to assess students' understanding.

Quick Check **Formative** Assessment

Estimate the product: 749 × 7 4,900

MDIS 2.0

ESTIMATING QUOTIENTS

Name _____

Estimating Quotients

The city soccer league has 47 children, between the ages of 8 and 10, signed up to play soccer. The people in charge of the soccer league want to put 9 children on each team. About how many teams should they make?

Estimate 47 ÷ 9 by answering 1 to 4.

1. What number is close to 47 and can be easily divided by 9? __45__

2. What is 45 ÷ 9? __5__

3. What is a good estimate of 47 ÷ 9? __5__

4. About how many soccer teams should the city make? __5__

You can use compatible numbers to help you estimate a quotient.

Estimate 543 ÷ 8 by answering 5 to 10.

5. Is 5 ÷ 8 a basic fact? __no__

6. Is 54 ÷ 8 a basic fact? __no__

7. What is a basic fact that is close to 54 ÷ 8? __56 ÷ 8__

8. Is 560 close to 543? __yes__

9. What is 560 ÷ 8? __70__

10. What is a good estimate of 543 ÷ 8? __70__

Estimate 615 ÷ 2 by answering 11 to 14.

11. Is 6 ÷ 2 a basic fact? __yes__

12. Is 600 close to 615? __yes__

13. What is 600 ÷ 2? __300__

14. What is a good estimate of 615 ÷ 2? __300__

15. **Reasoning** Show how you would estimate 2,398 ÷ 4? 2,400 ÷ 4

G43 (student p. 1)   MDIS 2.0

Name _____

Estimating Quotients (continued) Answers may vary.

Estimate each quotient. Write the numbers you used.

16. 75 ÷ 4 =
    80 ÷ 4 = 20

17. 31 ÷ 2 =
    30 ÷ 2 = 15

18. 824 ÷ 9 =
    810 ÷ 9 = 90

19. 465 ÷ 9 =
    450 ÷ 9 = 50

20. 230 ÷ 7 =
    210 ÷ 7 = 30

21. 630 ÷ 7 =
    630 ÷ 7 = 90

22. 56 ÷ 3 =
    60 ÷ 3 = 20

23. 181 ÷ 6 =
    180 ÷ 6 = 30

24. 414 ÷ 7 =
    420 ÷ 7 = 60

25. 564 ÷ 6 =
    540 ÷ 6 = 90

26. 729 ÷ 8 =
    720 ÷ 8 = 90

27. 311 ÷ 5 =
    300 ÷ 5 = 60

28. 3)923
    900 ÷ 3 = 300

29. 9)269
    270 ÷ 9 = 30

30. 5)345
    350 ÷ 5 = 70

31. 6)117
    120 ÷ 6 = 20

32. 2)81
    80 ÷ 2 = 40

33. 6)552
    540 ÷ 6 = 90

34. The Spencer family drove in their car to their favorite vacation spot. Mrs. Spencer likes to travel at a rate of 55 miles per hour. The Spencers traveled 849 miles in 3 days. Estimate the number of miles driven each day. _____ 300 miles

35. A manufacturer is packaging paper towels. If 6 rolls complete a package, about how many packages can be made from 327 rolls? _____ 50 packages

36. **Reasoning** Is 30 a reasonable quotient for 264 ÷ 9? Explain your reasoning.
    Yes, because 264 is close to 270 and 270 ÷ 9 = 30.

G43 (student p. 2)   MDIS 2.0

Objective Students will estimate quotients.
Vocabulary Quotient, estimate, compatible number

1 Conceptual Development
Use with Exercises 1–15.

In this lesson you will learn to estimate quotients.

Have students read the first problem. Review the terms *quotient* and *estimate* as needed. Have students complete Exercises 1–4. *How did you estimate the quotient?* I found a number close to 47 that is easier to divide by 9. *What is a compatible number?* A number that is close to another number but easier to work with. Have students complete Exercises 5–15.

2 Practice Use with Exercises 16–36.

Point out to students that they are looking for a compatible number for the greater of the two numbers. Remind them that they are looking for a number that is easy to divide by the single-digit number.

Error Intervention If students have difficulty estimating quotients, have them write out basic facts or use a multiplication table to find compatible basic facts.

If You Have More Time Have students solve the following problem and explain their methods: *To estimate 319 ÷ 6, should you round 319 to the nearest hundred or use compatible numbers? Explain.* You can do either, because 319 would round to 300, and 300 is a compatible number to use when dividing by 6.

3 Assessment

In this lesson students learned to estimate to find quotients. Use the **Quick Check** problem to assess students' understanding.

Quick Check   **Formative** Assessment

A scout troop is packing toothbrushes for military troops. If each supply kit has 7 toothbrushes, about how many supply kits can the scouts make from 359 toothbrushes? 50

G43   MDIS 2.0

Name _____

Multiplication and Arrays

Intervention
Lesson **G44**

Materials place-value blocks: 9 tens and 40 ones for
each group

To multiply 3 × 38, answer 1 to 7.

1. Show an array of 3 rows with 38 in each row, using
   place-value blocks.

2. How many tens in all? __9__ tens

3. 9 tens = __90__

4. How many ones in all? __24__

5. 24 ones = __24__

6. Add the tens and the ones together.

   9 tens + 24 ones = __90__ + __24__ = __114__

7. What is 3 × 38? __114__

To multiply 4 × 27, answer 8 to 11.

8. Show an array of 4 rows with 27 in each row, using
   place-value blocks.

9. How many tens in all? __8__ tens = __80__

10. How many ones in all? __28__

11. What is 4 × 27? 4 × 27 = __80__ + __28__ = __108__

G44 (student p. 1)   MDIS 2.0

Name _____

Multiplication and Arrays (continued)

Intervention
Lesson **G44**

Find each product. Draw a picture to help.

12. 3 × 16

    48

13. 5 × 21

    105

14. 2 × 23

    46

15. 3 × 18

    54

Find each product. Draw a picture to help you multiply with greater numbers.

16. 3 × 35 = __105__

17. 6 × 23 = __138__

18. 5 × 18 = __90__

19. 2 × 34 = __68__

20. 6 × 14 = __84__

21. 4 × 28 = __112__

22. 7 × 13 = __91__

23. 5 × 42 = __210__

24. **Reasoning** If you draw an array to find
    4 × 35, how many tens will you draw?   __12__ tens

    How many ones will you draw?   __20__ ones

    So, 4 × 35 = __140__.

G44 (student p. 2)   MDIS 2.0

Objective Students will use place-value blocks
and arrays to recognize multiplication as repeated
addition.

Vocabulary Product

Materials Place-value blocks, 9 tens and 40 ones
per group

❶ Conceptual Development
Use with Exercises 1–11.

*In this lesson, you will learn to multiply using place-
value blocks arranged in arrays.*

Have students work in groups of three. Distribute
place-value blocks to each group. Instruct each
student, one at a time, to put 3 tens blocks and 8 ones
blocks in a row. Students in the group should line their
rows up under each other. *What number does each
row show?* 38 *How many rows are there?* 3 Have
students do Exercises 2–5. *A product is the answer to
a multiplication problem. What product does the array
show?* 3 × 38 = 114 Have students do Exercises 6
and 7. Do Exercises 8–11 similarly.

❷ Practice Use with Exercises 12–24.

Encourage students to draw a picture to find the
products.

Error Intervention If students have trouble
drawing the arrays, allow them to work in pairs and
model the arrays using place-value blocks.

If You Have More Time Write 4 × 25 on
the board. Have students use place-value blocks to
model the problem and find the product. Then, have
students explain why finding the value of four quarters
is another way to solve this problem.

❸ Assessment

In this lesson, students multiplied using place-value
blocks. Use the **Quick Check** problem to assess
students' understanding.

Quick Check **Formative** Assessment

*To find 3 × 25, how many rows of place-value blocks
do you make?* 3 *How many tens blocks are in each
row?* 2 *How many ones blocks in each row?* 5

BREAKING APART NUMBERS TO MULTIPLY

Breaking Apart Numbers to Multiply

Materials place-value blocks: 16 tens and 48 ones per student or pair

Find 8 × 26 by answering 1 to 6.

1. Show an array of 8 rows with 26 in each row, using place-value blocks.

2. 26 = __2__ tens + __6__ ones

   = __20__ + __6__

3. Multiply the ones by 8 and write the product on the left.

   8 × __6__ ones = __48__ ones

   26
   × 8
   8 × 6 → 48
   8 × 20 → 160
   208

4. Multiply the tens by 8 and write the product on the left.

   8 × __2__ tens = __16__ tens = __160__

5. Add the products together and write the sum below the line, on the left.

6. So, 8 × 26 = __208__.

7. Find 3 × 45.

   45
   × 3
   3 × 5 → 15
   3 × 40 → 120
   135

8. Find 4 × 29. Use place-value blocks or draw pictures to help.

   29
   × 4
   4 × 9 → 36
   4 × 20 → 80
   116

G45 (student p. 1) MDIS 2.0

Breaking Apart Numbers to Multiply (continued)

Find each product.

9. 32
    × 3
    6   multiply ones
    + 90 multiply tens
    96 product

10. 42
    × 5
    10 multiply ones
    + 200 multiply tens
    210 product

11. $64
    × 3
    $192

12. 45
    × 2
    90

13. 64
    × 4
    256

14. $23
    × 5
    $115

15. 32
    × 6
    192

16. 53
    × 4
    212

17. 47
    × 3
    141

18. $38
    × 2
    $76

19. 67
    × 5
    335

20. 74
    × 3
    222

21. 18
    × 7
    126

22. 56
    × 4
    224

23. **Reasoning** Carlo wants to buy 3 model airplanes. If each airplane costs $29, how much money does he need? __$87__

24. Salvo called 5 friends and talked 34 minutes with each friend. How many minutes was Salvo on the phone? __170__ minutes

25. **Reasoning** James multiplied 5 × 54 by breaking 54 apart into 5 tens and 4 ones. Then he multiplied 5 × 4 and 5 × 5, and then added 20 + 25. Where did James make his mistake?
James should have multiplied 5 × 50, not 5 × 5, because 54 = 50 + 4 not 5 + 4.

G45 (student p. 2) MDIS 2.0

Objective Students will break apart numbers and use arrays to multiply 2-digit by 1-digit numbers.

Vocabulary Partial product

Materials Place-value blocks, 16 tens and 48 ones per pair

① Conceptual Development
Use with Exercises 1–8.

In this lesson, you will learn to break apart larger numbers to multiply.

Have students work in pairs. Give place-value blocks to each pair: 16 tens and 48 ones. *Use the place-value blocks to make an array of 8 rows of 26. What product does this show?* 8 × 26 Have students do Exercise 2. *Multiply the ones by 8. What is the product?* 8 × 6 = 48 *48 is called a partial product because it shows part of the product. The other part is found by multiplying the tens by 8. How many tens are there in each row?* 2 Have students do Exercise 4 and write each step in vertical form. *Add the partial products together and write the sum.* Have students do Exercises 5 and 6. Do Exercises 7 and 8 similarly.

② Practice Use with Exercises 9–25.

Allow students to work in pairs to do Exercises 9–14. Have them do the remaining exercises on their own.

Error Intervention If students have trouble putting the partial products in the correct place, encourage them to copy the format shown in Exercise 9 before they begin each problem.

If You Have More Time Have students make up and solve a story problem that involves multiplying a 2-digit number by a 1-digit number.

③ Assessment

In this lesson, students multiplied by breaking apart numbers. Use the **Quick Check** problem to assess students' understanding.

Quick Check **Formative** Assessment

What is 72 × 5? 360

Name _____

Multiplying Two-Digit Numbers
Intervention
Lesson **G46**

Materials place-value blocks: 6 tens and 24 ones per student

Jenny's Market has 4 boxes. Each box holds 16 cans of soup. Answer 1 to 7 to find the number of cans of soup Jenny's Market has altogether.

Find 4 × 16.

1. Show 4 groups of 16 using place-value blocks.

2. Multiply the ones. 4 × 6 ones = __24__ ones

3. Regroup the ones. Trade groups of ten ones for tens.

4. 24 = 2 tens and __4__ ones. Record the ones in the ones column of the Tens and Ones chart. Record the tens at the top of the tens column of the chart.

Tens	Ones
2	
1	6
×	4
6	4

5. Multiply the tens. 4 × 1 ten = __4__ tens

6. Add the regrouped tens to the 4 tens and record this value in the tens column of the chart.

4 tens + 2 tens = __6__ tens

7. So, 4 × 16 = __64__. How many cans of soup does Jenny's Market have altogether?

__64__

G46 (student p. 1)   MDIS 2.0

Name _____

Multiplying Two-Digit Numbers (continued)

Intervention
Lesson **G46**

Multiply.

8.	9.	10.	11.
17 ×2 = 34	25 ×3 = 75	21 ×7 = 147	34 ×4 = 136

12.	13.	14.	15.
22 ×6 = 132	48 ×3 = 144	37 ×5 = 185	47 ×4 = 188

16.	17.	18.	19.
14 ×6 = 84	18 ×3 = 54	23 ×4 = 92	31 ×5 = 155

20.	21.	22.	23.
27 ×7 = 189	43 ×4 = 172	52 ×2 = 104	65 ×3 = 195

24.	25.	26.	27.
57 ×5 = 285	62 ×3 = 186	75 ×3 = 225	37 ×8 = 296

28. Ron is 26 years old. His grandmother is 3 times his age. How old is his grandmother?   __78__ years

29. A basketball player usually scores 17 points in each game. How many points would she be expected to score in 5 games?   __85__ points

30. **Reasoning** Write a two-digit number multiplied by a one-digit number that does not require regrouping. Answers will vary. Sample answer: 4 × 21

G46 (student p. 2)   MDIS 2.0

Intervention
Lesson **G46**

Objective Students will use the standard algorithm to multiply a 2-digit number by a 1-digit number.
Vocabulary Regroup
Materials Place-value blocks, 6 tens and 24 ones per student

① Conceptual Development
Use with Exercises 1–7.

In this lesson, you will learn to regroup to find products.

Have students work in pairs. Have a volunteer read the story problem at the top of the page. Distribute place-value blocks: 6 tens and 24 ones to each student. *Use the place-value blocks to show 4 groups of 16. What product does this show?* 4 × 16 *Multiply the ones. How many ones in all?* 24 *You can regroup the ones by trading groups of 10 ones for tens. How many groups of 10 ones are there?* 2 *How many ones are left?* 4 Show students how to record the ones and tens in the chart in Exercise 4. *Next, multiply the tens and then add the two regrouped tens to the product: 4 + 2 is 6 tens in all.* Have students complete Exercises 6 and 7.

② Practice Use with Exercises 8–30.

Allow students to work in pairs to do Exercises 8–15.

Error Intervention If students consistently find products that are too large, make sure they are multiplying the tens digit before they add the regrouped tens.

If You Have More Time Have students work in pairs. Give each pair three number cubes. One partner rolls two cubes and writes a 2-digit number using the numbers rolled. The other partner rolls the third cube, and together the students find the product of the 2-digit number and the last number rolled.

③ Assessment

In this lesson, students multiplied using the standard algorithm. Use the **Quick Check** problem to assess students' understanding.

Quick Check   **Formative** Assessment

What is 24 × 8? 192

Worksheet (student p. 1)

Name _____

Intervention Lesson **G47**

Multiplying Three-Digit Numbers

A parking garage has 6 different levels. There are 128 parking spots on each level. Answer 1 to 13 to find the total number of parking spots.

Find 6 × 128.

1. 128 = __1__ hundred + __2__ tens + __8__ ones

2. Multiply the ones. 6 × 8 ones = __48__ ones

3. Do you need to regroup the ones? __yes__

4. 48 ones = __4__ tens + __8__ ones

5. Record the ones in the ones column of the chart at the right. Record the regrouped tens at the top of the tens column.

Hundreds	Tens	Ones
1	4	
1	2	8
×		6
7	6	8

6. Multiply the tens.

6 × 2 tens = __12__ tens

7. Now, add the regrouped tens.

__12__ tens + __4__ tens = __16__ tens = __160__

8. Do you need to regroup the tens? __yes__

9. 160 = __1__ hundred + __6__ tens

10. Record the tens in the tens column. Record the regrouped hundreds at the top of the hundreds column.

11. Multiply the hundreds. 6 × 1 hundred = __6__ hundreds

12. Now add the regrouped hundreds and record in the hundreds column.

__6__ hundreds + __1__ hundred = __7__ hundreds = __700__

13. So, 6 × 128 = __768__.
How many parking spots are in the garage? __768__

G47 (student p. 1) MDIS 2.0

Worksheet (student p. 2)

Name _____

Intervention Lesson **G47**

Multiplying Three-Digit Numbers (continued)

Multiply.

14.

Th	H	T	O
1	1	2	
	4	5	7
×			3
1	3	7	1

15.

Th	H	T	O
3	1	4	
	5	2	6
×			7
3	6	8	2

16. 223
× 4
892

17. 246
× 7
1,722

18. 117
× 5
585

19. 434
× 4
1,736

20. 519
× 2
1,038

21. 327
× 3
981

22. 572
× 5
2,860

23. 357
× 8
2,856

24. 323
× 4
1,292

25. 351
× 5
1,755

26. 217
× 7
1,519

27. 352
× 2
704

28. A company makes 352 boxes of cereal each day. How many boxes are made in 7 days? __2,464__ boxes

29. **Reasoning** Is 243 a reasonable product for 3 × 71?
Use estimation to explain why or why not.
No, 3 × 71 is very close to 3 × 70 = 210.
So, 243 is too large.

G47 (student p. 2) MDIS 2.0

Objective Students will multiply three-digit numbers.
Vocabulary Regroup

1 Conceptual Development
Use with Exercises 1–13.

In this lesson you will learn to multiply three-digit numbers.

Revisit the term *regroup* as needed. Have students read the problem and complete Exercises 1–5. *How do you know that you need to regroup ones as tens?* There are more than 9 ones. Have students complete Exercises 6–10. *How many regrouped hundreds did you record at the top of the hundreds column?* 1 Have students complete Exercises 11–13.

2 Practice Use with Exercises 14–29.

Remind students to break the larger number into its place-value values to make multiplying easier.

Error Intervention If students have difficulty multiplying three-digit numbers, suggest that they use place-value blocks to help them see why they need to regroup the tens and hundreds.

If You Have More Time Have students solve the following problem and explain their methods: *While solving this problem 174 × 7, Chase said he does not have to regroup the ones. Is he correct? Tell why or why not.* No; He does have to regroup the ones because there are 28 ones.

3 Assessment

In this lesson students learned to multiply three-digit numbers. Use the **Quick Check** problem to assess students' understanding.

Quick Check Formative Assessment

Find 501 × 7. What regrouping did you have to do? 3,507; Only the hundreds had to be regrouped.

MULTIPLYING MONEY

Name _____

Multiplying Money

Bryan wants to buy 4 posters. Each poster costs $3.95. Answer 1 to 14 to find how much money Bryan needs.

Find 4 × $3.95.

To find 4 × $3.95, multiply as you would with whole numbers.

1. $3.95 = __3__ dollars + __9__ dimes + __5__ pennies

2. Multiply the pennies. 4×5 pennies = __20__ pennies

3. Regroup the pennies.

   __20__ pennies = __2__ dimes and __0__ pennies

4. Record the pennies in the pennies column of the chart, even if there are zero. Record the regrouped dimes at the top of the dimes column.

Ten Dollars	Dollars	Dimes	Pennies
1	3	2	
	$3	. 9	5
×			4
$1	5	. 8	0

5. Multiply the dimes.

   4 × 9 dimes = __36__ dimes

6. Add the regrouped dimes. __36__ dimes + 2 dimes = __38__ dimes

7. Regroup the dimes. __38__ dimes = __3__ dollars and __8__ dimes

8. Record the dimes in the dimes column of the chart. Record the regrouped dollars at the top of the dollars column.

9. Multiply the dollars. 4 × 3 dollars = __12__ dollars

10. Add the regrouped dollars.

    __12__ dollars + __3__ dollars = __15__ dollars

11. Regroup the dollars.

    __15__ dollars = __1__ ten dollar and __5__ dollars

G48 (student p. 1)

MDIS 2.0

Name _____

Multiplying Money (continued)

12. Record the dollars and ten dollars in the chart.

13. Write the answer in dollars and cents by placing the dollar sign and decimal point.

14. How much money will Bryan need for the posters?   **$15.80**

Find each product.

15.	$1.25 × 5 $6.25	16.	$1.10 × 3 $3.30	17.	$8.15 × 7 $57.05	18.	$5.21 × 6 $31.26

19.	$8.39 × 4 $33.56	20.	$2.75 × 6 $16.50	21.	$2.25 × 3 $6.75	22.	$1.21 × 7 $8.47

23.	$2.46 × 7 $17.22	24.	$1.18 × 6 $7.08	25.	$3.62 × 3 $10.86	26.	$4.75 × 3 $14.25

27. **Reasoning** Ham is on sale for $3.21 per pound and chicken is on sale for $4.35 per pound. How much do 3 pounds of chicken cost?   **$13.05**

28. **Reasoning** Shanti has $35.00. She wants to buy 4 packs of baseball cards. Each packs costs $8.50. How much do 4 packs of cards cost? If she has enough money, how much change will Shanti get back? If she needs more money, how much more money does she need?

    Four packs cost $34.00. She will get $1.00 back in change.

G48 (student p. 2)

MDIS 2.0

Objective Students will multiply money amounts.
Vocabulary Regroup

1 Conceptual Development
Use with Exercises 1–14.

In this lesson you will learn to multiply money amounts.

Revisit the term *regroup* as needed. Have students read the problem and complete Exercise 1. *How is multiplying money amounts just like multiplying whole numbers?* You can separate the money amount into dollars, dimes, and pennies in the same way you can separate a whole number into hundreds, tens, and ones. Have students complete Exercises 2–10. *What is the maximum number of one-dollar bills you can have before you need to regroup to a ten-dollar bill?* 9 Have students complete Exercises 11–14.

2 Practice Use with Exercises 15–28.

Remind students to think of the money values as whole numbers when multiplying and then to use the dollar sign ($) and decimal point to show that they are using money.

Error Intervention If students have difficulty multiplying money, allow them to use play money to model regrouping and to determine where the decimal point should be placed to show the change.

If You Have More Time Have students solve the following problem and explain their methods: *Leo wants to buy 5 bracelets that cost $2.79 each. He has $10.89. Does he have enough money to buy all 5 bracelets? Explain why or why not.* No; 5 would cost $13.95, and he only has $10.89.

3 Assessment

In this lesson students learned to multiply money amounts. Use the **Quick Check** problem to assess students' understanding.

Quick Check   **Formative Assessment**

There are 8 bandanas left to sell at the school store. They sell for $1.79 each. How much money will the school make if all 8 are sold? $14.32

Name _____

Intervention
Lesson **G49**

**Multiplying One-Digit and
Four-Digit Numbers**

Each section of a parade float used 1,436 flowers. If the parade float had 4 different sections, how many flowers were used on the entire float?

Find 4 × 1,436 by answering 1 to 19.

1. Multiply the ones. 4 × 6 ones = __24__ ones

2. Do you need to regroup the ones? __yes__

3. Regroup the ones.

   __24__ ones = __2__ tens + __4__ ones

4. Record the ones in the ones column of the chart. Record the regrouped tens at the top of the tens column.

Thousands	Hundreds	Tens	Ones
1	1	2	
1	4	3	6
×			4
5	7	4	4

5. Multiply the tens.

   4 × 3 tens = __12__ tens

6. Add the regrouped tens.

   __12__ tens + __2__ tens = __14__ tens

7. Do you need to regroup the tens? __yes__

8. Regroup the tens. __14__ tens = __1__ hundred + __4__ tens

9. Record the tens in the tens column and record the regrouped hundreds at the top of the hundreds column.

10. Multiply the hundreds. 4 × 4 hundreds = __16__ hundreds

11. Add the regrouped hundreds.

   __16__ hundreds + __1__ hundred = __17__ hundreds

12. Do you need to regroup the hundreds? __yes__

G49 (student p. 1) MDIS 2.0

Name _____

Intervention
Lesson **G49**

Multiplying One-Digit and Four-Digit Numbers (continued)

13. Regroup the hundreds.

   __17__ hundreds = __1__ thousand + __7__ hundreds

14. Record the hundreds in the hundreds column. Record the regrouped thousands at the top of the thousands column.

15. Multiply the thousands. 4 × 1 thousand = __4__ thousands

16. Add the regrouped thousands.

   __4__ thousands + __1__ thousand = __5__ thousands

17. Do you need to regroup? __no__

18. Record the thousands in the thousands column.

19. How many flowers were used on the entire float? __5,744__

Find each product.

20. 2,356
   × 3
   ———
   7,068

21. 5,342
   × 4
   ———
   21,368

22. 1,081
   × 6
   ———
   6,486

23. 3,321
   × 4
   ———
   13,284

24. 1,431
   × 5
   ———
   7,155

25. 2,310
   × 3
   ———
   6,930

26. 8,211
   × 2
   ———
   16,422

27. 7,201
   × 4
   ———
   28,804

28. 1,121
   × 4
   ———
   4,484

29. 3,002
   × 3
   ———
   9,006

30. 4,610
   × 2
   ———
   9,220

31. 5,329
   × 5
   ———
   26,645

32. Last year 1,503 people attended a craft show. This year 3 times as many people attended. How many people attended the craft show this year? __4,509__ people

33. **Reasoning** Ramon estimated the product of 4,099 × 5 to be around 20,000. Is his estimate reasonable? Explain your reasoning.
   Yes, 4,099 is close to 4,000 and 4,000 × 5 = 20,000.

G49 (student p. 2) MDIS 2.0

Objective Students will multiply one-digit and four-digit numbers.

Vocabulary Regroup

① Conceptual Development
Use with Exercises 1–19.

In this lesson you will learn to multiply one-digit and four-digit numbers.

Revisit the term *regroup* as needed. Have students read the problem and complete Exercises 1–9. *Is there any difference between multiplying three-digit numbers and four-digit numbers?* No; You still multiply each place at a time, and, if there are more than 9 of any value, you regroup to the next place value. Have students complete Exercises 10–19.

② Practice Use with Exercises 20–33.

Remind students that multiplying four-digit numbers is just like multiplying three-digit numbers; if you need to regroup, you regroup to the place to the left.

Error Intervention If students have difficulty multiplying four-digit numbers, encourage them to use a place-value chart like the one on the first page.

If You Have More Time Have students solve the following problem and explain their methods: *There were 1,409 people at the park in the month of May. In July, there were 4 times that many people at the park. How many people were at the park in July?* 1,409 × 4 = 5,636 people

③ Assessment

In this lesson students learned to multiply one-digit and four-digit numbers. Use the **Quick Check** problem to assess students' understanding.

Quick Check Formative Assessment

The concession stand sells 2,097 pieces of chicken each month. How many pieces of chicken did they sell in 3 months? 6,291 pieces of chicken

---

G49 MDIS 2.0

DIVIDING WITH OBJECTS

Dividing with Objects

Materials 7 counters and 3 half sheets of paper for each student or pair

Andrew has 7 model cars to put on 3 shelves. He wants to put the same number of cars on each shelf. How many cars should Andrew put on each shelf? Answer 1 to 8.

Find $7 \div 3$.

1. Show 7 counters and 3 sheets of paper.

2. Put 1 counter on each piece of paper.

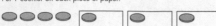

3. Are there enough counters to put another counter on each sheet of paper?   yes

4. Put another counter on each piece of paper.

5. Are there enough counters to put another counter on each sheet of paper?   no

6. How many counters are on each sheet?   2

7. How many counters are remaining, or left over?   1

So, $7 \div 3$ is 2 remainder 1, or $7 \div 3 = 2$ R1.

8. How many cars should Andrew put on each shelf? How many cars will be left over?

   Andrew can put 2 cars on each shelf with 1 car left over.

G50 (student p. 1)   MDIS 2.0

Dividing with Objects (continued)

Use counters or draw a picture to find each quotient and remainder.

9. $8 \div 3 =$ __2 R2__   10. $17 \div 3 =$ __5 R2__   11. $14 \div 3 =$ __4 R2__

12. $11 \div 4 =$ __2 R3__   13. $22 \div 4 =$ __5 R2__   14. $34 \div 4 =$ __8 R2__

15. $13 \div 5 =$ __2 R3__   16. $27 \div 5 =$ __5 R2__   17. $46 \div 5 =$ __9 R1__

18. $14 \div 6 =$ __2 R2__   19. $26 \div 6 =$ __4 R2__   20. $38 \div 6 =$ __6 R2__

21. $17 \div 7 =$ __2 R3__   22. $27 \div 7 =$ __3 R6__   23. $45 \div 7 =$ __6 R3__

24. $18 \div 8 =$ __2 R2__   25. $28 \div 8 =$ __3 R4__   26. $37 \div 8 =$ __4 R5__

27. $14 \div 9 =$ __1 R5__   28. $28 \div 9 =$ __3 R1__   29. $39 \div 9 =$ __4 R3__

30. $12 \div 8 =$ __1 R4__   31. $68 \div 7 =$ __9 R5__   32. $59 \div 8 =$ __7 R3__

33. $9 \div 4 =$ __2 R1__   34. $26 \div 5 =$ __5 R1__   35. $34 \div 6 =$ __5 R4__

36. $14 \div 5 =$ __2 R4__   37. $21 \div 6 =$ __3 R3__   38. $3 \div 2 =$ __1 R1__

39. **Reasoning** Grace is reading a book for school. The book has 26 pages and she is given 3 days to read it. How many pages should she read each day? Will she have to read more pages on some days than on others? Explain.

   She should read 8–9 pages each day; she will read 9 pages on 2 days and 8 pages on 1 day.

G50 (student p. 2)   MDIS 2.0

Objective Students will divide with objects.
Vocabulary Remainder
Materials 7 counters and 3 half sheets of paper for each student

❶ Conceptual Development
Use with Exercises 1–8.

In this lesson you will learn to divide with objects.

Revisit the term *remainder* as needed. Have students read the problem and complete Exercises 1–4. *How does using objects help you more clearly see what is happening when you divide?* When I use objects to divide, I can actually see the groups I am making when dividing up the objects rather than just remembering basic facts that fit the problems. Have students complete Exercises 5–8.

❷ Practice Use with Exercises 9–39.

Point out to students that they can draw a picture for each problem instead of using counters.

Error Intervention
If students have difficulty dividing with objects, provide them with various objects to use instead of counters. Help them to think of each problem in terms of sharing objects with x number of friends.

If You Have More Time
Have students solve the following problem and explain their methods: *Sandra shares 43 tokens with 3 other teammates. She hopes that each teammate will have 11 tokens. Will she have enough? Explain why or why not.* No; because $43 \div 4 = 10$ R3; She would need one more token, or 44 tokens, for each of the four teammates to have 11 tokens.

❸ Assessment

In this lesson students learned to divide with objects. Use the **Quick Check** problem to assess students' understanding.

Quick Check **Formative** Assessment

Find the quotient and remainder: $93 \div 9$ 10 R3

Name _____

Intervention
Lesson **G51**

Interpret the Remainder

Materials counters

Division is an operation that is used to find the number of equal groups or the number of objects that are in each group. Sometimes there is an extra amount. The leftover amount is called the **remainder**.

Can Leroy sort his collection of 14 sports cards into 3 equal piles?

○○   ○○   ○○   ○○
○○   ○○   ○○

Leroy can't sort 14 sports cards into 3 equal piles. He can put 4 cards in each of the 3 piles, but 2 sports cards are left. The remainder is 2 and can be written as R2; 14 ÷ 3 is 4 R2. Leroy can either give the extra sports cards to a friend or save them until he gets enough to make another pile of 4.

Use counters to solve the following problems.

1. 28 stickers, 5 stickers on a page
   How many pages are full? ____5____
   What is the remainder? ____3____
   What does the remainder mean? There are 3 stickers not on a page, so an additional page is needed.

2. 19 books, 6 books on a shelf
   How many shelves are full? ____3____
   What is the remainder? ____1____
   What does the remainder mean? There is 1 book not on a shelf, so an additional shelf is needed.

3. 34 marbles, 5 marbles in a group
   How many groups are complete? ____6____
   What is the remainder? ____4____
   What does the remainder mean? There are 4 marbles not in a group, so an additional group is needed.

G51 (student p. 1)   MDIS 2.0

Name _____

Intervention
Lesson **G51**

Interpret the Remainder (continued)

Solve each of the following problems.

4. 62 buttons, 7 buttons on a shirt
   How many shirts can be made? ____8____
   What is the remainder? ____6____
   What does the remainder mean? There are 6 extra buttons, which is not enough to make another shirt.

5. 95 pens, 10 pens in a package
   How many complete packages of pens are there? How many pens are extra?
   9 complete packages of pens; 5 pens are extra or R5

6. 40 action figures, 6 action figures in a row
   How many complete rows of action figures are there? How many action figures are extra?
   6 complete rows; 4 action figures are extra or R4

7. 74 apples, 9 apples in a bag
   How many bags are full? How many apples are extra?
   8 bags; 2 apples are extra or R2

8. Robert claims that 57 game tokens can be shared equally among himself and 5 friends without having any extra tokens. Is Robert correct? Explain.
   Robert Is Incorrect; 57 ÷ 6 is 9 R3, so there will be 3 game tokens

9. Mary is organizing her collection of 37 crayons in groups of 5. How many complete groups will she have? Are there any extra crayons? What can Mary do with any extra crayons?
   7 complete groups; 2 extra crayons; she can either start another incomplete group, or she can give them to a friend.

G51 (student p. 2)   MDIS 2.0

Objective Students will interpret remainders.
Vocabulary Remainder
Materials Counters

① Conceptual Development
Use with Exercises 1–3.

In this lesson you will interpret remainders.

Revisit the term *remainder* as needed. Have students read the paragraphs at the top of the page. *What does a remainder tell us?* A remainder tells us that there some left over when a large group of items has been divided into smaller equal groups. *How can you use counters to find a remainder?* Sort the counters into equal groups and see how many counters are left over. Have student complete Exercises 1–3.

② Practice Use with Exercises 4–9.

Remind students that if they cannot evenly divide all of the items into groups, the items left over are the remainder.

Error Intervention If students have difficulty understanding remainders, have them stand and act out a problem. After dividing into equal groups, some students will be "left over."

If You Have More Time Have students solve the following problem and explain their methods: *Aaron has 58 dog treats. He wants to give his dog 7 treats per week. He says he has enough treats for 7 weeks and has a remainder of 9. Is he correct? Explain why or why not.* No; He has enough treats for 8 weeks with a remainder of 2.

③ Assessment

In this lesson students learned to interpret remainders. Use the **Quick Check** problem to assess students' understanding.

Quick Check **Formative** Assessment

Candace has 41 bottles of nail polish. She can fit 5 bottles in a box. How many boxes will she fill? How many bottles are left over? 8 boxes with 1 bottle left over

USING OBJECTS TO DIVIDE

Name _____

Using Objects to Divide

Materials place-value blocks: 5 tens and 16 ones for each pair

Jaime has 56 swimming ribbons. He can display 4 ribbons in one frame.
How many frames will he need?
Find 56 ÷ 4 by answering 1 to 11.

1. Use place-value blocks to show the 56 ribbons.

2. Divide the tens evenly into 4 equal groups.

3. Are there any tens leftover? __yes__

   How many? __1__

4. Regroup the leftover ten as ones.

   __1__ ten = __10__ ones

5. Combine the regrouped ones with the
   other ones.

   __10__ ones + 6 ones = __16__ ones

6. Divide the 16 ones evenly into the
   4 equal groups.

7. How many ones are in each group?

   __4__

8. Are there any ones leftover? __no__

9. How many tens and ones are in each group?

   __1__ ten and __4__ ones

10. So 56 ÷ 4 = __14__. How many frames will Jaime
    need to display his swimming ribbons?   __14__ frames

11. **Reasoning** How can you check that the quotient is correct?
    Multiply 4 × 14 and see if the product is 56.

Name _____

Using Objects to Divide (continued)

Use place-value blocks or draw a picture to find each quotient.

12. 36 ÷ 3 = __12__   13. 42 ÷ 2 = __21__   14. 68 ÷ 4 = __17__

15. 60 ÷ 4 = __15__   16. 75 ÷ 5 = __15__   17. 54 ÷ 3 = __18__

18. 72 ÷ 6 = __12__   19. 57 ÷ 3 = __19__   20. 48 ÷ 3 = __16__

21. 52 ÷ 4 = __13__   22. 76 ÷ 4 = __19__   23. 38 ÷ 2 = __19__

24. Use place-value blocks or draw a picture to
    find how many nickels equal the number of
    pennies in the chart. (Remember: 1 nickel
    equals 5 pennies.)

Pennies	Nickels
70	14
65	13
90	18
85	17

25. **Reasoning** Write a division problem that
    does not require you to regroup the tens.
    The dividend must be two-digits and greater
    than 50. The divisor must be one-digit and
    greater than 5.

    Answers will vary. Sample answers: 60 ÷ 6,
    80 ÷ 8, or 90 ÷ 9

Objective Students will use objects to divide.
Vocabulary Quotient
Materials Place-value blocks: 5 tens and 16 ones
for each pair

① Conceptual Development
Use with Exercises 1–11.

In this lesson you will learn to use objects to divide.

Revisit the term *quotient* as needed. Have students
read the problem and complete Exercises 1–4 using
the place-value blocks. *Why did you need to regroup
1 ten as 10 ones?* So I can divide the 10 into groups.
How does using objects help you divide? Using
objects can help me to see how I can divide the
items into groups and to see whether I have any
items left over, or remaining. Have students complete
Exercises 5–11.

② Practice **Use with Exercises 12–25.**

Remind students that they are dividing the greater
number into equal groups.

Error Intervention If students have difficulty
using objects to divide, it may be easier to have
them use only ones cubes, count out their beginning
number, and then divide into groups.

If You Have More Time Have students solve
the following problem and explain their methods:
*Lynda was bagging bubble gum for a concession
stand. She has 56 pieces of bubble gum and wants
to make bags of 8 pieces each. How many bags can
she make?* 7 bags

③ Assessment

In this lesson students learned to use objects to divide.
Use the **Quick Check** problem to assess students'
understanding.

Quick Check **Formative** Assessment

*There are 78 sardines in a bucket. The zookeeper
wants to give each of the 6 penguins the same
number of sardines. How many sardines can each
penguin get?* 13 sardines

DIVIDING TWO-DIGIT NUMBERS

Name _____

Dividing Two-Digit Numbers

Materials place-value blocks: 6 tens and 15 ones for each pair

Find 65 ÷ 5 by answering 1 to 17.

1. Use place-value blocks to show 65.

2. Divide the 6 tens into 5 equal groups.

3. How many tens can go into each group? __1__

4. Record the 1 above the 6 in 65, at the right.

5. How many tens were used?

   5 × 1 ten = __5__ tens

6. Record the tens used below the 6 in 65, at the right.

7. How many tens are leftover?

   6 − 5 = __1__ ten

8. Record the tens left below the 5 and the line.

9. Regroup the tens into ones and add the other 5 ones.

   __1__ ten + 5 ones = __15__ ones

10. Bring down the 5 next to the 1, to show the 15 regrouped ones.

11. Divide the 15 ones evenly into the 5 groups. How many ones can go in each group? __3__

12. Record the 3 above the 5 in 65.

13. How many ones were used?

    5 × 3 ones = __15__ ones

$$
\begin{array}{r}
13 \\
5\overline{)65} \\
5 \leftarrow 5 \times 1 \\
\hline
6-5 \rightarrow 15 \\
15 \leftarrow 5 \times 3 \\
\hline
15-15 \rightarrow 0
\end{array}
$$

G53 (student p. 1)   MDIS 2.0

Name _____

Dividing Two-Digit Numbers (continued)

14. Record the ones used below the 15 regrouped ones.

15. How many ones are leftover? 15 − 15 = __0__ ones

16. Record the ones left below the 15 and the line.

17. What is 65 ÷ 5? __13__

Find each quotient.

18. $8\overline{)96}$ 12

19. $2\overline{)32}$ 16

20. $3\overline{)54}$ 18

21. $5\overline{)70}$ 14

22. $6\overline{)84}$ 14

23. $5\overline{)75}$ 15

24. $7\overline{)77}$ 11

25. $6\overline{)78}$ 13

26. $9\overline{)99}$ 11

27. $4\overline{)76}$ 19

28. $5\overline{)85}$ 17

29. $2\overline{)46}$ 23

30. Robert is writing a poem. The poem is divided into 5 stanzas and is on 2 pages. There are 60 lines in the poem. How many lines are in each stanza?   __12 lines__

31. **Reasoning** Yoko says that when you divide 75 by 5, the answer is 15. How can you check her answer? Is she correct? You can check her answer by multiplying 5 and 15. She is correct because 5 × 15 = 75.

G53 (student p. 2)   MDIS 2.0

Objective Students will divide two-digit numbers.

Vocabulary Quotient, regroup

Materials Place-value blocks: 6 tens and 15 ones for each pair

1 Conceptual Development
Use with Exercises 1–17.

In this lesson you will learn to divide two-digit numbers.

Revisit the terms *quotient* and *regroup* as needed. Have students read the problem and complete Exercises 1–10. *How does dividing the tens place first help you solve the problem?* When you start with the tens place, you can regroup any leftover tens with the ones. *What would you do if you subtracted the ones and there were some left?* I would leave the amount left over as a remainder. Have students complete Exercises 11–17.

2 Practice Use with Exercises 18–31.

Remind students to start with the tens place when they divide.

Error Intervention If students have difficulty solving division problems on paper, suggest that they write the problems on graph paper. Using graph paper helps assure that students line the numbers up vertically while they work through the problems.

If You Have More Time Have students solve the following problem and explain their methods: *Barb says if you divide 96 by 6, the answer is 16, but she isn't sure if she is correct. How can she check her answer?* She can multiply 16 × 6 to get 96.

3 Assessment

In this lesson students learned to divide two-digit numbers. Use the **Quick Check** problem to assess students' understanding.

Quick Check 🪷 **Formative** Assessment

Kourtney is getting bottled water ready for a class trip. She has 96 bottles of water and needs 4 bottles for each student. How many students does she have enough water for? 24 students

---

DIVIDING THREE-DIGIT NUMBERS

Name _____

Dividing Three-Digit Numbers

 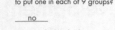

There are 324 baseball players at camp. If the camp counselors put them into 9 equal-sized living groups, how many players are in each group?

Find 324 ÷ 9 by answering 1 to 17.

The place-value blocks at the right show 324.

1. Are there enough hundreds in 324 to put one in each of 9 groups?

   __no__

2. Regroup the hundreds.

   3 hundreds + 2 tens = __32__ tens

3. How many tens can go into each of 9 groups? __3__

4. Record the 3 above the 2 in 324, at the right.

5. How many tens were used?

   9 × 3 tens = __27__ tens

6. Record the tens used below the 32 in 324, at the right.

7. How many tens are left over?

   32 − 27 = __5__ tens

8. Record the tens left below the 27 and the line.

9. Regroup the tens into ones and add the other 4 ones. Bring down the 4 to show the total ones.

   5 tens + 4 ones = __54__ ones

```
        36
     9)324
        27  ← 9 × 3
32 − 27 → 54
        54  ← 9 × 6
54 − 54 →  0
```

G54 (student p. 1)   MDIS 2.0

Name _____

Dividing Three-Digit Numbers (continued)

10. How many of the 54 ones can go in each of the 9 groups? __6__ ones

11. Record the 6 above the 4 in 324.

12. How many ones were used? 9 × 6 ones = __54__ ones

13. Record the ones used below the 54 regrouped ones.

14. How many ones are leftover? 54 − 54 = __0__ ones

15. Record the ones left below the 54 and the line.

16. What is 324 ÷ 9? __36__

17. How many players are in each living group? __36__ players

Find each quotient.

18. 8)656   **82**   19. 2)304   **152**   20. 9)828   **92**

21. 5)465   **93**   22. 7)238   **34**   23. 3)639   **213**

24. Nine friends are sharing a box of crackers. The box contains 135 crackers. How many crackers will each friend get if they are divided evenly?

    15 crackers

25. **Reasoning** In the division problem 432 ÷ 5, should the first step be to divide the hundreds or to regroup the hundreds to tens? Explain your reasoning.

    Begin by regrouping because 4 hundreds are not enough to put one hundred in each of 5 groups.

G54 (student p. 2)   MDIS 2.0

Objective Students will divide three-digit numbers.
Vocabulary Quotient, regroup
Materials Place-value blocks, if needed

1 Conceptual Development
Use with Exercises 1–17.

In this lesson you will learn to divide three-digit numbers.

Revisit the terms *quotient* and *regroup* as needed. Have students read the problem and complete Exercise 1. *What do you think you will have to do with the hundreds to be able to divide them into 9 groups?* We could regroup the hundreds into tens. Have students complete Exercises 2–4. *Why did you write the 3 above the tens place and not the hundreds place?* There are not enough hundreds, so when they are regrouped to tens, the hundreds place doesn't have a number in it. Have students complete Exercises 5–17.

2 Practice Use with Exercises 18–25.

Remind students that if they cannot divide into the hundreds, they can regroup and express the hundreds as tens.

Error Intervention
If students have difficulty dividing three-digit numbers, allow them to use place-value blocks or encourage them to create drawings that they can use to complete the problem.

If You Have More Time
Have students solve the following problem and explain their methods: *Scott is solving 638 ÷ 5. He says he needs to regroup the hundreds into 63 tens. Is he correct? Explain your answer.* No; The 6 hundreds can be divided by 5, so no regrouping is needed.

3 Assessment

In this lesson students learned to divide three-digit numbers. Use the **Quick Check** problem to assess students' understanding.

Quick Check   **Formative Assessment**

There are 9 teammates sharing the case of baseballs. There are 117 baseballs in the case. How many baseballs will each player get if the balls are divided evenly? 13 baseballs per player

---

Name _____

Intervention
Lesson **G55**

Zeros in the Quotient

Janice has 412 photographs. She wants to put them into 4 albums.
If she puts the same number of photographs in each album,
how many photographs will be in each album?

Find 412 ÷ 4 by answering 1 to 13.

The place-value blocks at the right
show 412.

1. Are there enough hundreds in 412
   to put one in each of 4 groups? ___yes___

2. How many hundreds can go into
   each of 4 groups? ___1___
   Record the 1 in the hundreds place of the quotient, below.

3. How many hundreds were used?

   4 × 1 hundred = ___4___ hundreds
   Record the hundreds used under the 4 in 412, below.

4. How many hundreds are leftover?

   4 − 4 = ___0___ hundreds

5. Bring down the 1 ten. How many
   tens can go into each of 4 groups? ___0___
   Record the 0 in the tens place of the quotient.

6. How many tens were used?

   4 × 0 tens = ___0___ tens
   Record this 0 below the 1.

7. How many tens are leftover? 1 − 0 = ___1___
   Record the tens left below the 0 and the line.

8. Regroup the tens into ones and add the other 2 ones.
   Bring down the 2 to show the total ones.

   1 ten + 2 ones = ___12___ ones

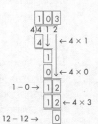

$$\begin{array}{r} 1\,0\,3 \\ 4\overline{)4\,1\,2} \\ 4\,\downarrow \leftarrow 4\times1 \\ \hline 1 \\ 0\,\downarrow \leftarrow 4\times0 \\ \hline 1\,2 \leftarrow 4\times3 \\ 0 \end{array}$$

1 − 0 → 12
12 − 12 → 0

G55 (student p. 1)   MDIS 2.0

Name _____

Intervention
Lesson **G55**

Zeros in the Quotient (continued)

9. How many ones can go into each of 4 groups? ___3___
   Record the 3 in the ones place of the quotient.

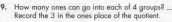

10. How many ones were used? 4 × 3 ones = ___12___ ones
    Record this 12 below the regrouped 12.

11. How many ones are leftover? 12 − 12 = ___0___
    Record the ones left below the 12 and the line.

12. What is 412 ÷ 4? ___103___

13. How many photographs will be
    in each of Janice's albums? ___103___ photographs

Find each quotient.

14. $\overset{103}{8\overline{)824}}$ 15. $\overset{305\ R1}{2\overline{)611}}$ 16. $\overset{1027}{9\overline{)9,243}}$

17. $\overset{109}{5\overline{)545}}$ 18. $\overset{303\ R3}{7\overline{)2,124}}$ 19. $\overset{205\ R2}{3\overline{)617}}$

20. $\overset{10\ R2}{3\overline{)32}}$ 21. $\overset{108\ R1}{5\overline{)541}}$ 22. $\overset{40\ R5}{7\overline{)285}}$

23. **Reasoning** Dante divided 642 by 8 and wrote the quotient as 8
    remainder 2. What error did Dante make? What is the correct answer?
    Sample answer: The student forgot to write the zero
    as a placeholder in the quotient. The correct answer
    is 80 R2.

G55 (student p. 2)   MDIS 2.0

Objective Students will understand zeros in the
quotient.
Vocabulary Quotient, regroup
Materials Place-value blocks, if needed

① Conceptual Development
Use with Exercises 1–13.

*In this lesson you will learn to understand zeros in the
quotient.*

Revisit the terms *quotient* and *regroup* as needed.
Have students read the problem and verbalize what
the problem is asking them to do. Divide 412 into 4
equal groups Guide students to complete Exercises
1–4. Draw attention to Exercise 5. Point out that there
is only one whole ten. *Do we have enough tens to
put ten in each of the four groups?* No Have students
complete Exercise 5. *What does the zero in your
quotient represent?* That means that there are not
enough tens to go into each of the 4 groups. Have
students complete Exercises 6–13.

② Practice Use with Exercises 14–23.

Remind students that when they use a zero in the
quotient as a placeholder, they have to remember to
regroup to the next place value.

Error Intervention If students have difficulty
with zeros in the quotient, have them use place-value
blocks to see what the zero represents and how it
helps with regrouping.

If You Have More Time Have students solve
the following problem and explain their methods:
*Divide 912 ÷ 3. Show all of your work and explain
your thinking.* 304; Check students' work.

③ Assessment

In this lesson students learned to understand zeros in
the quotient. Use the **Quick Check** problem to assess
students' understanding.

Quick Check   Formative
Assessment

*Marsha divided 3,256 by 8 and got 47 as her
quotient. What error did Marsha make? What is
the correct answer?* 3,256 ÷ 8 = 407; Marsha forgot
to use a zero to hold the tens place.

G55   MDIS 2.0

DIVIDING GREATER NUMBERS

Name _____

Dividing Greater Numbers

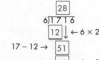
The Camara family wants to travel the same distance each of 6 days. They need to travel 1,716 miles in all. Answer 1 to 15 to find how far they should travel each day.

Find 1,716 ÷ 6.

1. Are there enough thousands to put one in each of 6 groups? ___no___

2. Regroup the thousand into hundreds and add the other 7 hundreds.

   1 thousand + 7 hundreds = __17__ hundreds

3. How many hundreds can go into each of 6 groups? ___2___
   Record the 2 in the hundreds place of the quotient, below.

4. How many hundreds were used?

   6 × 2 hundreds = __12__ hundreds
   Record the hundreds used below the 17 in 1,716, below.

5. How many hundreds are leftover?

   17 hundreds − 12 hundreds

   = __5__ hundreds
   Record the 5 under the 12.

```
        2 8
    6)1 7 1 6
      1 2  ↓ ← 6 × 2
   17 − 12 →  5 1
              4 8 ← 6 × 8
      51 − 48 →  3
```

6. Regroup the hundreds into tens and add the other 1 ten.

   5 hundreds + 1 ten = __51__ tens
   Bring down the 1 ten next to the 5 to show how many tens in all.

7. How many tens can go into each of 6 groups? __8__
   Record the 8 in the tens place of the quotient.

8. How many tens were used? 6 × 8 tens = __48__ tens
   Record 48 below the 51.

9. How many tens are leftover? __3__
   Record the tens left below the 48 and the line.

Name _____

Dividing Greater Numbers (continued)

10. Regroup the tens into ones and add the other 6 ones. Bring down the 6 to show the total ones.

    3 tens + 6 ones = __36__ ones

```
        2 8 6
    6)1 7 1 6
      1 2
        5 1
        4 8 ↓
          3 6
          3 6 ← 6 × 6
            0 ← 36 − 36
```

11. How many ones can go into each of 6 groups? ___6___
    Record the 6 in the ones place of the quotient.

12. How many ones were used?

    6 × 6 ones = __36__ ones
    Record the 36 below the regrouped 36.

13. How many ones are leftover? 36 − 36 = __0__
    Record the ones left below the 36 and the line.

14. What is 1,716 ÷ 6? __286__

15. How far should the Camara family travel each day? __286__ miles

Find each quotient.

16. 4)3,560 → 890

17. 6)1,836 → 306

18. 4)4,112 → 1,028

19. 2)2,246 → 1,123

20. 8)832 → 104

21. 7)6,510 → 930

22. **Reasoning** How can you use estimation to find out if the answer of 286 is reasonable for 1,716 ÷ 6?
    1,716 ÷ 6 is about 1,800 ÷ 6 = 300. Since 286 is close to 300, 286 is reasonable.

Objective Students will divide greater numbers.

1 Conceptual Development
Use with Exercises 1–15.

In this lesson you will learn to divide greater numbers.

Read the problem with students. *What do we know?* The family needs to travel the same distance each day for 6 days and cover 1,716 miles. *What do we need to find?* The number of miles the family will travel each day *How can we show that as an equation?* 1,716 ÷ 6 *When you divide, which digit will you begin with?* Thousands Read Exercise 1. *What digit is in the thousands place?* 1 *Are there enough thousands to put 1 in each of the 6 groups?* No *If there aren't enough thousands, what do you do next?* Regroup the thousand into hundreds Have students complete Exercises 2–15.

2 Practice Use with Exercises 16–22.

Discuss Exercise 22 together. Remind students that they can use compatible numbers and rounding to estimate.

Error Intervention If students have difficulty dividing, remind them to think about the fact families for each number. Provide fact tables as needed so students can continue to practice dividing longer numbers without being slowed by recalling facts.

If You Have More Time Have students solve the first problem again, using 1,932 miles as the total distance over 6 days. 322 miles

3 Assessment

In this lesson students learned to divide greater numbers. Use the **Quick Check** problem to assess students' understanding.

Quick Check **Formative** Assessment

Solve: 1,512 ÷ 4 378

Student Page 1

Name _____

Intervention
Lesson **G57**

Factoring Numbers

Materials color tiles or counters, 24 for each student

The arrays below show all of the factors of 12.

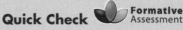

1×12

2×6 3×4 4×3 6×2

12×1

The order factors are listed may vary.
1. What are all the factors of 12?
   __1__, __2__, __3__, __4__, __6__, __12__

2. Create all the possible arrays you can with 17 color tiles.

3. What are the factors of 17? __1__, __17__

Numbers which have only 2 possible arrays and exactly 2 factors are prime numbers.

4. Is 17 a prime number? __yes__

5. Is 12 a prime number? __no__

Numbers which have more than 2 possible arrays and more than 2 factors are composite numbers.

6. Is 17 a composite number? __no__

7. Is 12 a composite number? __yes__
The order factors are listed may vary.
8. What are all the factors of 24? __1, 2, 3, 6, 8, 12, 24__

9. Is 24 a prime number or a composite number? __composite__

G57 (student p. 1)   MDIS 2.0

Student Page 2

Name _____

Intervention
Lesson **G57**

Factoring Numbers (continued)

Find all the factors of each number. Tell whether each is prime or composite.

10. 7
    __1, 7;__
    prime

11. 8
    __1, 2, 4, 8;__
    composite

12. 21
    __1, 3, 7, 21;__
    composite

13. 48
    __1, 2, 3, 4, 6, 8,__
    __12, 16, 24, 48;__
    composite

14. 51
    __1, 3, 17, 51;__
    composite

15. 9
    __1, 3, 9;__
    composite

16. 13
    __1, 13;__
    prime

17. 26
    __1, 2, 13, 26;__
    composite

18. 40
    __1, 2, 4, 5, 8,__
    __10, 20, 40;__
    composite

19. 55
    __1, 5, 11, 55;__
    composite

20. 70
    __1, 2, 5, 7, 10,__
    __14, 35, 70;__
    composite

21. 83
    __1, 83__
    prime

22. Mr. Lee has 18 desks in his room. He would like them arranged in a rectangular array. Draw all the different possible arrays and write a multiplication sentence for each.
    See answers on page 59.

23. **Reasoning** Lee says 53 is a prime number because it is an odd number. Is Lee's reasoning correct? Give an example to prove your reasoning.
    No; 53 is a prime number not because it is an odd number, but because it only has 2 factors: 1 and 53. A counterexample is 15 is an odd number but it is not a prime number because 15 has more than 2 factors: 1, 3, 5, 15.

G57 (student p. 2)   MDIS 2.0

Objective Students will factor numbers.
Vocabulary Prime number, composite number
Materials Color tiles or counters, 24 for each student

① Conceptual Development
Use with Exercises 1–9.

In this lesson you will learn to factor numbers.

Remind students that a number can have more than two factors. Read Exercise 1, and discuss the many factor pairs of 12 shown in the arrays. Have students write all the factors of 12. Read Exercise 2. Provide time for students to attempt to create arrays using 17. Revisit the terms *prime number* and *composite number* as needed. Have students paraphrase the difference between a prime number and a composite number. *What are the prime numbers less than 10?* 1, 2, 3, 5, 7 *What are the composite numbers less than 10?* 4, 6, 8, 9 Encourage students to use their counters to assess whether 12 and 17 are prime or composite numbers and complete Exercises 3–9.

② Practice Use with Exercises 10–23.

Remind students that a prime number has exactly two factors: itself and 1.

Error Intervention If students have difficulty finding all the factors of the numbers shown, have them first assess whether the number is divisible by 2, then 3, then 4, and continue up to 10.

If You Have More Time Have students share the strategies they used to determine the factors for each number and how they knew a particular number was prime or composite.

③ Assessment

In this lesson students learned to factor numbers. Use the **Quick Check** problem to assess students' understanding.

Quick Check 🍃 **Formative Assessment**

Find the factors of 36 and 19 and tell whether each is prime or composite. Factors of 36: 1×36, 2×18, 3×12, 4×9, 6×6; composite; Factors of 19: 1×19; prime

---

Name _____

Intervention
Lesson **G58**

Divisibility by 2, 3, 5, 9, and 10

A number such as 256 is divisible by a number like 2 if 256 ÷ 2 has no remainder. If 256 is a multiple of 2, then 256 is divisible by 2.

Use the divisibility rules and answer 1 to 10 to determine if 256 is divisible by 2, 3, 5, 9, or 10.

Divisibility Rules	
Number	**Rule**
2	The last digit is even: 0, 2, 4, 6, 8.
3	The sum of the digits is divisible by 3.
5	The last digit ends in a 0 or 5.
9	The sum of the digits is divisible by 9.
10	The ones digit is a 0.

1. Is the last digit in 256 an even number? _yes_

2. Is 256 divisible by 2? _yes_

3. Is the last digit in 256 a 0 or 5? _no_

4. Is 256 divisible by 5? _no_

5. Is 256 divisible by 10? _no_

6. What is the sum of the digits of 256? 2 + 5 + 6 = _13_

7. Is the sum of the digits of 256 divisible by 3? _no_

8. Is 256 divisible by 3? _no_

9. Is the sum of the digits of 256 divisible by 9? _no_

10. Is 256 divisible by 9? _no_

Use the divisibility rules to determine if 720 is divisible by 2, 5, 9, or 10.

11. Is 720 divisible by 2? _yes_   12. Is 720 divisible by 5? _yes_

13. Is 720 divisible by 10? _yes_   14. Is 720 divisible by 9? _yes_

G58 (student p. 1)   MDIS 2.0

Name _____

Intervention
Lesson **G58**

Divisibility by 2, 3, 5, 9, and 10 (continued)

Test each number to see if it is divisible by 2, 3, 5, 9, or 10. List the numbers each is divisible by.

15. 56
_____2_____

16. 78
_____2, 3_____

17. 182
_____2_____

18. 380
_____2, 5, 10_____

19. 105
_____3, 5_____

20. 126
_____2, 3, 9_____

21. 4,311
_____3, 9_____

22. 8,356
_____2_____

23. 2,580
_____2, 3, 5, 10_____

24. 7,265
_____5_____

25. 4,815
_____3, 5, 9_____

26. 630
_____2, 3, 5, 9, 10_____

27. Feliz has 225 baseball trophies. He wants to display his trophies on some shelves with an equal number of trophies on each. He can buy shelves in packages of 5, 9, or 10. Which shelf package should he NOT buy? Explain.
Feliz should not buy the package with 10 shelves.
225 is divisible by 5 and 9, but not by 10.

28. **Reasoning** Are all numbers that are divisible by 5 also divisible by 10? Explain your reasoning.
Not all numbers that are divisible by 5 are also divisible by 10. For example, 25 is divisible by 5 but not by 10.

29. **Reasoning** Are all numbers that are divisible by 10 also divisible by 5? Explain your reasoning.
All numbers that are divisible by 10 are divisible by 5. If a number ends in a zero, and thus is divisible by 10, it must end in either a zero or 5 and thus be divisible by 5.

G58 (student p. 2)   MDIS 2.0

Objective Students will determine divisibility by 2, 3, 5, 9, and 10.
Vocabulary Divisible

❶ Conceptual Development
Use with Exercises 1–14.

In this lesson you will learn to determine divisibility by 2, 3, 5, 9, and 10.

Remind students that if a number is *divisible* by another, it can be divided by that number without a remainder. *What number is 12 divisible by? 2 How do you know that so quickly? I know this fact from memory. What number is 243 divisible by? 3 Why is it more difficult to answer that question? Because the number is greater* Tell students that there are rules that make it easier to know the numbers that a greater number is divisible by. Discuss the Divisibility Rules table and then compare the first rule with 256 to respond to Exercises 1–2. Tell students that these rules will work for any number regardless of its size, or the number of digits. Have students complete Exercises 3–14.

❷ Practice Use with Exercises 15–29.

Remind students to test all the factors because many numbers have more than two factors.

Error Intervention If students have difficulty finding all factors of the numbers shown, have them go through the Divisibility Rules table in order each time, asking first whether the number is divisible by 2, then 3, then 5, then 9, and finally 10.

If You Have More Time Have students add 10 to Exercise 24 and add 12 to Exercise 25, and then re-evaluate for divisibility. Exercise 24: 7,275 is divisible by 3 and 5; Exercise 25: 4,827 is divisible by 3.

❸ Assessment

In this lesson students learned to determine divisibility by 2, 3, 5, 9, and 10. Use the **Quick Check** problem to assess students' understanding.

Quick Check 🌿 **Formative** Assessment

Test 1,215 to see whether it is divisible by 2, 3, 5, 9, or 10. 3, 5, 9

DIVISIBILITY

Name _____

Divisibility

A number such as 1,875 is divisible by a number like 5 if 1,875 ÷ 5 has no remainder. If 1,875 is a multiple of 5, then 1,875 is divisible by 5.

Use the divisibility rules to determine if 1,875 is divisible by 2, 3, 4, 5, 6, 9, or 10, by answering 1 to 15.

Divisibility Rules	
Number	**Rule**
2	The last digit is even: 0, 2, 4, 6, 8.
3	The sum of the digits is divisible by 3.
4	The last two digits of the number make a number that is divisible by 4.
5	The last digit ends in a 0 or 5.
6	The number is divisible by 2 and 3.
9	The sum of the digits is divisible by 9.
10	The ones digit is a 0.

1. Is the last digit in 1,875 an even number? _____ no
2. Is 1,875 divisible by 2? _____ no
3. Is the last digit in 1,875 a 0 or 5? _____ yes
4. Is 1,875 divisible by 5? _____ yes
5. Is 1,875 divisible by 10? _____ no
6. What is the sum of the digits of 1,875?

   1 + 8 + 7 + 5 = _21_

7. Is the sum of the digits divisible by 3? _____ yes
8. Is 1,875 divisible by 3? _____ yes
9. Is the sum of the digits divisible by 9? _____ no
10. Is 1,875 divisible by 9? _____ no
11. Is 1,875 divisible by both 2 and 3? _____ no

G59 (student p. 1)   MDIS 2.0

Name _____

Divisibility (continued)

12. Is 1,875 divisible by 6? _____ no
13. What number makes up the last two digits of 1,875? _____ 75
14. Is 75 divisible by 4? _____ no
15. Is 1,875 divisible by 4? _____ no

Test each number to see if it is divisible by 2, 3, 4, 5, 6, 9, or 10. List the numbers each is divisible by.

16. 214
    _2_
17. 313
    none
18. 425
    _5_
19. 670
    _2, 5, 10_

20. 2,312
    _2, 4, 8_
21. 773
    none
22. 470
    _2, 5, 10_
23. 847
    _7, 11_

24. 845
    _5_
25. 400
    _2, 4, 5, 10_
26. 900 _2, 3, 4, 5, 6, 9, 10_
27. 1,002
    _2, 3, 6_

28. 430
    _2, 5, 10_
29. 635
    _5_
30. 3,470
    _2, 5, 10_
31. 9,630 _2, 3, 5, 6, 9, 10_

32. 2,345
    _5_
33. 5,672
    _2, 4_
34. 1,236
    _2, 3, 4, 6_
35. 7,305
    _3, 5_

36. Camp Many Lakes has 198 campers registered this year. They are planning many activities and games which must be completed in groups of equal number of campers. What different sizes of groups can Camp Many Lakes divide the campers into? _2, 3, 6, or 9_

37. **Reasoning** Are all numbers that are divisible by 2 also divisible by 10? Explain your reasoning.
    Not all numbers that are divisible by 2 are also divisible by 10. For example, 24 is divisible by 2 but not by 10.

38. **Reasoning** Are all numbers that are divisible by 10 also divisible by 2? Explain your reasoning.
    All numbers that are divisible by 10 are divisible by 2. If a number ends in a zero, and thus is divisible by 10, it ends in an even number and thus is divisible by 2.

G59 (student p. 2)   MDIS 2.0

Objective Students will determine divisibility by 2, 3, 4, 5, 6, 9, and 10.

1 Conceptual Development
Use with Exercises 1–15.

In this lesson you will learn to determine divisibility by 2, 3, 4, 5, 6, 9, and 10.

Remind students that if a number is divisible by another, it can be divided by that number without a remainder. *What number is 100 divisible by?* 10 *What clues could tell you the answer if you did not already know?* Sample answer: The ones digit is a 0. Read the Divisibility Rules table together and complete Exercises 1–2. *How do you know that 1,875 is not divisible by 2?* The last digit is not even. Have students complete Exercises 3–15.

2 Practice Use with Exercises 16–38.

Remind students to test all the factors in the table because many numbers are divisible by more than two factors.

Error Intervention If students have difficulty finding the factors of the numbers shown, have them go through the Divisibility Rules table in order each time, asking first whether their number is divisible by 2, and then moving up through 10.

If You Have More Time Have students add together the numbers in Exercises 16–17 and write the sum. Then test the sum to see whether it is divisible by the numbers in the Divisibility Rules chart. *527 is not divisible by 2, 3, 4, 5, 6, 9, or 10.*

3 Assessment

In this lesson students learned to determine divisibility by 2, 3, 4, 5, 6, 9, and 10. Use the **Quick Check** problem to assess students' understanding.

Quick Check **Formative** Assessment

Test 2,958 to see whether it is divisible by 2, 3, 4, 5, 6, 9, or 10. 2, 3, 6

EXPONENTS

Name _____

Exponents

Scott is planning to run in a race and asked 2 friends to sponsor him. The following week, each friend asked 2 more friends to sponsor Scott. If this continued, how many sponsors did Scott have after seven weeks?

1. Complete the table.

Week	Number of Sponsors (Expanded Form)	Number of Sponsors (Exponential Form)	Number of Sponsors (Standard Form)
1	2	2^1	2
2	2×2	2^2	4
3	$2 \times 2 \times 2$	2^3	8
4	$2 \times 2 \times 2 \times 2$	2^4	16
5	$2 \times 2 \times 2 \times 2 \times 2$	2^5	32
6	$2 \times 2 \times 2 \times 2 \times 2 \times 2$	2^6	64
7	$2 \times 2 \times 2 \times 2 \times 2 \times 2 \times 2$	2^7	128

2. How many sponsors will Scott have on the 10th week?

Expanded form: $2 \times 2 \times 2 \times 2 \times 2 \times 2 \times 2 \times 2 \times 2 \times 2$

Exponential form: 2^{10} Standard form: 1,024

3. If Scott started by asking 3 friends to sponsor him and each of those friends asked three friends, how many sponsors would he have on the 4th week?

Expanded form: $3 \times 3 \times 3 \times 3$

Exponential form: 3^4 Standard form: 81

4. Use the table above to complete the following patterns. 16, 8, 4, 2, 1

$2^4, 2^3, 2^2, 2^1, 2^0$

$2^0 = 1$. Any number, except zero, to the zero power is 1.

5. What is 5^0? 1

G60 (student p. 1)   MDIS 2.0

Name _____

Exponents (continued)

Write each expression in exponential form.

6. $4 \times 4 \times 4$ **7.** $7 \times 7 \times 7 \times 7 \times 7$ **8.** $6 \times 6 \times 6$

    4^3 7^5 6^3

9. $10 \times 10 \times 10 \times 10$ **10.** 5×5 **11.** $3 \times 3 \times 3 \times 3$

    10^4 5^2 3^4

Write each expression in standard form.

12. 2^7 **13.** 1^7 **14.** 6^3

    128   1   216

15. 83^1 **16.** 4^3 **17.** 11^2

    83   64   121

18. 2^8 **19.** 10^4 **20.** 7^2

    256   10,000   49

21. 0^5 **22.** 3^3 **23.** 12^0

    0   27   1

Write each expression in expanded form.

24. 12^4 **25.** 8^3 **26.** 4^4

   $12 \times 12 \times 12 \times 12$ $8 \times 8 \times 8$ $4 \times 4 \times 4 \times 4$

27. 32^5 **28.** 3^4 **29.** 200^2

  $32 \times 32 \times 32 \times 32 \times 32$ $3 \times 3 \times 3 \times 3$ 200×200

30. **Reasoning** Is 2^5 the same as 5^2? Check by writing both numbers in standard form.
No, because $2^5 = 32$ and $5^2 = 25$.

G60 (student p. 2)   MDIS 2.0

Objective Students will work with exponents.
Vocabulary Exponent, exponential form

① Conceptual Development
Use with Exercises 1–5.

In this lesson you will learn to work with exponents.

Revisit the term *exponent* as needed. Have students read the word problem at the top of the page. *What do we know?* 2 friends are each asking 2 more friends to sponsor Scott each week. *What do we want to find?* The number of sponsors Scott will have after seven weeks Review each column and then discuss each row. *How is $2 \times 2 \times 2$ written in exponential form?* 2^3 *Using the format we see here, how would you write $5 \times 5 \times 5 \times 5$ in exponential form?* 5^4 *How do you know this?* 5 is being multiplied 4 times. Have students complete the table. *What does the exponent show?* The number of times 2 is multiplied. Have students complete Exercises 2–5.

② Practice Use with Exercises 6–30.

Remind students that any number, except zero, to the zero power is equal to 1.

Error Intervention If students have difficulty understanding how the word problems on the first page work, have them use counters to represent the friends and create a graphic interpretation of the problem.

If You Have More Time Have students find their age raised to the power of 5. Have students share their answers with their classmates. Check students' work.

③ Assessment

In this lesson students learned to work with exponents. Use the **Quick Check** problem to assess students' understanding.

Quick Check Formative Assessment

Write 9^3 in expanded form. $9 \times 9 \times 9$ *Write $6 \times 6 \times 6 \times 6$ in exponential form.* 6^4

PRIME FACTORIZATION

Name _____

Prime Factorization

1. Use the two factor trees shown to factor 240. For the first circle, think of what number times 6 is 24. For the next two circles, factor 10. Continue factoring each number. Do not use the number 1.

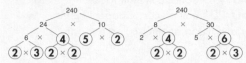

2. What are the numbers at the ends of the branches for each tree?

   2, 3, 2, 2, 2, 5   2, 2, 2, 5, 2, 3

3. **Reasoning** What do all the numbers at the end of each branch have in common?
   They are prime.

4. **Reasoning** What do you notice about the numbers in the two groups?
   They are the same.

5. Arrange the numbers from least to greatest and include a multiplication sign between each pair of numbers. $2 \times \underline{2} \times \underline{2} \times \underline{2} \times \underline{3} \times 5$

   Your answer to 5 above shows the prime factorization of 240.
   If you multiply all the factors back together, you get 240.

6. Write the prime factorization of 240 using exponents.
   $\underline{2^4} \times 3 \times 5$

G61 (student p. 1)   MDIS 2.0

Name _____

Prime Factorization (continued)

Complete each factor tree. Write the prime factorization with exponents, if you can. Do not use the number 1 as a factor.

7.   21
   7 × **3**

   3×7

8.   24
   6 × **4**
   2 × **3**   **2** × **2**

   $2^3 \times 3$

9.   81
   9 × **9**
   3 × **3**   **3** × **3**

   3^4

10.   56
   7 × **8**
   2 × **4**
   2 × **2**

   $2^3 \times 7$

For Exercises 11 to 22, if the number is prime, write <u>prime</u>.
If the number is composite, write the prime factorization of the number.

11. 11	12. 18	13. 41	14. 40
Prime	2×3^2	Prime	$2^3 \times 5$

15. 16	16. 17	17. 80	18. 95
2^4	Prime	$2^4 \times 5$	5×19

19. 35	20. 72	21. 48	22. 55
5×7	$2^3 \times 3^2$	$2^4 \times 3$	5×11

23. **Reasoning** Holly says that the prime factorization for 44 is 4×11. Is she right? Why or why not?
   No; 4 is not prime.

G61 (student p. 2)   MDIS 2.0

Objective Students will find the prime factorization of numbers.
Vocabulary Prime factorization

1 Conceptual Development
Use with Exercises 1–6.

In this lesson you will learn to find the prime factorization of a number.

Discuss the term *prime factorization*. Have students look at the two factor trees. *Why is there a line to 24 and to 10?* These are two factors of 240. *Why is there a line to 8 and to 30?* These are two factors of 240. *One factor of 24 is 6. What is the other factor?* 4 Have students fill in the factor trees and write the numbers at the ends of the branches of each. Discuss each row. *What do you notice about the list of factors for each factor tree?* They are the same. *How is $2 \times 2 \times 2 \times 2$ written using exponents?* 2^4 *What may be a reason to use exponents to show prime factorization?* It is shorter. Have students complete Exercises 2–6.

2 Practice Use with Exercises 7–23.

Remind students to list each factor, even if two or more of the factors are the same number.

Error Intervention If students have difficulty finding the prime factorization of a number, have them revisit the Divisibility Rules as a way to find two factors to begin their factor trees.

If You Have More Time Have students re-solve Exercises 8–9 using two other factors to begin their factor trees. Exercise 8: Start with 8×3; Exercise 9: Start with 3×27. Check students' work.

3 Assessment

In this lesson students learned to find the prime factorization of a number. Use the **Quick Check** problem to assess students' understanding.

Quick Check   **Formative** Assessment

Find the prime factorization of 100 using exponents.
$2^2 \times 5^2$

GREATEST COMMON FACTOR

Name _____

Greatest Common Factor

Materials 22 small pieces of paper, 12 in one color and 10 in another color, per pair

Find the greatest common factor of 48 and 60 by answering 1 to 5.

1. List the factors of 48.

    1, 2, 3, 4, 6, 8, 12, 16, 24, 48

    There should be 10 factors. Write the factors of 48, one on each piece of paper in one color.

2. List the factors of 60.

    1, 2, 3, 4, 5, 6, 10, 12, 15, 20, 30, 60

    There should be 12 factors. Write the factors of 60, one on each piece of paper in another color.

3. Group the factors into three groups: factors that appear only on one color of paper; factors that appear only on the other color of paper; and factors that appear on both colors of paper.

    Use your groups to fill in the Venn diagram shown. Factors that appear on both colors of paper go in the shaded area on the Venn diagram.

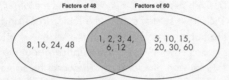

Factors of 48   Factors of 60

8, 16, 24, 48   1, 2, 3, 4, 6, 12   5, 10, 15, 20, 30, 60

4. Factors in the shaded area are common factors. List the common factors.   1, 2, 3, 4, 6, 12

5. What number is the greatest of these common factors?   12

    This is the greatest common factor (GCF) of 48 and 60.

G62 (student p. 1)   MDIS 2.0

Name _____

Greatest Common Factor (continued)

Find the greatest common factor of 16, 20 and 32 by answering 6 to 10.

6. List the factors of 16. ____ 1, 2, 4, 8, 16

7. List the factors of 20. ____ 1, 2, 4, 5, 10, 20

8. List the factors of 32. ____ 1, 2, 4, 8, 16, 32

9. List the common factors of 16, 20 and 32: ____ 1, 2, 4

10. What is the greatest common factor of 16, 20 and 32? ____ 4

Find the greatest common factor (GCF).

11. 8, 12	12. 16, 20	13. 15, 25	14. 18, 45
4	4	5	9

15. 35, 81	16. 21, 24	17. 34, 40	18. 7, 31
1	3	2	1

19. 6, 42	20. 8, 32, 40	21. 35, 42, 70	22. 10, 35, 75
6	8	7	5

23. A teacher has 35 desks in her room and 45 books. What is the greatest number of rows she can have if she wishes to have the same number of desks in each row and the same number of books for each row of desks?

    5

24. **Reasoning** Hope says the greatest common factor of 12 and 36 is 6. Is she right? Why or why not?

    No, 12 is a common factor that's bigger.

G62 (student p. 2)   MDIS 2.0

Objective Students will find the greatest common factor.

Vocabulary Greatest common factor

Materials 22 small pieces of paper, 12 in one color and 10 in another color, per pair

1 Conceptual Development
Use with Exercises 1–5.

In this lesson you will learn to find the greatest common factor.

Have students read the sentence at the top of the page, and then list the factors of 48 in Exercise 1. *What is a factor of a number?* A number that evenly divides the number Have students find the common factors of 48 and 60 by completing Exercises 2–4. *What is a common factor?* A number that is a factor of two or more numbers *What do you think the greatest common factor of two numbers might be?* The greatest number that is a factor of both numbers Have students complete Exercise 5.

2 Practice Use with Exercises 6–24.

Point out that the greatest common factor must be a factor of both numbers. If students have found a greatest common factor that does not evenly divide one of the numbers, they should check their work.

Error Intervention If students have difficulty finding the factors for a number, have them use a factor tree and compare the resulting factorization for the pair or group of numbers.

If You Have More Time Have students write in their own words how to find the greatest common factor for a pair of numbers. Check students' work.

3 Assessment

In this lesson students learned to find the greatest common factor. Use the **Quick Check** problem to assess students' understanding.

Quick Check **Formative Assessment**

Find the greatest common factor of 16 and 40. 8

Name _____

Intervention
Lesson **G63**

Least Common Multiple

A student group is having a large cookout. They wish to buy the same number of hamburgers and hamburger buns. Hamburgers come in packages of 12 and buns come in packages of 8. What is the least amount of each they can buy in order to have the same amount?

Follow 1 to 4 below to answer the question.

1. Complete the table.

Packages	1	2	3	4	5	6
Hamburgers	12	24	36	48	60	72
Buns	8	16	24	32	40	48

2. What are some common multiples from the table? **24, 48**

3. What is the least of these common multiples? **24**

   So, the least common multiple (LCM) of 12 and 8 is 24.

4. What is the least amount of hamburgers and buns that the students can buy and have the same amount of each? **24**

Find the least common multiple of 6 and 15 by following the steps below.

5. Complete the table.

	2 ×	3 ×	4 ×	5 ×	6 ×	7 ×	8 ×	9 ×	10 ×
6	12	18	24	30	36	42	48	54	60
15	30	45	60	75	90	105	120	135	150

6. What are the common multiples from the table? **30, 60**

7. What are the next three common multiples that are not in the table? **90, 120, 150**

8. What is the least common multiple of 6 and 15? **30**

G63 (student p. 1) MDIS 2.0

Name _____

Intervention
Lesson **G63**

Least Common Multiple (continued)

Find the least common multiple (LCM).

9. 30, 4
   _____**60**_____

10. 18, 9
   _____**18**_____

11. 12, 36
   _____**36**_____

12. 6, 12
   _____**12**_____

13. 8, 20
   _____**40**_____

14. 3, 14
   _____**42**_____

15. 6, 25
   _____**150**_____

16. 8, 12, 15
   _____**120**_____

17. 3, 4, 5
   _____**60**_____

18. Maria and her brother Carlos both got to be hall monitors today. Maria is hall monitor every 16 school days. Carlos is hall monitor every 20 school days. What is the least number of school days before they will both be hall monitors again?
    80 days

19. **Reasoning** Find two numbers whose least common multiple is 12.
    Answers will vary. Sample answer: 6, 12

20. **Reasoning** Can you find the greatest common multiple of 6 and 15? Explain.
    No, the common multiples will continue forever.

G63 (student p. 2) MDIS 2.0

Objective Students will find the least common multiple.
Vocabulary Least common multiple

1 Conceptual Development
Use with Exercises 1–8.

In this lesson you will learn to find the least common multiple.

Have students read the problem at the top of the page. *What do we know?* Hamburgers come in packages of 12; buns come in packages of 8. *What must we find?* The least number of packages to buy to have an equal number of hamburgers and buns Have students complete the table. *What multiples are common to both the hamburgers and the buns?* 24; 48 *How many packages of hamburgers would the students buy in order to have 24 hamburgers?* 2 *How many packages of buns?* 3 *What is a least common multiple?* The least number that is a multiple of both numbers Have students complete Exercises 5–8.

2 Practice Use with Exercises 9–20.

Point out that the least common multiple might be one of the numbers itself.

Error Intervention If students have difficulty finding the least common multiple, encourage them to use a table like the one on the first page.

If You Have More Time Have students write in their own words how to find the least common multiple for a pair of numbers. Check students' work.

3 Assessment

In this lesson students learned to find the least common multiple. Use the **Quick Check** problem to assess students' understanding.

Quick Check **Formative** Assessment

Find the least common multiple for 3 and 8. 24

MENTAL MATH: MULTIPLYING BY MULTIPLES OF 10

Name _____

Mental Math: Multiplying by Multiples of 10

A publishing company ships a particular book in boxes with 6 books each. How many books are in 20 boxes? How many in 2,000 boxes?

Find 20×6 and $2,000 \times 6$ by filling in the blanks.

1. $20 \times 6 = (10 \times 2) \times 6$

$= 10 \times (\underline{\ 2\ } \times 6)$

$= 10 \times \underline{\ 12\ }$

$= \underline{\ 120\ }$

2. $2,000 \times 6 = (1,000 \times 2) \times 6$

$= 1,000 \times (\underline{\ 2\ } \times 6)$

$= 1,000 \times \underline{\ 12\ }$

$= \underline{\ 12,000\ }$

3. How many books are in 20 boxes? $\underline{\ 120\ }$ books

4. How many books are in 2,000 boxes? $\underline{\ 12,000\ }$ books

The same publishing company ships a smaller book in boxes with 40 books each. How many books are in 50 boxes? How many are in 500 boxes?

Find 50×40 and 500×40 by filling in the blanks.

5. $50 \times 40 = (5 \times \underline{\ 10\ }) \times$

$(4 \times \underline{\ 10\ })$

$= 5 \times \underline{\ 4\ } \times 10 \times 10$

$= 20 \times \underline{\ 100\ }$

$= \underline{\ 2,000\ }$

6. $500 \times 40 = (5 \times \underline{\ 100\ }) \times$

$(4 \times \underline{\ 10\ })$

$= 5 \times \underline{\ 4\ } \times 100 \times 10$

$= 20 \times \underline{\ 1,000\ }$

$= \underline{\ 20,000\ }$

7. How many books are in 50 boxes? $\underline{\ 2,000\ }$ books

8. How many books are in 500 boxes? $\underline{\ 20,000\ }$ books

G64 (student p. 1)   MDIS 2.0

Name _____

Mental Math: Multiplying by Multiples of 10 (continued)

Notice the pattern when multiplying multiples of 10.

9. $7 \times 80 = \underline{\ 560\ }$

$70 \times 80 = \underline{\ 5,600\ }$

$70 \times 800 = \underline{\ 56,000\ }$

10. $4 \times 60 = \underline{\ 240\ }$

$40 \times 60 = \underline{\ 2,400\ }$

$40 \times 600 = \underline{\ 24,000\ }$

Multiply.

11. $30 \times 40 =$
$\underline{\ 1,200\ }$

12. $10 \times 600 =$
$\underline{\ 6,000\ }$

13. $70 \times 20 =$
$\underline{\ 1,400\ }$

14. $50 \times 400 =$
$\underline{\ 20,000\ }$

15. $700 \times 30 =$
$\underline{\ 21,000\ }$

16. $40 \times 800 =$
$\underline{\ 32,000\ }$

17. $600 \times 30 =$
$\underline{\ 18,000\ }$

18. $40 \times 90 =$
$\underline{\ 3,600\ }$

19. $90 \times 500 =$
$\underline{\ 45,000\ }$

20. $70 \times 500 =$
$\underline{\ 35,000\ }$

21. $30 \times 800 =$
$\underline{\ 24,000\ }$

22. $200 \times 70 =$
$\underline{\ 14,000\ }$

23. $800 \times 80 =$
$\underline{\ 64,000\ }$

24. $30 \times 600 =$
$\underline{\ 18,000\ }$

25. $40 \times 300 =$
$\underline{\ 12,000\ }$

26. A class of 30 students is collecting pennies for a school fundraiser. If each of them collects 400 pennies, how many have they collected all together? $\underline{\ 12,000\ }$ pennies

27. **Reasoning** Raul multiplied 60×500 and got 30,000. Since there are 4 zeros in the answer, he thought his answer was incorrect? Do you agree? Why or why not?
No, one of the zeros is from 6×5 which is 30.

G64 (student p. 2)   MDIS 2.0

Objective Students will use mental math to multiply by multiples of 10.

① Conceptual Development
Use with Exercises 1–8.

In this lesson you will learn to use mental math to multiply by multiples of 10.

Have students read the problem and the questions at the top of the page. *What do we know?* A company ships 6 books in a box. *What must we find?* The number of books in 20 boxes and the number of books in 2,000 boxes Have students complete the equations and find the answers in Exercises 1–4. *How are the answers to 20×6 and $2,000 \times 6$ similar?* Both begin with 12. *How are they different?* They have different numbers of zeros. *What do you notice about multiplying by 10?* When you add zeros to the factors, zeros are added to the products. Have students complete Exercises 5–8.

② Practice Use with Exercises 9–27.

Point out that students can find the product by multiplying the basic fact in the problem and then adding the total number of zeros in the factors.

Error Intervention If students have difficulty multiplying by multiples of 10, have them review the first two exercises and think about what is happening with each step. Then have them repeat each step as they complete the exercises.

If You Have More Time Have students solve the following problem and explain their methods: *Mila saved $80 in pennies. How many pennies did she save?* 8,000; $80 \times 100 = 8,000$

③ Assessment

In this lesson students learned to use mental math to multiply by multiples of 10. Use the **Quick Check** problem to assess students' understanding.

Quick Check   **Formative Assessment**

Multiply: 600×50 30,000

ESTIMATING PRODUCTS

Name _____

Estimating Products

Mrs. Wilson's class at Hoover Elementary School is collecting canned goods. Their goal is to collect 600 cans. There are 21 students in the class and each student agrees to bring in 33 cans. Answer 1 to 7 to find if the class will meet their goal.

Estimate 21 × 33 and compare the answer to 600.

Round each factor to get numbers you can multiply mentally.

1. What is 21 rounded to the nearest ten? __20__

2. What is 33 rounded to the nearest ten? __30__

3. Multiply the rounded numbers. 20 × 30 = __600__

The answer is the same as the number needed to meet the goal.

4. 21 was rounded to 20. Was it rounded up or down? __down__

5. 33 was rounded to 30. Was it rounded up or down? __down__

6. Is 21 × 33 more or less than 21 × 30? __more__

7. Will the goal be reached? __yes__

Hoover Elementary School had a goal to collect 12,000 canned goods. There are 18 classes and each class collects 590 cans. Answer 8 to 13 to find if the school will meet their goal.

Estimate 18 × 590 and compare the answer with 12,000.

Round each factor to get numbers you can multiply mentally.

8. What is 18 rounded to the nearest ten? __20__

9. What is 590 rounded to the nearest hundred? __600__

10. Multiply the rounded numbers. 20 × 600 = __12,000__

The answer is the same as the number needed to meet the goal.

G65 (student p. 1) MDIS 2.0

Name _____

Estimating Products (continued)

11. 18 was rounded to 20. Was it rounded up or down? __up__

   590 was rounded to 600. Was it rounded up or down? __up__

12. Is 18 × 590 more or less than 20 × 600? __less__

13. Will the goal be reached? __no__

Round each factor so that you can estimate the product mentally.

14. 71 × 382
   70 × 400
   28,000

15. 27 × 62
   30 × 60
   1,800

16. 45 × 317
   50 × 300
   15,000

17. 58 × 176
   60 × 200
   12,000

18. 831 × 24
   800 × 40
   32,000

19. 16 × 768
   20 × 800
   16,000

20. 87 × 67
   90 × 70
   6,300

21. 373 × 95
   400 × 100
   40,000

22. 57 × 722
   60 × 700
   42,000

23. Debra spends 42 minutes each day driving to work. About how many minutes does she spend driving to work each month? __1,200 minutes__

24. **Reasoning** If 64 × 82 is estimated to be 60 × 80, would the estimate be an overestimate or an underestimate? Explain.

   It would be an underestimate because you are rounding both factors down.

G65 (student p. 2) MDIS 2.0

Objective Students will estimate products.
Vocabulary Estimate

1 Conceptual Development
Use with Exercises 1–13.

In this lesson you will learn to estimate products.

Revisit the term *estimate* as needed. Have students read the paragraph at the top of the page. *What do we know?* A class wants to collect 600 cans. There are 21 students. Each student will bring in 33 cans. *What must we find?* Whether the class will meet the goal Have students complete Exercises 1–3. *What is the estimated product?* 600 *Will they meet their goal?* We don't know because the estimate is the same as the goal. Explain that students will discover whether they will meet their goal by determining whether they rounded up or down to find the answer. Have students complete Exercises 4–13.

2 Practice Use with Exercises 14–24.

Tell students to round two-digit numbers to the nearest 10 and three-digit numbers to the nearest 100.

Error Intervention If students have difficulty rounding to estimate products, have them review the rules for rounding numbers and write out each step as they find rounded factors and multiply by a multiple of 10.

If You Have More Time Have students revisit Exercise 23 and estimate how many minutes Debra spends driving to work in one year.
40 × 400 = 16,000 minutes

3 Assessment

In this lesson students learned to estimate products. Use the **Quick Check** problem to assess students' understanding.

Quick Check **Formative** Assessment

Round each factor and estimate mentally: 74 × 63.
70 × 60 = 4,200

USING ARRAYS TO MULTIPLY TWO-DIGIT FACTORS

Name _____

Using Arrays to Multiply Two-Digit Factors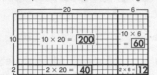

Intervention
Lesson **G66**

Materials crayons or markers

Find 12 × 26 by answering 1 to 4.

The array shows how to find each partial product.

1. Color the part of the array which shows 10 × 20 and write the product in the array and in the computation at the right.

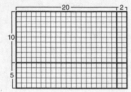

```
                20          6            26
                                       × 12
10    10 × 20 = |200|   10 × 6         |12| ← 2 × 6
                        = |60|         |40| ← 2 × 20
2      2 × 20 = |40|    2 × 6 = |12|   |60| ← 10 × 6
                                      |200| ← 10 × 20
                                       312
```

2. Use a different color for each of the other parts of the array. Color each and write the product in the array and in the computation above.

3. Each product you found is part of the product 12 × 26, so each is a partial product. Add the partial products.

4. What is 12 × 26? __312__

5. Use the grid to find the partial products and the product 15 × 22.

```
        20        2              2 2
                              ×  1 5
10                            |  1 0|
                             | 1 0 0|
                             |   2 0|
5                          + | 2 0 0|
                             | 3 0 0|

                    22 × 15 = __330__
```

Name _____

Using Arrays to Multiply Two-Digit Factors (continued)

Intervention
Lesson **G66**

Use an array to help complete the calculations.

6. 16 × 31

```
                              3 1
                            × 1 6
                            |    6|
                            |1 8 0|
                            |  1 0|
                          + |3 0 0|
                            |4 9 6|

                    31 × 16 = __496__
```

7.
```
    3 1
  × 1 4
  |    4|
  |1 2 0|
  |  1 0|
+ |3 0 0|
  |4 3 4|
```

8.
```
    2 4
  × 2 5
  |  2 0|
  |1 0 0|
  |  8 0|
+ |4 0 0|
  |6 0 0|
```

9.
```
    3 2
  × 2 1
  |  3 0|
  |  4 0|
  |6 0 0|
+ |6 7 2|
  |6 7 2|
```

10.
```
    1 9
  × 1 8
  |  7 2|
  |  8 0|
  |  9 0|
+ |1 0 0|
  |3 4 2|
```

11.
```
    2 6
  × 1 7
  |  4 2|
  |1 4 0|
  |  6 0|
+ |2 0 0|
  |4 4 2|
```

12.
```
    3 4
  × 2 6
  |  2 4|
  |1 8 0|
  |  8 0|
+ |6 0 0|
  |8 8 4|
```

13. Bob earns $25 per day at his job. How much does Bob earn in 15 days?

    __$375__

14. **Reasoning** What four simpler products can you use to find 32 × 27? 7 × 2 = 14, 7 × 30 = 210, 20 × 2 = 40, 20 × 30 = 600

Objective Students will use arrays to multiply two-digit factors.
Vocabulary Array, partial product
Materials Crayons or markers

1 Conceptual Development
Use with Exercises 1–5.

In this lesson you will learn to use arrays to multiply two-digit factors.

Have students read the problem and look at the array. Tell students that the *array* shows each part of the computations from the equation on the right. Have students follow the steps as outlined in Exercises 1–4. *How are the partial products shown on the array?* In different colors Have students complete Exercise 5.

2 Practice Use with Exercises 6–14.

Encourage students to use four different colors when completing Exercise 6.

Error Intervention If students have difficulty multiplying the factors in Exercises 7–12, encourage them to refer back to Exercise 1 and notice where each factor and partial product came from. Then have them follow that model as they work through the exercises.

If You Have More Time Have students calculate how much money Bob will earn in 35 days. $25 × 35 = $875

3 Assessment

In this lesson students learned to use arrays to multiply two-digit factors. Use the **Quick Check** problem to assess students' understanding.

Quick Check Formative Assessment

What is the product of 17 × 15? 255

Name _____

Intervention
Lesson **G67**

**Multiplying Two-Digit Numbers
by Multiples of 10**

A yearly membership to a museum costs $30. What is the total cost for
24 memberships, one for each student in Mr. Clark's class?

Find 24 × 30 by answering 1 to 10.

1. What is 24 × 0? __0__

2. Put a zero in the ones place of the product at the right.

    $$\begin{array}{r} \boxed{1} \\ 24 \\ \times\,30 \\ \hline \boxed{720} \end{array}$$

3. Multiply the 4 ones in 24 by the 3 tens in 30.

    What is 4 × 3 tens? __12__ tens

4. Regroup.

    12 tens = __1__ hundred + __2__ tens

5. Write the tens in the tens place and the hundred above the 24, in the
    computation above.

6. Multiply the 2 tens in 24 by the 3 tens in 30.

    What is 2 tens × 3 tens? __6__ hundreds

7. Add the regrouped hundreds.

    6 hundreds + 1 hundred = __7__ hundreds

8. Write the hundreds in the hundreds place of the product.

9. What is 24 × 30? __720__

10. How much do 24 memberships cost? $720

Find 43 × 50 by answering 11 to 17.

11. What is 43 × 0? __0__

    Put a zero in the ones place of the product at the right.

    $$\begin{array}{r} 43 \\ \times\,50 \\ \hline \boxed{0} \end{array}$$

12. What is 3 × 5 tens? __15__ tens

G67 (student p. 1)   MDIS 2.0

Name _____

Intervention
Lesson **G67**

Multiplying Two-Digit Numbers by Multiples of 10 (continued)

13. Regroup. 15 tens = __1__ hundred + __5__ tens
    Write the tens in the tens place of the product at the
    right and the hundred above the 43.

    $$\begin{array}{r} \boxed{1} \\ 43 \\ \times\,50 \\ \hline \boxed{215}0 \end{array}$$

14. What is 4 tens × 5 tens? __20__ hundreds

15. Add the regrouped hundreds.

    20 hundreds + 1 hundred = __21__ hundreds

16. Regroup. 21 hundreds = __2__ thousands + __1__ hundred
    Write the hundreds in the hundreds place of the product
    above and the thousands in the thousands place.

17. What is 43 × 50? __2,150__

Multiply.

18.	21	19.	35	20.	27	21.	34
	× 10		× 30		× 30		× 40
	210		1,050		810		1,360

22.	47	23.	23	24.	64	25.	19
	× 20		× 30		× 10		× 40
	940		690		640		760

26.	54	27.	72	28.	48	29.	28
	× 30		× 20		× 40		× 50
	1,620		1,440		1,920		1,400

30. Mr. Zacharias works 40 hours a week.
    How many hours does he work in 36 weeks?   __1,440__ hours

31. **Reasoning** When multiplying any number by a multiple of
    10, what is always the last digit of the product? Explain.
    0; If you are multiplying by a multiple of 10, the product is a
    multiple of 10 so the last digit is zero.

G67 (student p. 2)   MDIS 2.0

Objective Students will multiply two-digit numbers
by multiples of 10.

❶ Conceptual Development
Use with Exercises 1–17.

*In this lesson you will learn to multiply two-digit
numbers by multiples of 10.*

Have students read the problem at the top of the
page. *What do we know?* A membership to the
museum costs $30 per year. There are 24 students in
the class. *What must we find out?* The cost of
24 memberships Have the students follow the steps
in Exercises 1–10. *Why did you put a zero in the
ones place of the product?* Because 24 × 0 = 0 Have
students complete Exercises 11–17.

❷ Practice Use with Exercises 18–31.

Point out that the ones place of the product will always
be zero when one of the factors is 10.

Error Intervention If students have difficulty
correctly multiplying the factors in Exercises 18–29,
remind them of the importance of carrying the digit
in the tens place. Reinforce this multiplication step
by modeling it for Exercise 18 and having students
explain to you what you did.

If You Have More Time Have students
calculate how many hours Mr. Zacharias works in a
full year (52 weeks). 2,080 hours

❸ Assessment

In this lesson students learned to multiply two-digit
numbers by multiples of 10. Use the **Quick Check**
problem to assess students' understanding.

Quick Check **Formative**
Assessment

What is the product of 37 × 40? 1,480

MULTIPLYING BY TWO-DIGIT NUMBERS

Name _____

Multiplying by Two-Digit Numbers

On a cross-country trip, the Katz family drove an average of 58 miles each hour. How far did they drive in 26 hours?

Find 26 × 58 by answering 1 to 12.

1. What is 6 × 8? __48__

2. Regroup the ones.

   48 ones = __4__ tens +
   _____ __8__ ones

   Record the ones in the ones place of the first partial product in the chart at the right. Record the tens above the 58.

	Thousands	Hundreds	Tens	Ones
		1	4	
			5	8
×			2	6
		3	4	8
	1	1	6	0
	1	5	0	8

3. What is 6 × 5 tens? __30__ tens

4. Add the regrouped tens.

   30 tens + 4 tens = __34__ tens

5. Regroup the tens. 34 tens = __3__ hundreds + __4__ tens
   Record the tens in the tens place of the first partial product in the chart above. Record the hundreds in the hundreds place.

6. What is 2 tens × 8? __16__ tens

7. Regroup the tens. 16 tens = __1__ hundred + __6__ tens
   Record a zero as a place holder in the ones place of the second partial product in the chart above. Record the tens in the tens place of the second partial product. Record the hundred above the 58.

8. What is 2 tens × 5 tens? __10__ hundreds

9. Add the regrouped hundreds.

   10 hundreds + 1 hundred = __11__ hundreds

G68 (student p. 1)   MDIS 2.0

Name _____

Multiplying by Two-Digit Numbers (continued)

10. Regroup the hundreds.

    11 hundreds = __1__ thousand + __1__ hundred
    Record the hundred in the hundreds place of the second partial product in the chart. Record the thousand in the thousands place of the second partial product in the chart.

11. Add the partial products. What is 26 × 58? __1,508__

12. How far did the Katz family drive in 26 hours? __1,508__ miles

Multiply.

13.	27	14.	25	15.	21	16.	34
	× 15		× 13		× 27		× 24
	405		325		567		816

17.	37	18.	81	19.	62	20.	32
	× 33		× 46		× 44		× 65
	1,221		3,726		2,728		2,080

21.	61	22.	84	23.	72	24.	84
	× 53		× 42		× 77		× 34
	3,233		3,528		5,544		2,856

25.	17	26.	21	27.	32	28.	27
	× 17		× 14		× 22		× 35
	289		294		704		945

29. Jason's dad's car can go 27 miles on each gallon of gasoline. When the tank is full, the car holds 21 gallons of gasoline. If the car is going 55 miles per hour, how far can it go on one full tank of gasoline? __567 miles__

30. **Reasoning** How much greater is the product of 24 × 23 than the product of 24 × 21? Explain.
    It is 2 × 24 or 48 greater since 23 is 2 larger than 21.

G68 (student p. 2)   MDIS 2.0

Objective Students will multiply by two-digit numbers.
Vocabulary Partial product
Materials 2 number cubes

1 Conceptual Development
Use with Exercises 1–12.

In this lesson you will learn to multiply two-digit numbers.

Read the problem aloud with students. *What does an average of 58 miles each hour mean?* They drove about 58 miles each hour, although maybe a little more or a little less each hour. *What is meant by partial product?* One of the two products, after multiplying by the ones or by the tens *What will you multiply first?* 6 × 8 *How will regrouping affect how you enter the result?* You enter 8 ones and 4 tens are recorded to add to the tens when you multiply 6 × 5. Have students complete Exercises 1–4. Remind students to add the 4 tens to the product of 6 and 5 tens. *After you find the partial products, what do you do?* Add them. Have students complete Exercises 5–12.

2 Practice Use with Exercises 13–30.

Explain how partial products are obtained. Use expanded notation to rewrite the multiplication problem as two problems: for example, 34 × 69 = 34 × 9 and 34 × 60. Then show why there is a zero as a placeholder in the ones place in the chart.

Error Intervention If students have difficulty keeping their numbers aligned, give them grid paper on which they can write each digit.

If You Have More Time Have students roll two number cubes to make a two-digit number and repeat. Then have them multiply the two-digit numbers. Check students' work.

3 Assessment

In this lesson students learned to multiply two-digit numbers. Use the **Quick Check** problem to assess students' understanding.

Quick Check **Formative** Assessment

Multiply 69 × 78. 5,382

Name _____

Intervention
Lesson **G69**

Multiplying Greater Numbers

An airline company owns a plane that holds 267 passengers. How many passengers can the plane transport in 34 trips?

Find 34 × 267 by answering 1 to 17.

1. What is 4 × 7? __28__

2. Regroup the ones.

   28 ones = __2__ tens + __8__ ones

   Use the chart below. Record the ones in the ones place of the first partial product. Record the tens above the 267.

3. What is 4 × 6 tens? __24__ tens

4. Add the regrouped tens.

   24 tens + 2 tens = __26__ tens

5. Regroup the tens.

   26 tens = __2__ hundreds + __6__ tens

   Record the tens in the tens place of the first partial product in the chart. Record the hundreds above the 267.

Thousands	Hundreds	Tens	Ones
	2	2	
	2	6	7
×		3	4
1	0	6	8

6. What is 4 × 2 hundreds? __8__ hundreds

7. Add the regrouped hundreds.

   8 tens + 2 hundreds = __10__ hundreds

8. Regroup the hundreds.

   10 hundreds = __1__ thousand + __0__ hundreds

   Record the hundreds in the hundreds place of the first partial product above. Record the thousand in the thousands place.

9. What is 3 tens × 7? __21__ tens

10. Regroup the tens.

    21 tens = __2__ hundreds + __1__ ten

G69 (student p. 1) MDIS 2.0

Name _____

Intervention
Lesson **G69**

Multiplying Greater Numbers (continued)

Record a zero as a place holder in the second partial product in the chart at the right. Record the 1 ten in the tens place of the second partial product. Record the 2 hundreds above the 267.

Thousands	Hundreds	Tens	Ones
2	22	2	
	2	6	7
×		3	4
1	0	6	8
8	0	1	0
9	0	7	8

11. What is 3 tens × 6 tens?

    __18__ hundreds

12. Add the regrouped hundreds.

    18 hundreds + 2 hundreds = __20__ hundreds

13. Regroup the hundreds.

    20 hundreds = __2__ thousands + __0__ hundreds
    Record the hundreds in the hundreds place of the second partial product. Record the thousands above the 267.

14. What is 3 tens × 2 hundreds __6__ thousands

15. Add the regrouped thousands.

    6 thousands + 2 thousands = __8__ thousands
    Record the thousands in the thousands place of the second partial product in the chart.

16. Add the partial products. What is 34 × 267? __9,078__

17. How many passengers can the plane transport? __9,078__ passengers

Multiply.

18.	227	19.	425	20.	721	21.	534
	× 40		× 13		× 28		× 24
	9,080		5,525		20,188		12,816

22. **Reasoning** The school cafeteria prepares breakfast for 115 students each morning. In purchasing food for the week, they will need 2 apples and 35 ounces of juice for each student. How much juice will the cafeteria need for the week? __4,025 ounces__

G69 (student p. 2) MDIS 2.0

Objective Students will multiply greater numbers.
Vocabulary Partial product

① Conceptual Development
Use with Exercises 1–17.

In this lesson you will learn to multiply greater numbers.

Revisit the term *partial product* as needed. Read the problem aloud with students. *What operation will you use to solve the problem?* Multiplication *How can you use the chart to regroup?* The regrouped value can be recorded in the box above that place value. *Why is regrouping common in multiplication problems?* There are not many multiplication facts that have a product less than 10. Have students complete Exercises 1–8. Review place values, making sure students know that 10 hundreds is the same as 1 thousand. *How will you find the number of passengers?* Add the partial products. Have students complete Exercises 9–17.

② Practice Use with Exercises 18–22.

Review when to use a zero as a placeholder in the partial products. Explain why a zero must be used based on the place value of the digits being multiplied.

Error Intervention If students have difficulty tracking their regrouping, have them highlight the numbers that have been regrouped and write a plus sign in the front of the number to remind them to add it.

If You Have More Time Have students write a word problem that can be solved by multiplying greater numbers. Then have them show their solution. Check students' work.

③ Assessment

In this lesson students learned to multiply greater numbers. Use the **Quick Check** problem to assess students' understanding.

Quick Check 🌸 **Formative Assessment**

Multiply 97 × 486. 47,142

MENTAL MATH: USING PROPERTIES

Name _____

Mental Math: Using Properties

---

1. Use the Distributive Property to complete the number sentence and make it true.

   $23 \times (15 + 12) = (23 \times 15) + (23 \times \underline{12})$

The Distributive Property can be used to break apart numbers and make it easier to multiply.

2. Use the Distributive Property to find 4×17 by filling in the blanks.

   $4 \times 17 = 4 \times (10 + \underline{7})$
   $= (4 \times \underline{10}) + (4 \times \underline{7})$
   $= \underline{40} + 28 = \underline{68}$

3. Use the Commutative Property of Multiplication to complete the number sentence and make it true.

   $19 \times 12 = \underline{12} \times 19$

4. Use the Associative Property of Multiplication to complete the number sentence and make it true.

   $(38 \times 4) \times 25 = 38 \times (\underline{4} \times 25)$

The Commutative and Associative Properties can be used to make computations easier when there are compatible numbers in the factors.

5. Use the Commutative and Associative Properties to find $4 \times (287 \times 25)$ by filling in the blanks.

   $4 \times (287 \times 25) = 4 \times (\underline{25} \times 287)$ Which property? <u>Commutative</u>
   $= (\underline{4} \times 25) \times 287$ Which property? <u>Associative</u>
   $= \underline{100} \times 287$
   $= \underline{28,700}$

6. Use the Identity Property of Multiplication to complete the number sentence and make it true.

   $573 \times 1 = \underline{573}$

7. Use the Identity Property of Multiplication to find $793 \times (238 - 237)$ by filling in the blanks.

   $793 \times (238 - 237) = 793 \times \underline{1} = \underline{793}$

G70 (student p. 1)   MDIS 2.0

Name _____

Mental Math: Using Properties (continued)

---

8. Use the Zero Property of Multiplication to complete the number sentence and make it true.

   $489 \times 0 = \underline{0}$

9. Use the Zero Property of Multiplication. $793 \times 0 \times 83 = \underline{0}$

Fill in the blanks to show how to use mental math to find the product. Name the property or properties used.

10. $5 \times (83 \times 2) = 5 \times (\underline{2} \times 83)$ Which property? <u>Commutative</u>
    $= (5 \times \underline{2}) \times 83$ Which property? <u>Associative</u>
    $= \underline{10} \times 83$
    $= \underline{830}$

11. $35 \times 128 \times 0 = \underline{0}$ Which property? <u>Zero</u>

12. $12 \times 1 \times 4 = 12 \times 4$ Which property? <u>identity</u>
    $= \underline{48}$

13. $3 \times 45 = (3 \times 40) + (3 \times \underline{5})$ Which property? <u>Distributive</u>
    $= \underline{120} + \underline{15}$
    $= \underline{135}$

14. $(70 \times 4) \times 25 = 70 \times (\underline{4} \times 25)$ Which property? <u>Associative</u>
    $= 70 \times \underline{100}$
    $= \underline{7,000}$

15. **Reasoning** A bookcase has 4 shelves. Each shelf has 5 hard-cover books and 23 paperback books. How many books are on the shelves? Explain how to find the total number of books mentally.
    112 books; $5 + 23 = 28$. Sample answers for finding 4×28:
    $4 \times 28 = 4 \times (25 + 3) = (4 \times 25) + (4 \times 3) = 100 + 12 = 112$
    $4 \times 28 = 4 \times (20 + 8) = (4 \times 20) + (4 \times 8) = 80 + 32 = 112$
    $4 \times 28 = 4 \times (30 - 2) = (4 \times 30) - (4 \times 2) = 120 - 8 = 112$

G70 (student p. 2)   MDIS 2.0

Objective Students will use properties with mental math.
Vocabulary Distributive Property, Commutative Property, Associative Property, Identity Property, Zero Property

① Conceptual Development
Use with Exercises 1–9.

In this lesson you will learn to use properties with mental math.

Explain that properties can be used to make mental math, especially multiplication, possible. *Which property allows you to multiply a factor by each term in a sum?* Distributive Property Have students complete Exercises 1–2. *What is the difference between the Commutative Property and the Associative Property?* The Commutative Property is about the order of the factors. The Associative Property is about grouping the factors differently. Have students complete Exercises 3–5. *What is the multiplicative identity?* 1 *What does the Zero Property state?* Anything times 0 equals 0. Have students complete Exercises 6–9.

② Practice Use with Exercises 10–15.

Use common language to help students remember the meaning of each of the properties. For example: *How does* distribute *relate to the Distributive Property? What is an* identity *and how does it relate to the Identity Property?*

Error Intervention
If students have difficulty identifying the property, have them verbally describe what changes in the equation.

If You Have More Time
Have students make a poster that teaches each property. Have them include in their own words what each property states and give an example. Check students' work.

③ Assessment

In this lesson students learned to use properties with mental math. Use the **Quick Check** problem to assess students' understanding.

Quick Check Formative Assessment

Identify the property that you can use in order to use mental math to find the product: $(5 \times 3) \times 2 = (3 \times 5) \times 2$ Commutative Property

---

MDIS 2.0

Name _____

Dividing by Multiples of 10

Intervention
Lesson **G71**

Use the multiplication sentences to find each quotient. Look
for a pattern.

1. $4 \times 20 =$ __80__ $80 \div 20 =$ __4__

   $40 \times 20 =$ __800__ $800 \div 20 =$ __40__

   $400 \times 20 =$ __8,000__ $8,000 \div 20 =$ __400__

2. What basic division fact is used in each quotient above?

   __8__ $\div$ __2__ $=$ __4__

Use basic facts and a pattern to find $2,400 \div 80$. Answer 3 to 5.

3. What basic division fact can be used to find $2,400 \div 80$?

   __24__ $\div$ __8__ $=$ __3__

In $24 \div 8 = 3$, 24 is the dividend, 8 is the divisor, and 3 is the quotient.

4. Look for a pattern.

Number Sentence	Zeros in the Dividend	Zeros in the Divisor	Zeros in the Quotient
$240 \div 80 =$ __3__	1	1	0
$240 \div 8 =$ __30__	1	0	1
$2,400 \div 8 =$ __300__	2	0	2
$2,400 \div 80 =$ __30__	2	1	1

Complete.

Zeros in the dividend − Zeros in the divisor = __zeros__ in the quotient

5. **Reasoning** Use the pattern to explain why $2,400 \div 80$ has one zero.
2,400 has 2 zeros and 80 has one zero.
$2 - 1 = 1$, so the quotient has 1 zero.

G71 (student p. 1)   MDIS 2.0

Name _____

Dividing by Multiples of 10 (continued)

Intervention
Lesson **G71**

Divide. Use mental math.

6. $300 \div 30 =$ __10__   7. $60 \div 20 =$ __3__   8. $200 \div 40 =$ __5__

9. $240 \div 60 =$ __4__   10. $490 \div 70 =$ __7__   11. $450 \div 90 =$ __5__

12. $100 \div 50 =$ __2__   13. $2,700 \div 90 =$ __30__   14. $1,800 \div 60 =$ __30__

15. $3,500 \div 70 =$ __50__   16. $1,500 \div 30 =$ __50__   17. $800 \div 40 =$ __20__

18. $640 \div 80 =$ __8__   19. $3,600 \div 60 =$ __60__   20. $140 \div 70 =$ __2__

21. $1,200 \div 20 =$ __60__   22. $8,100 \div 90 =$ __90__   23. $560 \div 80 =$ __7__

24. $600 \div 30 =$ __20__   25. $400 \div 20 =$ __20__   26. $2,400 \div 60 =$ __40__

27. $1,200 \div 40 =$ __30__   28. $2,500 \div 50 =$ __50__   29. $2,100 \div 70 =$ __30__

30. $4,500 \div 90 =$ __50__   31. $480 \div 80 =$ __6__   32. $450 \div 50 =$ __9__

33. Dan has a coin collection. His sister Michaela has just started collecting. Michaela has 20 coins, and Dan has 400 coins. About how many times larger is Dan's collection?

     __20 times larger__

34. Hector must store computer CDs in cartons that hold 40 CDs each. How many cartons will he need to store 2,000 CDs?

     __50 cartons__

35. **Reasoning** Write another division problem with the same answer as $2,700 \div 90$.
Sample answer: $270 \div 9$

G71 (student p. 2)   MDIS 2.0

Objective Students will divide by multiples of ten.
Vocabulary Multiple, quotient

1 Conceptual Development
Use with Exercises 1–5.

In this lesson you will learn to divide by multiples of ten.

Explain that the pattern for dividing by multiples of ten can be useful with mental math. *What is the relationship between multiplication and division?* They are opposites. Have students complete Exercises 1–2. *How can you find the basic fact related to a quotient involving a multiple of ten?* Look at the numbers and ignore the zeros *How do you decide how many zeros are in the quotient?* Zeros in the dividend minus zeros in the divisor Have students complete Exercises 3–5.

2 Practice Use with Exercises 6–35.

Review the pattern that comes from multiplying by multiples of ten. Compare it to the pattern related to division by multiples of ten.

Error Intervention If students have difficulty determining the number of zeros in the quotient, have them cross through pairs of zeros, one from each of the dividend and divisor.

If You Have More Time Have students write a word problem involving dividing by multiples of ten and solve it. Then have them find a partner and solve each other's problems. Check students' work.

3 Assessment

In this lesson students learned to divide by multiples of ten. Use the **Quick Check** problem to assess students' understanding.

Quick Check **Formative** Assessment

Use mental math to solve: $4,200 \div 60$ 70

     G71   MDIS 2.0

ESTIMATING QUOTIENTS WITH TWO-DIGIT DIVISORS

Name _____

Estimating Quotients with Two-Digit Divisors

Intervention Lesson **G72**

A charity needs to mail 209 boxes. The workers can mail 28 boxes each day. About how many days do they need to mail all the boxes?

Estimate the quotient of 209 ÷ 28 by answering 1 to 7.

1. What is 28 rounded to the nearest ten? _____30_____

2. To find compatible numbers for 209 and 30, list some of the multiples of 3.

   3, 6, __9__, __12__, __15__, __18__, __21__, __24__

3. Which multiple of 3 is closest to the first digit or two of 209? _____21_____

4. What is 209 rounded to the nearest compatible number? _____210_____

5. What is 210 ÷ 30? _____7_____

6. What is a good estimate for 209 ÷ 28? _____7_____

7. About how many days do the workers need to mail all the boxes? _____7_____ days

Estimate the quotient of 4,156 ÷ 72 by answering 8 to 10.

8. What is 72 rounded to the nearest ten? _____70_____

9. What is 4,156 rounded to the nearest compatible number? _____4,200_____

10. What is a good estimate for 4,156 ÷ 72?

    __4,200__ ÷ __70__ = __60__

Estimate the quotient of 8,273 ÷ 43 by answering 11 to 13.

11. What is 43 rounded to the nearest ten? _____40_____

12. What is 8,273 rounded to the nearest compatible number? _____8,000_____

13. What is a good estimate for 8,273 ÷ 47?

    __8,000__ ÷ __40__ = __200__

G72 (student p. 1) MDIS 2.0

Name _____

Estimating Quotients with Two-Digit Divisors (continued)

Intervention Lesson **G72**

Estimate each quotient. Write the compatible numbers you used.

14. 465 ÷ 89 =

    __450 ÷ 90__

    __5__

15. 2,304 ÷ 74 =

    __2,100 ÷ 70__

    __30__

16. 637 ÷ 82 =

    __640 ÷ 80__

    __8__

17. 3,561 ÷ 37 =

    __3,600 ÷ 40__

    __90__

18. 181 ÷ 61 =

    __180 ÷ 60__

    __3__

19. 4,149 ÷ 73 =

    __4,200 ÷ 70__

    __60__

20. 564 ÷ 62 =

    __540 ÷ 6__

    __90__

21. 7,198 ÷ 82 =

    __7,200 ÷ 80__

    __90__

22. 3,118 ÷ 57 =

    __3,000 ÷ 60__

    __50__

23. 1,590 ÷ 42 =

    __1,600 ÷ 40__

    __40__

24. 1,235 ÷ 19 =

    __1,200 ÷ 20__

    __60__

25. 7,118 ÷ 77 =

    __7,200 ÷ 80__

    __90__

26. 32)902

    __900 ÷ 30__

    __30__

27. 62)1,130

    __1,200 ÷ 60__

    __20__

28. 28)2,112

    __2,100 ÷ 30__

    __70__

29. The school band is raising money to go on a trip. The 68 members hope to raise $6,400. The trip will be 4 days in length. Estimate the amount that each member should raise.

    __$6,300 ÷ 70 = $90__

G72 (student p. 2) MDIS 2.0

Objective Students will estimate quotients with two-digit divisors.

Vocabulary Quotient, compatible number

1 Conceptual Development
Use with Exercises 1–13.

In this lesson you will learn to estimate quotients with two-digit divisors.

Read the problem aloud with students. *What operation would you use to solve the problem?* Division *What key word in the problem indicates that estimating the quotient is acceptable? About What is a compatible number?* Compatible numbers are numbers that form basic division facts. Have students complete Exercises 1–7. *Why do you use compatible numbers instead of rounding when estimating a quotient?* Traditional rounding may not result in numbers that are easy to divide. Have students complete Exercises 8–13.

2 Practice Use with Exercises 14–29.

Review multiplication facts with students. Also review dividing by multiples of ten. Explain that these two skills will be combined as students estimate quotients with two-digit divisors.

Error Intervention If students have difficulty finding compatible numbers, allow them to refer to a multiplication table to identify facts that could be used.

If You Have More Time Give students two compatible numbers and have them write a quotient that could be estimated using those compatible numbers. Check students' work.

3 Assessment

In this lesson students learned to estimate quotients with two-digit divisors. Use the **Quick Check** problem to assess students' understanding.

Quick Check **Formative** Assessment

Estimate the quotient: 3,142 ÷ 83 40

G72 MDIS 2.0

DIVIDING BY TWO-DIGIT DIVISORS

A carpenter cut a board that is 144 inches long. He cut pieces 32 inches long. How many pieces did he get and how much of the board was left?

Find 144 ÷ 32 by answering 1 to 11.

1. First, estimate to find the approximate number of pieces.

    150 ÷ 30 = ___5___

2. Write the estimate in the ones place of the quotient, on the right.

    $32\overline{)144}$ 5

3. Multiply. 32 × 5 = ___160___   1 6 0

4. Compare the product to the dividend. Write > or <.

    160 ⊙ 144

    Since 160 is too large, 5 was too large. Try 4.

5. Multiply. 32 × 4 = ___128___

6. Compare the product to the dividend. Write > or <.

    128 < 144

    Since 128 is less than 144, 4 is not too large. Write 4 in the ones place of the quotient on the right. Write 128 below 144.

    $32\overline{)144}$ 4   1 2 8   1 6

7. Subtract. 144 − 128 = ___16___

8. Compare the remainder to the divisor. Write > or <.

    16 ⊙ 32

    Since the remainder is less than the divisor, the division is finished.

9. What is 144 ÷ 32? ___4___ R ___16___

10. How many 32-inch pieces did the carpenter cut? ___4___ pieces

11. How much of the board was left? ___16___ inches

   G73 (student p. 1)   MDIS 2.0

Divide.

12. 6 R10 $32\overline{)202}$
13. 2 R72 $94\overline{)260}$
14. 7 R30 $45\overline{)345}$

15. 2 R13 $62\overline{)137}$
16. 7 R16 $28\overline{)212}$
17. 9 R30 $58\overline{)552}$

18. 8 R1 $82\overline{)657}$
19. 4 R3 $32\overline{)131}$
20. 8 R80 $93\overline{)824}$

21. 5 R20 $89\overline{)465}$
22. 2 R56 $74\overline{)204}$
23. 8 R13 $78\overline{)637}$

24. 7 R22 $77\overline{)561}$
25. 2 R59 $61\overline{)181}$
26. 5 R54 $73\overline{)419}$

27. 8 R60 $63\overline{)564}$
28. 8 R62 $82\overline{)718}$
29. 5 R33 $57\overline{)318}$

30. A vegetable stand sells 192 cucumbers and 224 squash during the month of July. About how many cucumbers did they sell each day? ___Between 6 and 7___

31. **Reasoning** To start dividing 126 by 23, Miranda used the estimate 120 ÷ 20 = 6. How could she tell 6 is too high?
    6 × 23 = 138 and 138 > 120.

   G73 (student p. 2)   MDIS 2.0

Objective Students will divide by two-digit divisors.
Vocabulary Quotient

1 Conceptual Development
Use with Exercises 1–11.

In this lesson you will learn to divide by two-digit divisors.

Read the problem aloud with students and draw a picture modeling it. *Why should you first estimate the quotient?* So that you can get a good idea what value to start with for the quotient *How will you know whether your estimate is too big?* The product will be greater than the dividend. *How will you know if your estimate is too small?* The remainder will be greater than the divisor. Have students complete Exercises 1–10. *What does the remainder represent in this problem?* How many inches of board are left over after the pieces have all been cut Have students complete Exercise 11.

2 Practice Use with Exercises 12–31.

Explain to students that keeping their numbers aligned is extremely important when dividing. Remind them that if, at any time, the divisor does not divide into the other number, that means the result is 0, and the 0 must be recorded.

Error Intervention
If students have difficulty dividing by two-digit divisors, have them first estimate their solution using compatible numbers so that they can know approximately what the quotient should be.

If You Have More Time
Have students use estimation with compatible numbers to check each of their quotients.

3 Assessment

In this lesson students learned to divide by two-digit divisors. Use the **Quick Check** problem to assess students' understanding.

Quick Check   Formative Assessment

Divide 528 ÷ 75. 7 R3

   G73   MDIS 2.0

ONE- AND TWO-DIGIT QUOTIENTS

Name _____

One- and Two-Digit Quotients

Trinity wants to buy a computer which costs $802. With her part-time job, she can save $37 a week. How many weeks does she need to save to have enough money to buy the computer?

Find 802 ÷ 37 by answering 1 to 11.

1. Begin by estimating the quotient.

   800 ÷ 40 = __20__

Since the estimate has two digits, begin by dividing the tens.

2. Write the first digit of the estimate in the tens
   place of the quotient.

3. What is 37 × 2 tens? __74__ tens
   Write the product below the 80.

4. What is 80 tens − 74 tens? __6__ tens
   Write the difference below the 74 and the line.

```
    2
37)8 0 2
  7 4
    6
```

5. Regroup. 6 tens and 2 ones = __62__ ones
   Bring down the ones to show the total ones.

6. How many groups of 37 are there in 62? __1__
   Write this number in the ones place of the quotient.

7. What is 37 × 1? __37__ Write the product below the 62.

8. What is 62 − 37? __25__
   Write the difference below the 37 and the line.

```
      2 1
37)8 0 2
  7 4
    6 2
    3 7
    2 5
```

9. Compare the remainder to the divisor. Write > or <.

   25 (<) 37

Since the remainder is less than the divisor, the division is finished.

10. 802 ÷ 37 = __21__ R __25__

11. **Reasoning** How many weeks does Trinity need to save to have enough money to buy the computer? Explain.
    Trinity needs to save 21 weeks and part of another week. After 22 weeks, she will have enough money.

G74 (student p. 1)   MDIS 2.0

Name _____

One- and Two-Digit Quotients (continued)

Find 516 ÷ 63 by answering 12 to 17.

12. Begin by estimating the quotient: 480 ÷ 60 = __8__

Since the estimate has one digit, begin by dividing the ones.

13. Write the estimate in the ones place of the quotient.

14. What is 63 × 8? __504__
    Write the product below the 516.

15. What is 516 − 504? __12__
    Write the difference below the 504 and the line.

```
      8
63)5 1 6
  5 0 4
    1 2
```

16. Compare the remainder to the divisor. Write > or <.

    12 (<) 63

Since the remainder is less than the divisor, the division is finished.

17. 516 ÷ 63 = __8__ R __12__

Divide.

18. 32)602   18 R26
19. 94)960   10 R20
20. 25)545   21 R20

21. 43)285   6 R27
22. 28)147   5 R7
23. 61)485   7 R58

24. 35)993   28 R13
25. 19)213   11 R4
26. 31)558   18

27. The local museum's records indicate that 874 people participated in the guided tours in June. There were 38 guided tours in the month of June and each tour had the same number of people. How many people were on each tour?   __23__

28. **Reasoning** Is 25 R32 a reasonable answer for the problem 607 ÷ 23? Why or why not?
    No, the remainder is larger than the divisor.

G74 (student p. 2)   MDIS 2.0

Objective Students will divide with one- and two-digit quotients.
Vocabulary Quotient

① Conceptual Development
Use with Exercises 1–17.

In this lesson you will learn to divide with one- and two-digit quotients.

Read the problem aloud with students. *Why is division the appropriate operation to use to solve this problem?* You are given a whole, how much she needs, and an equal part, how much she saves each week. *What will an estimate of the quotient tell you?* Whether to divide the tens or the ones first *How do you regroup in division?* When you subtract and "bring down," you are regrouping into ones. Have students complete Exercises 1–11. *What does the remainder represent in this problem? What fraction of a week she must also save to have enough money How does this affect the actual answer to the problem?* You have to add 1 to the quotient because after 21 weeks, she still will not have enough. Have students complete Exercises 12–17.

② Practice Use with Exercises 18–28.

Review the meaning of remainders with students using simpler division problems. Give students examples of problems where the answer is the quotient, one more than the quotient, or the remainder.

Error Intervention If students have difficulty lining up numbers correctly while dividing, suggest that they use graph paper to solve the problems.

If You Have More Time Have students find the number of people on each museum tour if there had been 19 tours in the month of June. 46

③ Assessment

In this lesson students learned to divide with one- and two-digit quotients. Use the **Quick Check** problem to assess students' understanding.

Quick Check   Formative Assessment

Divide 823 ÷ 61. 13 R30

DIVIDING GREATER NUMBERS

Dividing Greater Numbers

A charity collected 5,782 cans of food. They put 28 cans in each box.
How many boxes were full and how many cans were left over?

Find 5,782 ÷ 28 by answering 1 to 16.

1. Begin by estimating the quotient.   6,000 ÷ 30 = __200__

Since the estimate has three digits, begin by dividing the hundreds.

2. Write the first digit of the estimate in the hundreds place of the quotient.

$$\begin{array}{r} 2 \\ 28\overline{)5\ 7\ 8\ 2} \\ 5\ 6\downarrow \\ \hline 1\ 8 \end{array}$$

3. What is 28 × 2 hundreds? __56__ hundreds
Write the product below 5,782.

4. What is 57 hundreds − 56 hundreds? __1__ hundred
Write the difference below the 56 and the line.

5. Regroup. 1 hundred + 8 tens = __18__ tens
Bring down the tens to show the total tens.

6. How many groups of 28 are there in 18? __0__
Write the 0 in the tens place of the quotient below.

7. Multiply 28 × 0 tens and write the product below 18, in the computation at the right.

$$\begin{array}{r} 2\ 0\ 6 \\ 28\overline{)5\ 7\ 8\ 2} \\ 5\ 6 \\ \hline 1\ 8 \\ 0 \\ \hline 1\ 8\ 2 \\ 1\ 6\ 8 \\ \hline 1\ 4 \end{array}$$

8. Subtract 18 − 0 and write the difference below the 0 and the line.

9. Regroup. 18 tens + 2 ones = __182__ ones
Bring down the ones to show the total ones.

10. How many groups of 28 are there in 182? __6__
Write the 6 in the ones place of the quotient.

11. What is 28 × 6? __168__
Write the product below 182.

12. What is 182 − 168? __14__
Write the difference below the 168 and the line.

G75 (student p. 1)   MDIS 2.0

Dividing Greater Numbers (continued)

13. Compare the remainder to the divisor. Write > or < .

   14 (<) 28

Since the remainder is less than the divisor, the division is finished.

14. 5,782 ÷ 28 __206__ R __14__

15. How many of the charity's boxes are full?   __206__ boxes

16. How many cans are left over?   __14__ cans

Divide.

17. $32\overline{)9,602}$ **300 R2**

18. $94\overline{)1,960}$ **20 R80**

19. $25\overline{)5,345}$ **213 R20**

20. $22\overline{)6,257}$ **284 R9**

21. $32\overline{)5,731}$ **179 R3**

22. $43\overline{)8,024}$ **186 R26**

23. $89\overline{)9,565}$ **107 R42**

24. $58\overline{)6,237}$ **107 R31**

25. $33\overline{)4,219}$ **127 R28**

26. $35\overline{)9,093}$ **259 R28**

27. $19\overline{)2,213}$ **116 R9**

28. $31\overline{)4,558}$ **147 R1**

29. A book distributor orders 5,175 books on anthropology that it will distribute to 23 bookstores. The book is listed at $26. How many books will each store receive?   __225__ books

30. **Reasoning** Kwan says that 2,162 ÷ 12 equals 180. Is she correct? Why or why not?
No; she forgot the remainder of 2.

G75 (student p. 2)   MDIS 2.0

Objective Students will divide greater numbers.
Vocabulary Quotient

1 Conceptual Development
Use with Exercises 1–16.

In this lesson you will learn to divide greater numbers.

Read the problem aloud with students. *What parts of the quotient will give you the answers to each question?* The whole number will tell you how many boxes are full. The remainder will tell you how many cans are left over. Have students complete Exercises 1–5. *When will the quotient have a zero as a digit?* When the divisor does not divide into the regrouped number *Do you need to write a zero? Why or why not?* Yes, because it shows there are none of that place value *How do you know when the division is finished?* When there is a digit in the ones place of the quotient and the remainder is less than the divisor Have students complete Exercises 6–16.

2 Practice Use with Exercises 17–30.

Review estimating quotients with compatible numbers. Explain that estimating the quotient is a good way to begin the division process because it gives you a number to start with.

Error Intervention
If students have difficulty dividing greater numbers, have them write their problems on grid paper, putting one digit in each square. This will help them keep their digits aligned and ensure that each digit in the quotient is filled.

If You Have More Time
Have students use estimation with compatible numbers to check each of their quotients. Check students' work.

3 Assessment

In this lesson students learned to divide greater numbers. Use the **Quick Check** problem to assess students' understanding.

Quick Check **Formative** Assessment

Divide 4,261 ÷ 32. 133 R5

G75   MDIS 2.0

USING MENTAL MATH TO MULTIPLY

Name _____

Using Mental Math to Multiply

Intervention
Lesson **G76**

Jeremy needs to order one uniform for each player in the Millwood baseball league. There are 6 teams in the league, and each team has 19 players. How many uniforms should Jeremy order?

Use this information to answer 1 to 7.

1. How many teams are in the league? <u>There are 6 teams</u>

   How many players are on each team? <u>There are 19 players on each team</u>

2. What are you asked to find? <u>The total number of uniforms</u>

3. What is one way you can use mental math to find the answer?
   Sample answer: Use compensation. Substitute a number for 19 that is easy to multiply.

4. What number is close to 19 and easy to multiply? <u>20</u>

   Did you add or subtract to find the new number? <u>add</u>

   How many did you add or subtract? <u>1</u>

5. What multiplication sentence will you write using the new number?
   6 × <u>20</u> = <u>120</u>

6. How will you adjust the answer? Subtract 1 group of 6; 120 − 6 = 114.

   What is the solution? <u>Jeremy should order 114 uniforms.</u>

7. When you adjusted, how did you know whether to add or subtract?
   Sample answer: When I substituted a number for 19, I added, so when I adjusted, I needed to subtract.

G76 (student p. 1)   MDIS 2.0

Name _____

Using Mental Math to Multiply (continued)

Intervention
Lesson **G76**

In 8 through 13, use compensation to find each product.

8. 5 × 38
   Substitute: 5 × <u>40</u> = 200
   Adjust: <u>200</u> − 10 = <u>190</u>

9. 3 × 42
   Substitute: 3 × <u>40</u> = 120
   Adjust: <u>120</u> + 6 = <u>126</u>

10. 59 × 4
    Substitute: <u>60</u> × 4 = <u>240</u>
    Adjust: <u>240</u> − <u>4</u> = <u>236</u>

11. 3 × 94
    Substitute: 3 × <u>90</u> = <u>270</u>
    Adjust: <u>270</u> + <u>12</u> = <u>282</u>

12. 4 × 32
    Substitute: 4 × <u>30</u> = <u>120</u>
    Adjust: <u>120</u> + <u>8</u> = <u>128</u>

13. 6 × 41
    Substitute: 6 × <u>40</u> = <u>240</u>
    Adjust: <u>240</u> + <u>6</u> = <u>246</u>

For Exercises 14 through 20, find each product mentally.

14. 5 × 33 = <u>165</u>

15. 4 × 18 = <u>72</u>

16. 8 × 43 = <u>344</u>

17. 31 × 7 = <u>217</u>

18. 39 × 4 = <u>156</u>

19. 53 × 3 = <u>159</u>

20. 6 × 27 = <u>162</u>

G76 (student p. 2)   MDIS 2.0

Objective Students will use compensation to find products mentally.
Vocabulary compensation

1 Conceptual Development
Use with Exercises 1–7.

In this lesson you will learn to use compensation to find products mentally.

Have students read the problem at the top of the page and complete Exercise 1. *How many teams are in the league?* 6 *How many players are on each team?* 19 Revisit the term *compensation* if necessary. *How can compensation help you solve this problem?* You can choose numbers that are easy to multiply mentally. Have students complete Exercises 2–7.

2 Practice Use with Exercises 8–20.

Remind students that they need to add or subtract groups of numbers when they adjust. For example, for Exercise 11, students need to add 3 groups of 4, not just the number 4.

Error Intervention If students have difficulty determining whether they should add or subtract when they adjust, encourage them to ask themselves, "Did I add or subtract when I substituted?" If they added, they need to compensate by subtracting. If they subtracted, they need to compensate by adding.

If You Have More Time Have students solve the following problem and explain their methods: *Mr. Gerard plants 5 rows of trees every day. There are 17 trees in each row. How many trees does he plant in 10 days?* 850

3 Assessment

In this lesson students learned to use compensation to find products mentally. Use the **Quick Check** problem to assess students' understanding.

Quick Check Formative Assessment

Explain how to use compensation to find the product 4 × 37. Sample answer: Substitute 40 for 37. 4 × 40 = 160. Adjust by subtracting 4 groups of 3. 160 − 12 = 148.

Name _____

Intervention
Lesson **G77**

Adding and Subtracting on a Number Line

At the beginning of June, 62 children arrived at Camp Firefly. A week later, 17 more children arrived. At the end of June, 25 children went home. How many children were at Camp Firefly at the end of June? Find $62 + 17 - 25$.

Use this information to answer 1 to 6.

1. What are you asked to find? How many children arrived at the camp at the beginning of June?
   The number of children at Camp Firefly at the end of June; 62

2. How can you use a number line to find the answer? How do you show addition? How do you show subtraction?
   Sample answer: Draw arrows to show addition and subtraction; Draw arrows going to the right to show addition; Draw arrows going to the left to show subtraction

3. Which number is added? 17

   Why is it added? 17 more children arrived.

4. Which number is subtracted? 25

   Why is it subtracted? 25 children went home.

5. Use the number line to solve the problem.
   $62 + 17 - 25 =$ 54

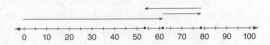

6. How did you know where the second and third arrows should begin?
   Each arrow begins where the last arrow ended.

G77 (student p. 1)   MDIS 2.0

Name _____

Intervention
Lesson **G77**

Adding and Subtracting on a Number Line (continued)

In 7 through 11, use the number line to solve the problem.

7. $45 + 28 =$ 73

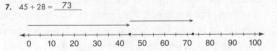

8. $22 + 73 =$ 95

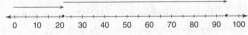

9. $98 - 77 =$ 21

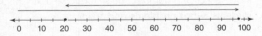

10. $167 - 55 + 30 =$ 142

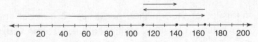

11. $95 + 90 - 65 =$ 120

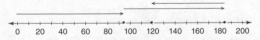

G77 (student p. 2)   MDIS 2.0

Objective Students will add and subtract numbers on a number line.

Vocabulary number line

1 Conceptual Development
Use with Exercises 1–6.

In this lesson you will learn to add and subtract numbers on a number line.

Have students read the problem at the top of the page. Revisit the term *number line* if necessary. Have students complete Exercise 1. *What happened during the month of June at Camp Firefly?* Sample answer: Some children arrived, and some went home. *How does the last sentence of the problem help you find the answer?* We are asked to find $62 + 17 - 25$. *How will you solve this problem?* Use a number line Have students complete Exercises 2–6.

2 Practice Use with Exercises 7–11.

Point out to students that the numbers on a number line increase from left to right. Therefore, students should use an arrow going to the right to add and an arrow going to the left to subtract.

Error Intervention If students have difficulty adding and subtracting on a number line, have them begin with a simpler example. Ask students to use a number line numbered from 0 to 100 to find $80 - 30$. Have them draw an arrow from 0 to 80. Then have them draw an arrow that starts at 80 and goes to the left 30 units.

If You Have More Time Have students complete the following exercise: *Write and solve a word problem that is modeled with the number line in Exercise 11.* Sample answer: Monday morning, a bookstore had 95 posters for sale. Later that day, it received a shipment of 90 additional posters. Tuesday, it sold 65 posters. How many posters did the bookstore have at the end of the day Tuesday? $95 + 90 - 65 = 120$ posters

3 Assessment

In this lesson students learned to add and subtract numbers on a number line. Use the **Quick Check** problem to assess students' understanding.

Quick Check   **Formative Assessment**

Use a number line to solve $72 - 39$. 33

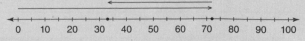

Name ______________________

Skip Counting on the Number Line

Intervention Lesson G78

Caroline is setting up tables for a party. She sets up 4 tables. If she puts 4 chairs at each table, how many chairs will there be in all?

Use this information to answer 1 to 9.

1. How many tables is Caroline setting up for the party?

   There are __4__ tables.

2. How many chairs does Caroline put at each table?

   She will put __4__ chairs at each table.

3. What are you asked to find? The total number of chairs

4. How many people will be able to sit at 1 table? __4__

Draw 1 jump on the number line to show the number of chairs at 1 table.

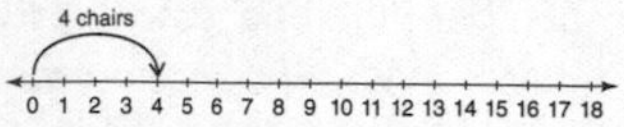

5. How can you use skip counting to find the number of chairs at 2 tables?

   __4__, __8__

Use the number line to show the number of chairs at 2 tables.

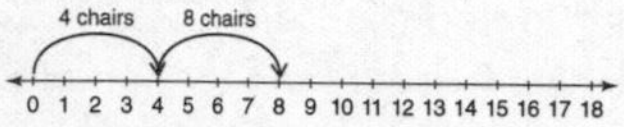

6. Explain in words how you can use a number line to find the number of chairs at 4 tables.

   Sample answer: Draw arrows on the number line to show the number of chairs at each table; Draw 4 arrows, each with a length of 4 units

7. Use a number line to solve the problem.

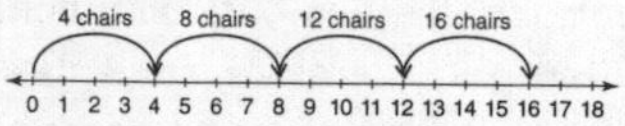

   There will be __16__ chairs in all.

Copyright © Pearson Education, Inc., or its affiliates. All Rights Reserved. G78 (student p. 1) MDIS 2.0

Name ______________________

Skip Counting on the Number Line (continued)

Intervention Lesson G78

8. How can you use skip counting to find the total number of chairs?

   __4__, __8__, __12__, __16__

9. What multiplication sentence does the number line show?

   __4__ × __4__ = __16__

In 10 and 11, find each solution on the number line.

10. Trevor reads 3 books a week. How many books can he read in 5 weeks? Draw jumps on the number line to show how many books he can read.

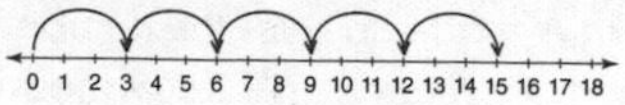

   Trevor can read __15__ books in 5 weeks.

11. Ms. Light's students worked on a science project in groups of 4. How many students were in 3 groups? Draw jumps on the number line to show the number of students.

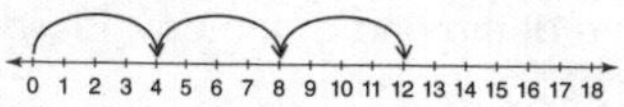

   There were __12__ students in 3 groups.

In 12 and 13, show the multiplication fact on the number line. Write the product.

12. 8 × 2 = __16__

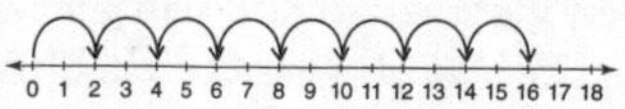

13. 6 × 3 = __18__

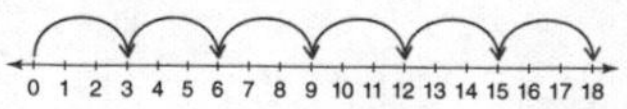

Copyright © Pearson Education, Inc., or its affiliates. All Rights Reserved. G78 (student p. 2) MDIS 2.0

Objective Students will use a number line and skip counting to show multiplication.
Vocabulary skip count

1 Conceptual Development
Use with Exercises 1–9.

In this lesson you will learn to use a number line and skip counting to show multiplication.

Have students read the problem at the top of the page. Revisit the term *skip count* if necessary. Have students complete Exercises 1–2. *How many tables does Caroline set up?* 4 *Will she put the same number of chairs at each table?* Yes; she will put 4 chairs at each table. *How can you use skip counting to find the answer?* Skip count 4 times by 4. *How can a number line help you solve the problem?* You can draw 4 jumps, each 4 units long. Have students complete Exercises 2–9.

2 Practice **Use with Exercises 10–13.**

Encourage students to think of jumps on the number line as groups: groups of 3 books, groups of 4 students, and so on. For Exercise 12, they are finding 8 groups of 2.

Error Intervention If students have difficulty using a number line to represent each problem, encourage them to first answer the question using skip counting. For example, for Exercise 10, to find the number of books Trevor can read in 5 weeks, have students skip count by 3s 5 times: *3, 6, 9, 12, 15.* Then have them show the answer on the number line.

If You Have More Time Have students complete the following exercise and explain their methods: *Write and solve a word problem that is modeled by the number line in Exercise 13.* Check students' word problems and solutions.

3 Assessment

In this lesson students learned to use a number line and skip counting to show multiplication. Use the **Quick Check** problem to assess students' understanding.

Quick Check Formative Assessment

There are 8 bowls. Eddie puts 3 strawberries in each bowl. How can Eddie draw a number line to find the total number of strawberries? Draw 8 jumps, each 3 units long. How can he use skip counting to find the total? 3, 6, 9, 12, 15, 18, 21, 24

Copyright © Pearson Education, Inc., or its affiliates. All Rights Reserved.

Name _____

Addition Properties

Materials 4 half sheets of paper, 24 color tiles (8 each of
3 colors) per pair

1. Show 2 + 5 and 5 + 2 by placing the tiles on the paper.

 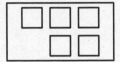 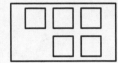 

2. Add. 2 + 5 = _____ and 5 + 2 = _____

3. The Commutative Property says that you can change the
order of the addends and the sum will be the same.

So, 2 + 5 = 5 + _____.

4. Use the tiles to show (4 + 3) + 1. Use 3 different colors of tiles.

 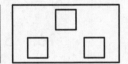 

5. Add. Remember the parentheses show which numbers to add first.

(4 + 3) + 1 = _____ + 1 = _____

6. Move the paper with 3 tiles closer to the paper with 1 tile to
show 4 + (3 + 1).

 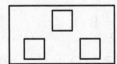 

7. Add. 4 + (3 + 1) = 4 + _____ = _____

8. The Associative Property says that you can group addends
in any way and the sum will be the same.

So, (4 + 3) + 1 = 4 + (_____ + _____).

         MDIS 2.0

Addition Properties (continued)

9. Use tiles to show $3 + 0$.

10. Add: $3 + 0 =$ _____.

11. The Identity Property says that the sum of any number and 0
is that number.

So, $3 + 0 =$ _____.

Find each sum.

12. $(4 + 6) + 2 =$ _____ $+ 2 =$ _____

$4 + (6 + 2) = 4 +$ _____ $=$ _____

13. $(7 + 1) + 2 =$ _____ $+ 2 =$ _____

$7 + (1 + 2) = 7 +$ _____ $=$ _____

14. $9 + 3 =$ _____

$3 + 9 =$ _____

15. $5 + 8 =$ _____

$8 + 5 =$ _____

16. $6 + 9 =$ _____

$9 + 6 =$ _____

17. $7 + 0 =$ _____

18. $0 + 13 =$ _____

19. $5 + 0 =$ _____

Write each missing number.

20. $4 + 6 = 6 +$ _____

21. $7 + 4 =$ _____ $+ 7$

22. $6 + 9 = 9 +$ _____

23. $4 +$ _____ $= 4$

24. $0 +$ _____ $= 8$

25. $7 +$ _____ $= 7$

26. $(7 + 8) + 2 = 7 + (8 +$ _____$)$

27. $9 + (1 + 8) = (9 + 1) +$ _____

28. **Reasoning** Carla ate 2 bananas and 10 raisins. The next day
she ate 10 raisins and 2 bananas. Did Carla eat the same number
of pieces of fruit each day? Explain.

MDIS 2.0

Name _____

Relating Addition and Subtraction

Materials 16 counters per student

1. Use counters to show each number sentence in the table.
    Find the missing number. Draw the counters you used in
    the table.

Addition	Subtraction
3 + _____ = 8	8 − 5 = _____
Addition	**Subtraction**
_____ + 3 = 8	_____ − 3 = 5

2. Related addition and subtraction facts have
    the same numbers. These same numbers
    are called a fact family. What three numbers
    were used in the fact family above?   _____

3. Fill in the blanks to complete the fact family.

    _____ + 7 = 13   13 − 7 = _____

    _____ + 6 = _____   _____ − 6 = 7

4. What three numbers were used in the fact family
    in Question 3?   _____

Relating Addition and Subtraction (continued)

Complete the related addition and subtraction facts.

5.

$3 + 7 =$ _____ $7 + 3 =$ _____

$10 - 3 =$ _____ $10 - 7 =$ _____

6.

_____ $+ 7 = 12$ $7 +$ _____ $= 12$

$12 - 7 =$ _____ $12 -$ _____ $= 7$

Complete each fact family. You may use counters to help.

7. $4 + 8 =$ _____ $12 -$ _____ $= 8$ 8. $5 + 9 =$ _____   _____ $- 5 = 9$

    _____ $+ 4 = 12$ _____ $- 8 = 4$ $9 +$ _____ $= 14$ $14 -$ _____ $= 5$

9. $8 + 3 =$ _____ $11 - 8 =$ _____   10. $6 +$ _____ $= 13$ $13 -$ _____ $= 7$

    $3 +$ _____ $= 11$ _____ $- 3 = 8$ $7 +$ _____ $= 13$ _____ $- 7 = 6$

11.   **Reasoning** John has 14 pencils. He gives
some to Sonja. He has 8 left. How many
pencils did John give to Sonja?   _____

12.   Write two facts that are related to the subtraction
fact $14 - 8 = 6$.

    G2 (student p. 2)   MDIS 2.0

Name _____

Using Mental Math to Add

Materials place-value blocks: 6 tens and 12 ones per pair

Find the sum of 26 and 42 by breaking apart each addend.

1. Show 26 with place value blocks.

   2 tens = _____ 6 ones = _____

2. Show 42 with place value blocks.

   4 tens = _____ 2 ones = _____

3. Add the tens. 20 + _____ = _____

   Add the ones. 6 + _____ = _____

4. Add the tens and the ones together. _____ + 8 = _____

   So, 26 + 42 = _____.

Find the sum of 18 and 34 by breaking apart the second addend.

5. Show 18 with place value blocks.

   1 ten = _____ 8 ones = _____

6. Show 34 with place value blocks.

   3 tens = _____ 4 ones = _____

7. Take 2 ones from the 34 and add them to 18. What sum do you have now?

   18 + 34 = _____ + _____

8. Add. 20 + 32 = _____

   So, 18 + 34 = _____.

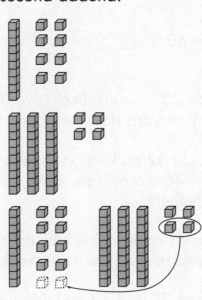

G3 (student p. 1) MDIS 2.0

Name _____

Using Mental Math to Add (continued)

Find each sum using mental math.

9. 22 + 56 = _____   **10.** 37 + 24 = _____   **11.** 43 + 36 = _____

12. 55 + 32 = _____   **13.** 23 + 21 = _____   **14.** 43 + 44 = _____

15. 44 + 34 = _____   **16.** 52 + 32 = _____   **17.** 45 + 4 = _____

18. 45 + 34 = _____   **19.** 37 + 51 = _____   **20.** 23 + 46 = _____

21. 64 + 23 = _____   **22.** 26 + 73 = _____   **23.** 35 + 63 = _____

24. 88 + 26 = _____   **25.** 39 + 45 = _____   **26.** 57 + 16 = _____

Fill in the blanks to show how to add mentally.

27. 35 + 12 = 40 + _____ = _____   **28.** 83 + 46 = _____ + 9 = _____

29. 49 + 16 = 50 + _____ = _____   **30.** 78 + 24 = 80 + _____ = _____

31. Reggie has 25 crayons. Brett gives him 14 more.
How many crayons does he have now?   _____

32. Darla bought 32 stickers on Monday. Two days later
she bought 46 more. How many stickers does she
have altogether?   _____

33. Rafael has 41 rocks in his rock collection. His friend gave
him 18 more rocks. How many rocks does he have now?   _____

34. **Reasoning** To add 59 and 16, Juan took one from the 16
to make the 59 a 60. What number should he add to 60?

35. **Reasoning** To add 24 and 52, Ashley first added 24 and
50. What numbers should she add next?

G3 (student p. 2)   MDIS 2.0

Name _____

Intervention
Lesson   **G4**

Using Mental Math to Subtract

20 21 22 23 24 25 26 27 28 29 30 31 32 33 34 35 36 37 38 39 40 41 42 43 44 45 46 47 48 49 50

Find the difference of 46 − 27 one way, by doing the following.

1. Round the number being subtracted.

   27 rounded to the nearest ten is _____.

2. Solve the new problem.

   46 − 30 = _____

3. Since you rounded 27 to 30, did you
   subtract too much or too little from 46?   _____

4. How much more is 30 than 27? _____

5. Since 30 is 3 **more than** 27, you subtracted too much. You must now
   add 3 to the difference in Question 2.

   16 + 3 = _____

6. So, 46 − 27 = _____.

Find the difference of 46 − 27 another way, by doing the following.

7. How much needs to be added to the 27
   so that it forms a ten?   27 + _____ = 30

8. Since you added 3 to 27, you need to add 3 to 46.   46 + 3 = _____

9. Solve the new problem.   49 − 30 = _____

10. So, 46 − 27 = _____.

11. How can you change 52 − 18 to make it easier to subtract mentally?

   52 − 18 = _____ − 20 = _____

       MDIS 2.0

Using Mental Math to Subtract (continued)

Find each difference using mental math.

12. 57 − 38 = _____   **13.** 32 − 17 = _____   **14.** 61 − 26 = _____

15. 85 − 29 = _____   **16.** 43 − 28 = _____   **17.** 67 − 42 = _____

18. 32 − 18 = _____   **19.** 52 − 46 = _____   **20.** 41 − 18 = _____

21. 28 − 16 = _____   **22.** 55 − 33 = _____   **23.** 86 − 23 = _____

24. 39 − 26 = _____   **25.** 57 − 28 = _____   **26.** 93 − 34 = _____

27. 62 − 47 = _____   **28.** 33 − 16 = _____   **29.** 84 − 35 = _____

30. **Reasoning** To find 56 − 48, add the same amount to both numbers to make it easier to subtract. Explain what you did to solve the problem.

56 − 48

31. Lupe has $32. She buys a present for her mother and gets $9 in change. How much money did she spend on the present?

_____

32. **Reasoning** Becca subtracts 73 − 26 mentally by thinking: "73 − 30 = 43, and 43 − 4 = 39. The answer is 39." What did she do wrong? Explain.

G4 (student p. 2)   MDIS 2.0

Estimating Sums

When Joseppi added 43 and 28, he got a sum of 71. To check that this answer is reasonable, use estimation.

1. Round each addend to the nearest ten.

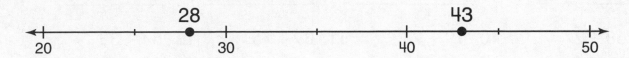

43 rounded to the nearest ten is _____.

28 rounded to the nearest ten is _____.

2. Add the rounded numbers.

40 + 30 = _____

Since 71 is close to 70, the answer is reasonable.

When Ling added 187 and 242, she got a sum of 429. To check that this answer is reasonable, use estimation.

3. Round each addend to the nearest hundred.

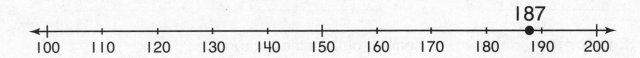

187 rounded to the nearest hundred is _____.

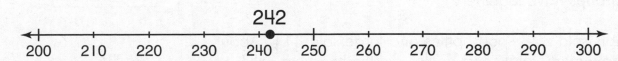

242 rounded to the nearest hundred is _____.

4. Add the rounded numbers.

200 + 200 = _____

Since 429 is close to 400, the answer is reasonable.

 MDIS 2.0

Name _____

Estimating Sums (continued)

Estimate by rounding to the nearest ten.

5. 71 + 36   6. 24 + 81   7. 43 + 91   8. 54 + 66

   _____   _____   _____   _____

9. 68 + 27   10. 19 + 93   11. 89 + 75   12. 54 + 33

   _____   _____   _____   _____

Estimate by rounding to the nearest hundred.

13.   367   14.   791   15.   506   16.   458
    + 141   + 632   + 249   + 891

   _____   _____   _____   _____

17. 940 + 190   18. 675 + 460   19. 531 + 776

   _____   _____   _____

20. 369 + 481   21. 151 + 260   22. 705 + 936

   _____   _____   _____

23. **Reasoning** Jaime was a member of the school chorus
    for 3 years. Todd was a member of the school band for
    2 years. The chorus has 43 members and the band has
    85 members. About how many members do the two
    groups have together?   _____

24. Luis sold 328 sport bottles and Jorge sold 411. About
    how many total sport bottles did the two boys sell?   _____

25. **Reasoning** What is the largest number that can be added to
    46 so that the sum is 70 when both numbers are rounded to the
    nearest ten? Explain.

G5 (student p. 2)   MDIS 2.0

Estimating Differences

When Jarvis subtracted 41 − 29, he got a difference of 12.
To check that this answer is reasonable, use estimation.

1. Round each number to the nearest ten.

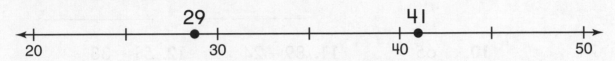

41 rounded to the nearest ten is _____.

29 rounded to the nearest ten is _____.

2. Subtract the rounded numbers.

40 − 30 = _____

Since 12 is close to 10, the answer is reasonable.

DaNitra subtracted 685 − 279 and got a difference of 406.
To check that this answer is reasonable, use estimation.

3. Round each number to the nearest hundred.

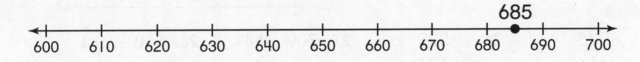

685 rounded to the nearest hundred is _____.

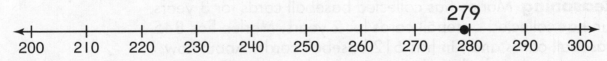

279 rounded to the nearest hundred is _____.

4. Subtract the rounded numbers.

700 − 300 = _____

Since 406 is close to 400, the answer is reasonable.

Estimating Differences (continued)

Estimate by rounding to the nearest ten.

5. 47
− 19

6. 82
− 34

7. 67 − 51

_____

8. 94 − 48

_____

9. 71
− 12

10. 65
− 49

11. 89 − 24

_____

12. 51 − 38

_____

13. 93
− 45

14. 88
− 32

15. 57 − 18

_____

16. 28 − 17

_____

Estimate by rounding to the nearest hundred.

17. 586
− 195

18. 941
− 362

19. 442 − 181

_____

20. 861 − 298

_____

21. 418
− 125

22. 546
− 234

23. 945 − 119

_____

24. 681 − 132

_____

25. 935
− 464

26. 322
− 176

27. 709 − 649

_____

28. 550 − 214

_____

29. Reasoning Marlee has collected baseball cards for 3 years.
Kin has collected baseball cards for 2 years. Marlee has 845
baseball cards and Kin has 612 baseball cards. About how
many more baseball cards does Marlee have than Kin? _____

30. Reasoning What is the smallest number that can be
subtracted from 723 so that the difference is 200 when both
numbers are rounded to the nearest hundred? Explain.

MDIS 2.0

Adding Two-Digit Numbers

Materials place-value blocks: 6 tens and 13 ones per pair

There are 25 boys and 38 girls at the library. How many students total?

1. Show 25 using place-value blocks.

2. Show 38 using place-value blocks.

3. Add 25 + 38 to find the total students.

    Add the ones. 5 + 8 = _____

4. Do you have more then 10 ones? _____

5. Since you have 13 ones, regroup them into tens and ones

    13 ones = _____ ten and _____ ones

6. Record the 3 ones at the bottom of the ones column of the Tens and Ones chart. Record the 1 ten at the top of the tens column.

7. Add the tens. Add the 1 ten that you regrouped, the 2 tens from the 25, and the 3 tens from the 38.

    1 ten + 2 tens + 3 tens = _____ tens

8. Record the tens at the bottom of the tens column of the Tens and Ones chart.

9. So, 25 + 38 = _____

    How many students are at the library? _____.

10. Use place value-blocks and the Tens and Ones chart to add 46 + 29.

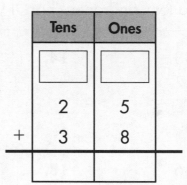

	Tens	Ones
	2	5
+	3	8

	Tens	Ones
	4	6
+	2	9

MDIS 2.0

Adding Two-Digit Numbers (continued)

Add.

11.

Tens	Ones
1	3
+ 2	8

12.

Tens	Ones
2	4
+ 2	9

Add. Use a tens and ones chart if you like.

13. 58
        + 17
        ___
         75

14. 56
        + 11

15. 18
        + 19

16. 20
        + 28

17. 46
        + 45

18. 36
        + 17

19. 17
        + 49

20. 45
        + 14

21. 32
        + 66

22. 26
        + 37

23. 22
        + 65

24. 33
        + 33

25. 21
        + 39

26. 17
        + 29

27. 36
        + 16

28. 64
        + 27

29. A puppy weighs 15 pounds. His mother weighs 65 pounds. How much do the puppy and his mother weigh together?   _____

30. **Reasoning** What number do you add to 19 to get 30?   _____

G7 (student p. 2)   MDIS 2.0

Name _____

Subtracting Two-Digit Numbers

Materials place-value blocks: 3 tens and 20 ones per pair

There are 34 kittens and 16 puppies. How many more kittens than puppies are there?

1. Show 34 with place-value blocks.

2. Do you have enough ones to take away 6 ones?   _____

3. Regroup 1 ten into 10 ones. Show this with your place-value blocks.

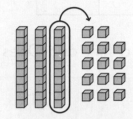

3 tens and 4 ones = _____ tens and 14 ones

4. Cross out the 3 tens in the Tens and Ones chart and write 2 above it. Cross out the 4 ones and write 14 above it.

5. Now, take away 6 ones and write the difference at the bottom of the ones column.

14 ones − 6 ones = _____ ones

Tens	Ones
3	4
− 1	6

6. Subtract the tens and write the difference at the bottom of the tens column.

2 tens − 1 ten = _____ ten

7. So, 34 − 16 = _____.

How many more kittens than puppies are there?   _____

8. Use place-value blocks and the Tens and Ones chart to subtract 56 − 27.

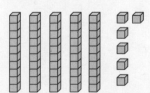

Tens	Ones
5	6
− 2	7

         MDIS 2.0

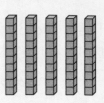

Subtracting Two-Digit Numbers (continued)

Subtract.

9.

Tens	Ones
4	2
− 1	9

10.

Tens	Ones
5	0
− 2	4

Subtract. Use a Tens and Ones chart if you like.

11. 35
      − 17

12. 80
      − 38

13. 45
      − 39

14. 61
      − 13

15. 74
      − 45

16. 22
      − 18

17. 50
      − 32

18. 48
      − 20

19. 95
      − 69

20. 34
      − 7

21. 61
      − 26

22. 90
      − 74

23. Thompson has 32 flowers. If he plants 18 flowers in
the front yard, how many will he have left? _____

24. **Reasoning** In which problem do you need to regroup to
subtract, 53 − 28 or 58 − 23? Explain.

G8 (student p. 2) MDIS 2.0

Name _____

Mental Math Strategies

You can add or subtract mentally by breaking apart numbers.

Find the difference of 647 − 235.

1. Break apart each number into its expanded form.

647 = 600 + _____ + _____   235 = _____ + 30 + _____

2. Subtract the hundreds in both numbers.   600 − 200 = _____

3. Subtract the tens in both numbers.   40 − _____ = _____

4. Subtract the ones in both numbers.   _____ − 5 = _____

5. Add the differences of the hundreds, tens, and ones.

400 + 10 + 2 + = _____

6. So, 647 − 235 = _____.

You can also add or subtract mentally by using compensation.

Find the sum of 235 + 197.

7. Find the number closest to a multiple of 100 and round.

197 rounded to the nearest hundred is _____.

8. Solve the new problem.   235 + 200 = _____

9. Since you rounded 197 to 200, did
you add too much or too little to 235?   _____

10. How much more is 200? _____

11. Since 200 is 3 more than 197, you added too
much. You now must subtract 3 from the sum
to compensate for adding 3.   435 − 3 = _____

12. So, 235 + 197 = _____.

 MDIS 2.0

Name _____

Mental Math Strategies (continued)

Add or subtract mentally. Use breaking apart.

13. 313 + 216   **14.** 842 + 115   **15.** 283 + 114   **16.** 254 + 621

_____   _____   _____   _____

17. 365 + 423   **18.** 457 + 222   **19.** 947 − 516   **20.** 786 − 314

_____   _____   _____   _____

21. 466 − 325   **22.** 579 − 256   **23.** 688 − 232   **24.** 875 − 231

_____   _____   _____   _____

Add or subtract mentally. Use compensation.

25. 462 + 399   **26.** 618 + 296   **27.** 256 + 195   **28.** 326 + 295

_____   _____   _____   _____

29. 145 + 197   **30.** 328 + 598   **31.** 540 − 298   **32.** 742 − 394

_____   _____   _____   _____

33. 916 − 497   **34.** 732 − 296   **35.** 867 − 395   **36.** 683 − 499

_____   _____   _____   _____

37. On vacation, the Gonzales family traveled
595 miles in one day. Their destination is
949 miles from their home. How much farther
do they need to travel to get there?   _____

38. **Reasoning** To subtract 767 − 496, Wang
first found 767 − 500 = 267. Now should
he add 4 to 267 or subtract 4 from 267?

   G9 (student p. 2)   MDIS 2.0

Adding Three-Digit Numbers

Materials place-value blocks: 4 hundreds, 12 tens,
15 ones per pair or group

There are 176 trucks and 249 cars. How many vehicles total?

1. Show 176 using place-value blocks.

2. Show 249 using place-value blocks.

3. Add 176 + 249 to find the total vehicles.

   Add the ones. 6 + 9 = _____

4. Do you have more then 9 ones? _____

5. Regroup the 15 ones into tens and ones.

   15 ones = _____ ten and _____ ones

6. Record the 5 ones at the bottom of the
   ones column of the Hundreds, Tens, and
   Ones chart. Record the 1 ten at the top
   of the tens column.

7. Add the tens.

   1 ten + 7 tens + 4 tens = _____ tens

8. Regroup the 12 tens into hundreds and tens.

   12 tens = _____ hundred and _____ tens

9. Record the 2 tens in the tens column of the chart. Record the 1 hundred at the top
   of the hundreds column.

10. Add the hundreds.

    1 hundred + 1 hundred + 2 hundreds = _____ hundreds

11. Record the 4 hundreds in the hundreds column of the chart.

12. How many total vehicles are there? _____ .

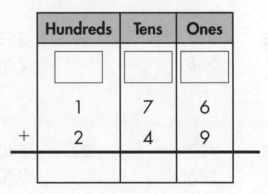

Hundreds	Tens	Ones
☐	☐	☐
1	7	6
+ 2	4	9

MDIS 2.0

Name _____

Adding Three-Digit Numbers (continued)

Add.

13.

Hundreds	Tens	Ones
3	4	8
+ 1	8	4

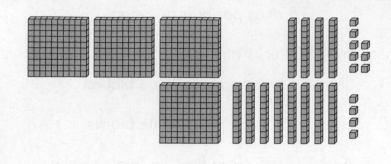

Add. Use place-value blocks if you like.

14. 135
       + 168

15. 149
       + 370

16.   23
       + 388

17. 136
       + 215

18. 217
       + 548

19. 353
       + 274

20. 731
       + 85

21. 636
       + 271

22. 407
       + 175

23. 540
       + 370

24.   84
       + 555

25. 811
       + 109

26. Kelvin has 526 pennies in one jar and 378 pennies
in another jar. How many pennies does he have total? _____

27. LaTasha picked 281 cherries from a tree. Liz picked
237 cherries. How many cherries did they pick together? _____

28. **Reasoning** How many times do you need to regroup to
add 347 to 276? Explain.

G10 (student p. 2) MDIS 2.0

Name _____

Subtracting Three-Digit Numbers

Materials place-value blocks: 3 hundreds, 14 tens, 13 ones per pair or group

There are 353 students at lunch. After 165 students
went back to class, how many are still at lunch?

1. Subtract 353 − 165 to find how many
   students are still at lunch

   Show 353 using place-value blocks.

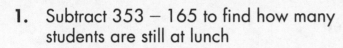

2. You have 3 ones. Do you have
   enough ones to take away 5 ones?   _____

3. Regroup 1 ten as 10 ones. Show this
   with your place-value blocks.

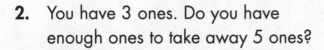

   5 tens and 3 ones = 4 tens and _____ ones

4. Cross out the 5 tens in the Hundreds, Tens,
   and Ones chart and write 4 above it. Cross
   out the 3 ones and write 13 above it.

Hundreds	Tens	Ones
3	5	3
− 1	6	5

5. Now, take away 5 ones and write the
   difference at the bottom of the ones
   column.

   13 ones − 5 ones = _____ ones

6. You now have 4 tens. Is this enough tens to take away 6 tens? _____

7. Regroup 1 hundred into 10 tens. Show this with your place-value blocks.

   3 hundreds and 4 tens = _____ hundreds and 14 tens.

8. Record the regrouping in the chart. Cross out the 3 hundreds and write 2
   above it. Make the 4 tens, 14 tens.

9. Subtract the tens and write the difference in the chart.

   14 tens − 6 tens = _____ tens

       MDIS 2.0

Subtracting Three-Digit Numbers (continued)

10. You now have 2 hundreds. Is this enough hundreds to take away 1 hundred? _____

11. Subtract the hundreds and write the difference in the chart.

2 hundreds − 1 hundred = _____ hundred

12. So, 353 − 165 = _____.

How many students are still at lunch? _____.

Subtract.

13. 436
       − 167

14. 564
       − 285

15. 826
       − 593

16. 332
       − 151

17. 731
       − 256

18. 443
       − 175

19. 561
       − 299

20. 253
       − 167

21. 438 − 244 = _____

22. 826 − 539 = _____

23. 165 − 146 = _____

24. 336 − 277 = _____

25. Reasoning The school has 646 students. On Tuesday, 177 students left the school to go to an art museum. How many students remained in school that day?

26. Number Sense How many times do you need to regroup to subtract 316 from 624? Explain.

 MDIS 2.0

Adding and Subtracting Money

To find $2.67 + $3.25, add as you would with whole numbers.

1. Add the pennies.

2. Since you have 12 pennies, regroup them into dimes and pennies.

12 pennies = _____ dime

and _____ pennies

3. Record the 2 pennies at the bottom of the pennies column of the chart. Record the 1 dime at the top of the dimes column.

4. Add the dimes. $1 + 6 + 2 =$ _____ dimes
Record this value at the bottom of the dimes column.

5. Add the dollars. $2 + 3 =$ _____ dollars
Record this value at the bottom of the dollars column.

6. Write the answer in dollars and cents by placing the dollar sign and decimal point.

So, $2.67 + $3.25 = _____.

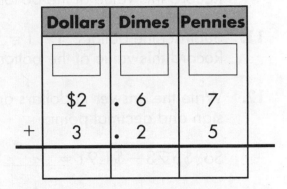

Dollars	Dimes	Pennies
$2 .	6	7
+ 3 .	2	5

To find $5.73 − $1.91, subtract as you would with whole numbers.

7. Subtract the pennies. $3 - 1 =$ _____
Record this value at the bottom of the pennies column.

8. Since you cannot subtract 9 dimes from 7 dimes, regroup 1 dollar into 10 dimes.

5 dollars and 7 dimes = 4 dollars

and _____ dimes

9. Record this regrouping in the chart. Cross out the 5 dollars and write 4 above it. Change the 7 dimes to 17 dimes.

Dollars	Dimes	Pennies
$5 .	7	3
− 1 .	9	1

 MDIS 2.0

Adding and Subtracting Money (continued)

10. Subtract the dimes. $17 - 9 =$ _____ dimes
Record this value at the bottom of the dimes column.

11. Subtract the dollars. $4 - 1 =$ _____ dollars
Record this value at the bottom of the dollars column.

12. Write the answer in dollars and cents by placing the dollar
sign and decimal point.

So, $5.73 - $1.91 =$ _____.

Add or subtract.

13. $2.92
       $+ 0.74$

14. $2.78
       $+ 0.94$

15. $0.99
       $+ 2.49$

16. $5.70
       $- 1.35$

17. $2.30
       $+ 1.95$

18. $7.15
       $- 5.09$

19. $4.84
       $- 1.36$

20. $6.65
       $+ 3.25$

21. $8.42
       $- 2.08$

22. $9.11
       $+ 0.09$

23. $5.03
       $+ 3.58$

24. $6.45
       $- 1.26$

25. $3.58
       $+ 0.29$

26. $7.40
       $- 1.26$

27. $5.68
       $+ 0.90$

28. $4.41
       $- 4.17$

29. **Reasoning** Which is easier for you to subtract,
$3.87 - $1.63 or $4.15 - $2.89? Explain.

     MDIS 2.0

Name _____

Estimating Sums and Differences
of Greater Numbers

When Juanita added 4,287 and 4,683, she got a sum of 8,970.
To check that this answer is reasonable, use estimation.

1. Round each addend to the nearest thousand.

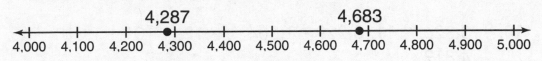

4,287 rounded to the nearest thousand is _____.

4,683 rounded to the nearest thousand is _____.

2. Add the rounded numbers.

4,000 + 5,000 = _____

Since 8,970 is close to 9,000, the answer is reasonable.

Martin subtracted 8,319 − 3,910 and got a difference of 4,409.
To check that this answer is reasonable, use estimation.

3. Round each number to the nearest thousand.

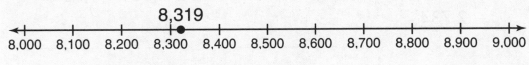

8,319 rounded to the nearest thousand is _____.

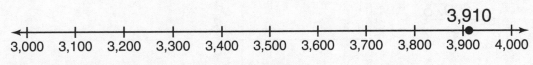

3,910 rounded to the nearest thousand is _____.

4. Subtract the rounded numbers.

8,000 − 4,000 = _____

Since 4,409 is close to 4,000, the answer is reasonable.

G13 (student p. 1) MDIS 2.0

Estimating Sums and Differences of Greater Numbers (continued)

Estimate each sum by rounding to the nearest thousand.

5.   6,729
     + 2,490

6.   4,919
     + 1,834

7. 2,886 + 2,341 _____

8. 5,098 + 3,921 _____

9.   972
     + 6,127

10.   3,326
     + 4,812

11. 8,229 + 1,304 _____

12. 1,101 + 1,010

13.   7,825
     + 2,481

14.   4,444
     + 3,333

15. 5,907 + 1,856 _____

16. 2,298 + 6,371 _____

Estimate each difference by rounding to the nearest thousand.

17.   5,986
     − 1,595

18.   9,341
     − 3,662

19. 4,142 − 1,981 _____

20. 8,761 − 2,985

21.   4,018
     − 1,825

22.   5,746
     − 2,734

23. 9,945 − 1,119 _____

24. 6,881 − 1,732

25.   8,935
     − 4,164

26.   3,222
     − 1,076

27. 7,009 − 6,049 _____

28. 5,850 − 2,314

29. **Reasoning** The theater sold 7,893 tickets on Friday night. There were 5,123 tickets sold on Saturday night. About how many more tickets were sold on Friday night than Saturday night? _____

30. **Reasoning** What is the smallest number that can be added to 2,791 so that the sum is 7,000 when both numbers are rounded to the nearest thousand? Explain.

G13 (student p. 2)   MDIS 2.0

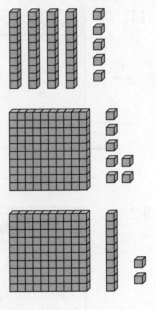
Name _____

Adding Three Numbers

Materials place-value blocks: 2 hundreds, 6 tens, and 14 ones per pair or group

How many total pieces of fruit are in a box containing
45 apples, 107 oranges, and 112 bananas?

1. Show 45, 107, and 112 using place-value blocks.

2. Add 45 + 107 + 112 to find the total pieces of
fruit in the box.

3. Do you have more then 10 ones? _____
Add the ones.

5 ones + 7 ones + 2 ones = _____ ones

4. Since you have 14 ones, regroup them into
tens and ones.

14 ones = _____ ten and _____ ones

5. Record the 4 ones at the bottom of the
ones column of the Hundreds, Tens,
and Ones chart. Record the 1 ten at
the top of the tens column.

6. Add the tens.

1 ten + 4 tens + 1 ten = _____ tens

7. Do you have more than 10 tens? _____

8. Record the tens at the bottom of the tens column of the chart.

9. Add the hundreds and record the value at the bottom of the
hundreds column.

1 hundred + 1 hundred = _____ hundreds

10. So, 45 + 107 + 112 = _____.

How many total pieces of fruit are in the box? _____

Hundreds	Tens	Ones
	4	5
1	0	7
+ 1	1	2

MDIS 2.0

Name _____

Adding Three Numbers (continued)

Add.

11.

Hundreds	Tens	Ones
2	5	4
1	2	9
+	6	2

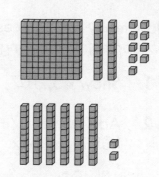

12.

Hundreds	Tens	Ones
1	1	7
1	0	6
+	7	4

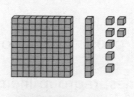

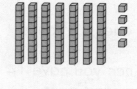

13.   123
          365
        + 50

14.   211
          423
        + 23

15.   23
          45
        + 14

16.   322
          43
        + 16

17.   335
          125
        + 32

18.   543
          144
        + 46

19.   613
          205
        + 64

20.   851
          32
        + 40

21. There were 234 books returned to the library on
Monday, 109 books returned on Tuesday, and
41 books returned on Wednesday. How many
books were retuned to the library in the three days?   _____

22. **Reasoning** Write the smallest 2-digit number that
when added to 345 and 133 would require
regrouping of both the ones and the tens.   _____

G14 (student p. 2)   MDIS 2.0

Subtracting Four-Digit Numbers

The Pacific Crest Trail is 2,655 miles long. The California Coastal Trail is 1,294 miles long. How much longer is the Pacific Coast Trail than the California Coastal Trail?

1. Write 2,655 – 1,294 in the chart.

Thousands	Hundreds	Tens	Ones
2	6	5	5
− 1	2	9	4

2. Look at the ones column. Do you have enough ones to subtract 4 ones? _____

3. Subtract the ones and record this value at the bottom of the ones column.

  5 ones − 4 ones = _____ one

4. Look at the tens column. Do you have enough tens to subtract 9 tens? _____

5. Regroup 1 hundred into 10 tens. Cross out the 6 hundreds and write 5 above it. Cross out the 5 tens and write 15 above it.

6. Subtract the tens. Record this value at the bottom of the tens column.

  15 tens − 9 tens = _____ tens

7. Do you have enough hundreds to subtract 2 hundreds? _____

8. Subtract the hundreds. Record this value at the bottom of the hundreds column.
  5 hundreds − 2 hundred = _____ hundreds

9. Subtract the thousands. Record this value at the bottom of the thousands column.
  2 thousands − 1 thousand = _____ thousand

10. How much longer is the Pacific Crest Trail than the California Coast Trail? _____ miles

MDIS 2.0

Name _____

Subtracting Four-Digit Numbers (continued)

Subtract.

11.

Thousands	Hundreds	Tens	Ones
☐	☐	☐	☐
4	2	1	3
− 1	8	5	7

12.   8,156
        − 5,948

13.   14,951
        − 8,965

14.   7,811
        − 2,766

15.   9,056
        − 4,128

16.   7,510
        − 3,295

17.   8,152
        − 965

18.   5,874
        − 2,287

19.   4,213
        − 1,464

20.   6,182
        − 2,741

21.   5,623
        − 1,278

22.   2,132
        − 856

23.   3,814
        − 1,735

24. At its greatest depth, the Atlantic Ocean is
9,219 meters deep, the Indian Ocean is
7,455 meters deep, and the Caribbean Sea is
6,946 meters deep. How much deeper is the
Indian Ocean than the Caribbean Sea?

25. Reasoning Explain how to find 1,500 − 499 using
mental math.

G15 (student p. 2)   MDIS 2.0

Name _____

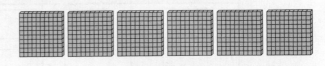

Subtracting Across Zero

Materials place-value blocks: 6 hundreds; 10 tens and 10 ones for each group

There were 600 students at school. After lunch, 245 students went on a field trip. How many students were left at school?

1. Subtract 600 − 245 to find the number of students left at school. Show 600 using place-value blocks.

2. You have 0 ones. Do you have enough ones to take away 5 ones? _____

3. Do you have tens to regroup? _____

4. Go to the hundreds. Regroup 1 hundred into 10 tens. Show this with your place-value blocks.

    6 hundreds = 5 hundreds and _____ tens

5. Record this in the Hundreds, Tens, Ones chart: Cross out the 6 hundreds and write 5 above it. Cross out the 0 tens and write 10 above it.

6. Now, regroup 1 ten into 10 ones. Show this with your place-value blocks.

    1 hundred = _____ tens and 10 ones.

7. Record this in the chart: Cross out the 10 tens and write 9 above it. Cross out the 0 ones and write 10 above it.

8. Subtract. Write each difference in the bottom row of the chart.

    10 ones − 5 ones = _____ ones   9 tens − 4 tens = _____ tens

    5 hundreds − 2 hundreds = _____ hundreds

9. How many students were left at school? _____

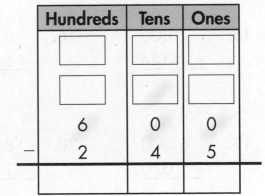

Hundreds	Tens	Ones
6	0	0
− 2	4	5

          MDIS 2.0

Subtracting Across Zero (continued)

Subtract

10. Use the place value chart to find 4,000 − 2,512.

Thousands	Hundreds	Tens	Ones
☐	☐	☐	☐
☐	☐	☐	☐
4	0	0	0
− 2	5	1	2

11. 802
      − 561

12. 760
      − 395

13. 400
      − 254

14. 500
      − 298

15. 7,800
      − 4,324

16. 8,050
      − 6,045

17. 6,000
      − 4,560

18. 3,000
      − 1,875

19. 6,000
      − 2,020

20. 8,500
      − 1,362

21. 700
      − 222

22. 660
      − 387

23. **Reasoning** What is the missing number?
4,000 − ■ = 3,200   _____

24. There are 500 students at an elementary school.
Of those students, 229 are involved in sports.
How many students are not involved in sports?   _____

                  MDIS 2.0

Adding 4-Digit Numbers

On Friday, 2,931 people attended the school play. On Saturday, 3,246 people attended the school play. How many total people attended the school play?

Thousands	Hundreds	Tens	Ones
□	□	□	□
2	9	3	1
+ 3	2	4	6

1. Write 2,931 and 3,246 in the place value chart.

2. Add the ones and record the sum in the ones column.

    1 one + 6 ones = _____ ones

3. Add the tens and record the value in the tens column.

    3 tens + 4 tens = _____ tens

4. Add the hundreds and record the value in the hundreds column.

    9 hundreds + 2 hundreds = _____ hundreds

5. Since you have 11 hundreds, regroup them.

    11 hundreds = _____ thousand and 1 hundred

6. Record the hundred in the hundreds column and record the thousand at the top of the thousands column.

7. Add the thousands and record the value in the thousands column.

    1 thousand + 2 thousands + 3 thousands = _____ thousands

8. So, 2,931 + 3,246 = _____

9. How many total people attended the school play on Friday and Saturday?

    _____

 MDIS 2.0

Adding 4-Digit Numbers (continued)

Add

10.

Thousands	Hundreds	Tens	Ones
☐	☐	☐	☐
4	8	2	9
+ 3	5	6	7

11.   4,687
      + 3,250

12.   2,479
      + 1,431

13.   6,354
      + 2,125

14.   3,218
      + 5,673

15.   5,927
      + 3,073

16.   1,032
      + 4,668

17.   3,640
      + 5,270

18.   3,063
      + 4,137

19.   9,135
      + 681

20.   6,754
      + 137

21.   2,136
       4,021
      + 1,345

22.   3,275
       1,342
      + 5,123

23. 2,124 + 4,205   **24.** 7,126 + 2,574   **25.** 3,025 + 1,975

26. A truck driver traveled 2,175 miles in June and 1,745 miles in July.
      How many total miles did the truck driver travel?

      _____ miles

27. **Reasoning** Sara wrote 5,236 + 2,673 = 7,809.
      What mistake did Sara make? Write the correct sum.

      _____

      _____

         MDIS 2.0

Adding Greater Numbers

On Monday, 26,833 tickets sold for a concert. On Tuesday, 35,106 tickets were sold. What is the total number of tickets sold?

1. Write 26,833 and 35,106 in the place value chart.

2. Add the ones and record the sum in the ones column.

   3 ones + 6 ones

   = _____ ones

Ten Thousands	Thousands	Hundreds	Tens	Ones
2	6	8	3	3
+ 3	5	1	0	6

3. Add the tens and record the value in the tens column.

   3 tens + 0 tens = _____ tens

4. Add the hundreds and record the value in the hundreds column.

   8 hundreds + 1 hundred = _____ hundreds

5. Add the thousands.

   6 thousands + 5 thousands = _____ thousands

6. Since you have 11 thousands, regroup them.

   11 thousands = _____ ten thousand and 1 thousand

7. Record the thousand in the thousands column and record the ten thousands at the top of the ten thousands column.

8. Add the ten thousands and record the value.
   1 ten thousand + 2 ten thousands + 3 ten thousands

   = _____ ten thousands

9. So, 26,833 + 35,106 = _____.
   How many total concert tickets were sold on Monday and Tuesday?   _____

 MDIS 2.0

Adding Greater Numbers (continued)

Add

10.

Ten Thousands	Thousands	Hundreds	Tens	Ones
5	4	3	2	7
+ 1	7	5	4	8

11.   7,169
        + 1,943

12.   4,275
        + 2,786

13.   5,184
        + 2,936

14.   2,943
        + 178

15. $38.64
        + 19.98

16. $475.98
        + 269.23

17.   12,975
        + 8,166

18.   42,973
        + 17,127

19. $245.89
          174.03
        + 108.25

20.   71,043
           9,481
        + 6,055

21.   4,379
        + 2,851

22.   5,612
        + 3,399

23.   1,102 + 6,931

24.   11,070 + 982

25.   62,800 + 3,225

26. Louisiana has an area of 49,651 square miles.
Mississippi has an area of 48,286 square miles.
What is their combined area?   _____ square miles

27. **Reasoning** Alex wrote 33,123 + 56,879 = 80,002.
What mistake did Alex make? Write the correct sum.

       MDIS 2.0

Subtracting Greater Numbers

The local grocery made $341,272 profit this year and $298,432 last year. How much more profit did they make this year than last year?

1. Subtract $341,272 − $298,432 to find the difference in profit. The numbers are shown in the place-value chart below.

Hundred Thousands	Ten Thousands	Thousands	Hundreds	Tens	Ones
3	4	1	2	7	2
− 2	9	8	4	3	2

2. Subtract the ones and record the value in the place-value chart.

   2 ones − 2 ones = _____ ones

3. Subtract the tens and record the value in the chart.

   7 tens − 3 tens = _____ tens

4. Since you only have 2 hundreds, regroup one thousand as 10 hundreds.

   How many thousands do you now have? _____

   How many hundreds? _____ Record this value in the chart.

5. Subtract the hundreds and record the value in the chart.

   12 hundreds − 4 hundreds = _____ hundreds

6. Since you have 0 thousands, regroup one ten thousand as 10 thousands.

   How many ten thousands do you now have? _____

   How many thousands? _____

7. Subtract the thousands and record the value in the chart.

   10 thousands − 8 thousands = _____ thousands

Subtracting Greater Numbers (continued)

8. Since you only have 3 ten thousands, regroup one hundred thousand for 10 ten thousands.

   How many hundred thousands do you now have? _____

   How many ten thousands? _____
   Record this value in the chart.

9. Subtract the ten thousands and record the value in the chart.

   13 ten thousands − 9 ten thousands = _____ ten thousands

10. Subtract the hundred thousands.

    2 hundred thousands − 2 hundred thousands = _____ hundred
    thousands

11. How much more profit did the grocery
    make this year than last year?   _____

Subtract.

| 12. | 25,049 − 12,651 | 13. | 30,675 − 21,599 | 14. | $261.05 − 95.14 | 15. | $745.16 − 394.29 |

| 16. | $809.47 − 152.68 | 17. | 68,714 − 59,856 | 18. | 220,915 − 114,876 | 19. | 172,560 − 143,695 |

20. Gretta has $250 to spend on supplies for a dance. If the
    table decorations cost $188.65, how much money will
    she have left to spend on balloons?   _____

21. **Reasoning** Explain how to regroup in order to subtract
    22,000 − 10,452.

G19 (student p. 2)   MDIS 2.0

Name _____

Multiplication as Repeated Addition

Materials 24 counters and 4 half-sheets of paper per student or pair

Freyja has 4 plates. Each plate has 5 cherries. Answer 1 to 6 to find how many cherries she has in all.

You can use multiplication to find how many in all when you have equal groups.

1. Show 4 plates with 5 cherries on each using counters.

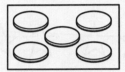 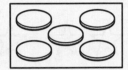 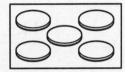 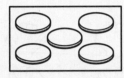

2. Use addition to find how many cherries Freyja has.

_____ + _____ + _____ + _____ = 20

3. How many plates? _____

4. How many cherries on each plate? _____

5. Use multiplication to find how many cherries Freyja has in all.

_____ × _____ = 20

    Number   Number of
    of Plates   Cherries on
                Each Plate

6. How many cherries does Freyja have in all? _____

7. Use counters and repeated addition to find 3×8.

$3 \times 8 = 8 +$ _____ $+$ _____

           $=$ _____

 MDIS 2.0

Multiplication as Repeated Addition (continued)

Add. Then multiply. Use counters if you like.

8.

$3 + 3 = $ _____

$2 \times 3 = $ _____

9.

$2 + 2 + 2 + 2 = $ _____

$4 \times 2 = $ _____

Use the pictures to fill in the blanks.

10.

3 groups of _____

$4 + $ _____ $ + $ _____ $ = $ _____

$3 \times $ _____ $ = $ _____

11.

3 groups of _____

$6 + $ _____ $ + $ _____ $ = $ _____

$3 \times $ _____ $ = $ _____

Fill in the blanks to make each number sentence true.

12. _____ $ + $ _____ $ + $ _____ $ + $ _____ $ + $ _____ $ + $ _____ $ = 6 \times 8$

13. $9 + 9 + $ _____ $ + $ _____ $ = $ _____ $ \times 9$

14. **Reasoning** Melissa says that $5 + 5 + 5 + 3$ is the same thing as 4×5. Explain why Melissa is wrong.

 MDIS 2.0

Name _____

Arrays and Multiplication

Materials 16 counters per student

1. Show an array of 4 rows with 2 counters in each row.

2. Write a multiplication sentence for the array.

   _____ × _____ = _____

   | Number of Rows | Number of Counters in Each Row | Total Number of Counters |

3. How many counters are in the array? _____

4. Show an array of 2 rows with 4 counters in each row.

5. Write a multiplication sentence for this array.

   _____ × _____ = _____

   | Number of Rows | Number of Counters in Each Row | Total Number of Counters |

6. How many counters are in this array? _____

7. Both arrays have 8 counters.

   So, $4 \times 2 = 2 \times$ _____.

8. Since both arrays have 8 counters then you can say,

   $4 \times 2 = 8$, and $2 \times 4 =$ _____.

Knowing one multiplication fact means you know another.

9. If you know $3 \times 8 = 24$, then you know $8 \times 3 =$ _____.

G21 (student p. 1)   MDIS 2.0

Name _____

Arrays and Multiplication (continued)

Write a multiplication sentence for each array.

10.

☆ ☆ ☆ ☆ ☆
☆ ☆ ☆ ☆ ☆
☆ ☆ ☆ ☆ ☆
☆ ☆ ☆ ☆ ☆
☆ ☆ ☆ ☆ ☆
☆ ☆ ☆ ☆ ☆

11.

❀ ❀ ❀ ❀ ❀ ❀ ❀
❀ ❀ ❀ ❀ ❀ ❀ ❀
❀ ❀ ❀ ❀ ❀ ❀ ❀
❀ ❀ ❀ ❀ ❀ ❀ ❀
❀ ❀ ❀ ❀ ❀ ❀ ❀

_____   _____

Draw an array to find each multiplication fact. Write the product.

12. $3 \times 5 =$ _____

13. $2 \times 6 =$ _____

Fill in the blanks.

14. $4 \times 8 = 32$, so $8 \times 4 =$ _____

15. $9 \times 2 = 18$, so _____ $\times 9 = 18$

16. $5 \times 7 = 35$, so $7 \times$ _____ $= 35$

17. $3 \times 6 = 18$, so _____ $\times 3 = 18$

18. $2 \times 4 = 8$, so $4 \times$ _____ $= 8$

19. $1 \times 6 = 6$, so $6 \times 1 =$ _____

20. Reasoning How does an array show equal groups?

    MDIS 2.0

Using Multiplication to Compare

Materials 12 counters per student

Alicia has 2 stickers. Pedro has 3 times as many stickers as Alicia. How many stickers does Pedro have?

1. Show Alicia's stickers with counters.

2. Show Pedro's stickers with counters.

3. Write a multiplication sentence.

3	times	as many as Alicia has	equals	number Pedro has
↓	↓	↓	↓	↓
_____	× _____	_____	=	_____

4. How many stickers does Pedro have? _____

Mia has 4 yo-yos. Flo has twice as many as Mia. How many yo-yos does Flo have?

The word **twice** in a word problem means 2 times as many.

5. Show Mia's yo-yos with counters.

6. Show Flo's yo-yos with counters.

7. Write a multiplication sentence.

2	times	as many as Mia has	equals	number Flo has
↓	↓	↓	↓	↓
_____	× _____	_____	=	_____

8. How many yo-yos does Flo have? _____

     MDIS 2.0

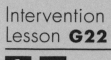

Name _____

Using Multiplication to Compare (continued)

Solve. You may use drawings or counters to help.

9. Janos has 3 stickers. Lucy has twice as many stickers as Janos. How many stickers does Lucy have?

_____

10. Rob has 4 model airplanes. Julio has 3 times as many model airplanes as Rob. How many model airplanes does Julio have?

_____

11. Mr. King has 5 apples left in his store. Ruth needs twice as many apples to bake apple pies. How many apples does Ruth need?

_____

Use the recipe to answer Exercises 12–15.

12. The recipe serves 5 people. Joan wants to make the recipe for 15 people. How many times more is this?

_____

13. How many bananas will Joan need to make the recipe for 15 people?

_____

14. How many cups of strawberries will Joan need to make the recipe for 15 people?

_____

15. Reasoning If Joan wants to make twice as much as the recipe in the chart, what will she need to do to all of the ingredients?

Fruit Smoothie
3 large bananas
2 cups strawberries
1 cup orange juice
1 cup cranberry juice
1 cup ice cubes
Blend until smooth. Makes 5 servings.

G22 (student p. 2) MDIS 2.0

Name _____

Writing Multiplication Stories

Follow 1 to 5 below to write a multiplication story for 5 × 4 that is about hamburgers and pickle slices.

1. 5 × 4 means _____ groups of _____.

2. So, 5 × 4 might mean _____ hamburgers with _____ pickle slices each.

3. Write a story about 5 hamburgers with 4 pickle slices each.

   Mrs. _____ went through a drive thru and

   bought _____ hamburgers. Each hamburger had _____

   pickle slices. How many _____ were there in all?

4. Draw a picture to find how many pickle slices there were in all.

   5 × 4 = _____

5. How many pickle slices were there in all? _____

6. Write a multiplication story for 6 × 3 about nests and eggs.

   Mr. _____ found _____ nests. Each nest had

   _____ eggs. How many _____ did he find in all?

7. Draw a picture to find how many eggs he found in all.

   6 × 3 = _____

8. How many eggs did he find in all? _____

 MDIS 2.0

Writing Multiplication Stories (continued)

Write a multiplication story. Then find the product.

9.

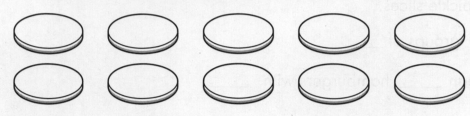

$2 \times 5 =$ _____

Write a multiplication story for Exercises 10 and 11.
Draw a picture to find each product.

10. $6 \times 6 =$ _____

11. $4 \times 5 =$ _____

12. There are 4 houses on Oak Street. Four people live in each house. How many people live on Oak Street?

G23 (student p. 2) MDIS 2.0

Multiplying by 2 and 5

1. Continue skip counting by 2s on the number line below.

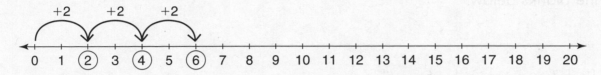

2. Each number that a hop lands on is a **multiple** of two. Circle each multiple of 2 on the number line. Then list them in the blanks below.

_____ _____ _____ _____ _____ _____ _____ _____ _____ _____

3. To find 6 × 2, count by 2s until you have said 6 numbers.

2, 4, _____, _____, 10, _____

So, 6 × 2 = _____.

2s Facts

0 × 2 = 0	5 × 2 = _____
1 × 2 = _____	6 × 2 = 12
2 × 2 = _____	7 × 2 = _____
3 × 2 = _____	8 × 2 = _____
4 × 2 = _____	9 × 2 = _____

4. Repeat 3 above for each of the 2s facts in the table. Complete the table.

5. Reasoning What is the pattern in the products of the 2s facts?

All of the multiples of 2 end in 0, 2, _____, _____, or _____.

6. Continue skip counting by 5s on the number line below. Circle each multiple of 5 on the number line.

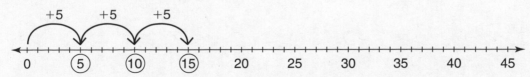

 MDIS 2.0

Name _____

Multiplying by 2 and 5 (continued)

---

7. Circle each multiple of 5 on the number line. Then list them
in the blanks below.

_____ _____ _____ _____ _____ _____ _____ _____ _____

8. To find 7×5, count by 5s until
you have said 7 numbers.

5, 10, 15, _____, _____,

_____, _____

So, $7 \times 5 =$ _____.

9. Repeat 8 above for each of
the 5s facts in the table.

10. **Reasoning** What is the pattern in
the products of the 5s facts?

All of the multiples of 5 end in _____ or _____.

5s Facts

$0 \times 5 = 0$	$5 \times 5 =$ _____
$1 \times 5 =$ _____	$6 \times 5 =$ _____
$2 \times 5 =$ _____	$7 \times 5 = 35$
$3 \times 5 =$ _____	$8 \times 5 =$ _____
$4 \times 5 =$ _____	$9 \times 5 =$ _____

Complete each multiplication problem.

11.   2
  $\times 3$

12.   2
  $\times 6$

13.   2
  $\times 2$

14.   2
  $\times 1$

15.   7
  $\times 2$

16.   7
  $\times 5$

17.   5
  $\times 3$

18.   8
  $\times 5$

19.   5
  $\times 4$

20.   1
  $\times 5$

21.   2
  $\times 4$

22.   5
  $\times 2$

23. **Reasoning** Movie tickets are on sale for $5 each. Ross, Emily, and John
want to see the movie. Is $18 enough for all of their tickets? Explain.

G24 (student p. 2) MDIS 2.0

Name _____

Multiplying by 9

Learn how to multiply by 9 by answering 1 to 5.

1. Complete the table.

Fact	Product	Two Digits in the Product	Sum of the Two Digits in the Product
$0 \times 9 =$	0	0 and 0	$0 + 0 = 0$
$1 \times 9 =$	9	0 and 9	$0 + 9 = 9$
$2 \times 9 =$	18		
$3 \times 9 =$	27	2 and 7	$2 + 7 = 9$
$4 \times 9 =$	36		
$5 \times 9 =$	45	4 and 5	
$6 \times 9 =$	54		
$7 \times 9 =$	63		
$8 \times 9 =$	72		
$9 \times 9 =$	81		$8 + 1 = 9$

2. **Reasoning** Besides the product of 0×9, what pattern do you see in the sums of the digits of each product?

3. Look at the number being multiplied by 9 in each product and the tens digit of that product.

When 3 is multiplied by 9, what is the tens digit of the product? _____.

When 6 is multiplied by 9, what is the tens digit of the product? _____.

 MDIS 2.0

Multiplying by 9 (continued)

4. **Reasoning** Complete to describe the pattern you see in the tens digits of the products when a factor is multiplied by 9.

The tens digit of the product is _____ less than the other factor.

5. Complete the following to find 7×9.

The tens digit is $7 - 1 =$ _____.

The ones digit is $9 - 6 =$ _____.

So, $7 \times 9 =$ _____ and $9 \times 7 =$ _____.

Find each product.

6. $\begin{array}{r} 1 \\ \times 9 \\ \hline \end{array}$ 7. $\begin{array}{r} 9 \\ \times 2 \\ \hline \end{array}$ 8. $\begin{array}{r} 9 \\ \times 4 \\ \hline \end{array}$ 9. $\begin{array}{r} 9 \\ \times 0 \\ \hline \end{array}$

10. $\begin{array}{r} 6 \\ \times 9 \\ \hline \end{array}$ 11. $\begin{array}{r} 9 \\ \times 9 \\ \hline \end{array}$ 12. $\begin{array}{r} 8 \\ \times 9 \\ \hline \end{array}$ 13. $\begin{array}{r} 5 \\ \times 9 \\ \hline \end{array}$

14. $\begin{array}{r} 9 \\ \times 7 \\ \hline \end{array}$ 15. $\begin{array}{r} 3 \\ \times 9 \\ \hline \end{array}$ 16. $\begin{array}{r} 2 \\ \times 9 \\ \hline \end{array}$ 17. $\begin{array}{r} 9 \\ \times 6 \\ \hline \end{array}$

18. **Reasoning** Joshua and his sister have each saved $9. They wish to buy a new game that costs $20. If they put their savings together, do they have enough money to buy the game?

19. **Reasoning** Jane said that $7 \times 9 = 62$. Explain how you know this is incorrect.

                    MDIS 2.0

Name _____

Multiplying by 1 or 0

Materials 9 counters and 9 half sheets of paper per student

Complete 1 to 6 to discover that when you multiply any number by 1, the product is the other number.

Use the paper to show groups and the counters to show the number in each.

1. Show 5×1.

2. How many counters in all? _____ $5 \times 1 =$ _____

3. Show 4×1.

4. How many counters in all? _____ $4 \times 1 =$ _____

5. Use the paper and counters to complete the table on the right.

6. **Reasoning** What pattern do you see in the table?

1s Facts

$0 \times 1 = 0$	$5 \times 1 = 5$
$1 \times 1 =$ _____	$6 \times 1 =$ _____
$2 \times 1 =$ _____	$7 \times 1 =$ _____
$3 \times 1 =$ _____	$8 \times 1 =$ _____
$4 \times 1 = 4$	$9 \times 1 =$ _____

Complete 7 to 12 to discover that when you multiply any number by 0, the product is 0.

7. Show 3×0.

8. How many counters in all? _____

9. Show 6×0.

10. How many counters in all? _____

G26 (student p. 1)

Multiplying by 1 or 0 (continued)

0s Facts

$0 \times 0 = 0$	$5 \times 0 = $ _____
$1 \times 0 = $ _____	$6 \times 0 = 0$
$2 \times 0 = $ _____	$7 \times 0 = $ _____
$3 \times 0 = 0$	$8 \times 0 = $ _____
$4 \times 0 = $ _____	$9 \times 0 = $ _____

11. Use the paper and counters to complete the table on the right.

12. **Reasoning** What pattern do you see in the table?

Find each product.

13. $2 \times 1 = $ _____

14. $4 \times 0 = $ _____

15. $6 \times 1 = $ _____

16. $1 \times 9 = $ _____

17. $1 \times 2 = $ _____

18. $4 \times 1 = $ _____

19. $\begin{array}{r} 3 \\ \times\,0 \\ \hline \end{array}$

20. $\begin{array}{r} 0 \\ \times\,9 \\ \hline \end{array}$

21. $\begin{array}{r} 8 \\ \times\,1 \\ \hline \end{array}$

22. $\begin{array}{r} 1 \\ \times\,8 \\ \hline \end{array}$

23. $\begin{array}{r} 9 \\ \times\,1 \\ \hline \end{array}$

24. $\begin{array}{r} 5 \\ \times\,1 \\ \hline \end{array}$

25. $\begin{array}{r} 5 \\ \times\,0 \\ \hline \end{array}$

26. $\begin{array}{r} 1 \\ \times\,1 \\ \hline \end{array}$

27. $\begin{array}{r} 1 \\ \times\,0 \\ \hline \end{array}$

28. $\begin{array}{r} 7 \\ \times\,1 \\ \hline \end{array}$

29. **Reasoning** Explain why $1 \times 0 = 0$.

 MDIS 2.0

Name _____

Multiplying by 3

Materials 18 counters, 6 inch piece of yarn per student

Use 1s facts and 2s facts to multiply by 3.

1. Show a 3 × 6 array.

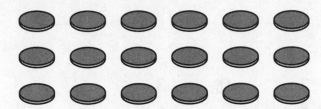

2. Place the piece of yarn between the first and second row of the array.
Fill in the blanks.

1 × _____ = _____

_____ × 6 = _____

3. So, 3 × 6 = 6 + 12 = _____.

4. Use 1s and 2s facts to find 3 × 7 by doing the following.

1 × 7 = _____

2 × 7 = _____

So, 3 × 7 = _____ + _____ = _____.

5. Use 1s and 2s facts to find 3 × 8 by doing the following.

1 × 8 = _____

2 × 8 = _____

So, 3 × 8 = _____ + _____ = _____.

 MDIS 2.0

Name _____

Multiplying by 3 (continued)

Find each product.

6. $2 \times 3 =$ _____

7. $1 \times 3 =$ _____

8. $7 \times 3 =$ _____

9. $3 \times 4 =$ _____

10. $3 \times 6 =$ _____

11. $3 \times 7 =$ _____

12. $\begin{array}{r} 5 \\ \times 3 \\ \hline \end{array}$

13. $\begin{array}{r} 8 \\ \times 3 \\ \hline \end{array}$

14. $\begin{array}{r} 3 \\ \times 8 \\ \hline \end{array}$

15. $\begin{array}{r} 3 \\ \times 6 \\ \hline \end{array}$

16. $\begin{array}{r} 3 \\ \times 1 \\ \hline \end{array}$

17. $\begin{array}{r} 3 \\ \times 2 \\ \hline \end{array}$

18. $\begin{array}{r} 3 \\ \times 3 \\ \hline \end{array}$

19. $\begin{array}{r} 4 \\ \times 3 \\ \hline \end{array}$

20. $\begin{array}{r} 3 \\ \times 5 \\ \hline \end{array}$

21. $\begin{array}{r} 9 \\ \times 3 \\ \hline \end{array}$

22. The weatherman says the temperature is rising 3 degrees every hour. How much hotter is it after 2 hours have passed?

_____

23. Mrs. Hernandez's class is raising money by selling boxes of cookies for $3 each. Alex sold 4 boxes to her mother and 2 more to her neighbor. How much money did Alex raise?

_____

24. **Reasoning** If 3×6 can be solved by separating an array into a 1×6 and a 2×6 array, explain how 4×6 can be separated so that it can be solved with known facts? Then find 4×6.

 MDIS 2.0

Multiplying by 4

Materials 24 counters, 6 inch piece of yarn per student

Use 2s facts to multiply by 4.

1. Show a 4 × 6 array.

2. Place the piece of yarn between the second and third row of the array.
Fill in the blanks.

_____ × 6 = _____

2 × _____ = _____

3. So, 4 × 6 is double the product of 2 × 6.

2 × 6 = _____

Double the product: 12 + 12 = _____   So, 4 × 6 = _____.

4. Use 2s facts to find 4 × 7 by doing the following.

Find the product of 2 × 7.   2 × 7 = _____

Double the product: 14 + 14 = _____   So, 4 × 7 = _____.

5. Use 2s facts to find 4 × 4 by doing the following.

Find the product of 2 × 4.   2 × 4 = _____

Double the product: 8 + 8 = _____   So, 4 × 4 = _____.

       MDIS 2.0

Multiplying by 4 (continued)

Find each product.

6. $8 \times 4 =$ _____

7. $3 \times 4 =$ _____

8. $1 \times 4 =$ _____

9. $\begin{array}{r} 4 \\ \times\ 4 \\ \hline \end{array}$

10. $\begin{array}{r} 4 \\ \times\ 8 \\ \hline \end{array}$

11. $\begin{array}{r} 9 \\ \times\ 4 \\ \hline \end{array}$

12. $\begin{array}{r} 7 \\ \times\ 4 \\ \hline \end{array}$

13. $\begin{array}{r} 6 \\ \times\ 4 \\ \hline \end{array}$

14. $\begin{array}{r} 4 \\ \times\ 6 \\ \hline \end{array}$

15. $\begin{array}{r} 4 \\ \times\ 1 \\ \hline \end{array}$

16. $\begin{array}{r} 4 \\ \times\ 2 \\ \hline \end{array}$

17. $\begin{array}{r} 4 \\ \times\ 5 \\ \hline \end{array}$

18. $\begin{array}{r} 5 \\ \times\ 4 \\ \hline \end{array}$

19. $\begin{array}{r} 4 \\ \times\ 7 \\ \hline \end{array}$

20. $\begin{array}{r} 2 \\ \times\ 4 \\ \hline \end{array}$

21. $\begin{array}{r} 4 \\ \times\ 3 \\ \hline \end{array}$

22. **Reasoning** If $9 \times 4 = 36$, then $4 \times$ _____ $= 36$.

23. Helen is planting a garden. She buys 3 trays of tomato plants. Each tray has 4 plants and costs $2. How many tomato plants did Helen buy? _____

24. Jean reads 5 pages in a book before bedtime each night. Bedtime is at 9:00 P.M. How many pages does Jean read in 4 nights? _____

25. How can you find 4×8 without using two 4×4 arrays?

MDIS 2.0

Name _____

Multiplying by 6 or 7

Materials 56 counters, 6 inch piece of yarn per student or pair

Use 1s facts and 5s facts to multiply by 6.

1. A 6 × 7 array is 6 rows of _____.

2. Draw a line to separate the 6 × 7 array into 1 row of 7 and 5 rows of 7.

   1 × 7 = _____   5 × 7 = _____

   So, 6 × 7 = 7 + _____ = _____.

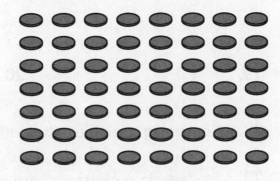

Use 2s facts and 5s facts to multiply by 7.

3. A 7 × 8 array is 7 rows of _____.

4. Draw a line to separate the 7 × 8 array into 2 rows of 8 and 5 rows of 8.

   2 × 8 = _____   5 × 8 = _____

   So, 7 × 8 = 16 + _____ = _____.

5. 6 × 8 = 8 + _____ = _____

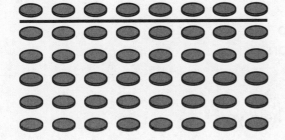

6. 7 × 7 = 14 + _____ = _____

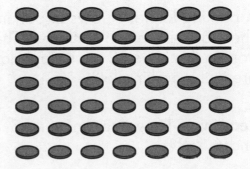

G29 (student p. 1)   MDIS 2.0

Name _____

Multiplying by 6 or 7 (continued)

Find each product.

7. $\begin{array}{r} 1 \\ \times 7 \\ \hline \end{array}$

8. $\begin{array}{r} 6 \\ \times 3 \\ \hline \end{array}$

9. $\begin{array}{r} 6 \\ \times 8 \\ \hline \end{array}$

10. $\begin{array}{r} 9 \\ \times 7 \\ \hline \end{array}$

11. $\begin{array}{r} 6 \\ \times 9 \\ \hline \end{array}$

12. $\begin{array}{r} 7 \\ \times 4 \\ \hline \end{array}$

13. $\begin{array}{r} 4 \\ \times 6 \\ \hline \end{array}$

14. $\begin{array}{r} 3 \\ \times 7 \\ \hline \end{array}$

15. $\begin{array}{r} 7 \\ \times 7 \\ \hline \end{array}$

16. $\begin{array}{r} 2 \\ \times 7 \\ \hline \end{array}$

17. $\begin{array}{r} 6 \\ \times 6 \\ \hline \end{array}$

18. $\begin{array}{r} 6 \\ \times 2 \\ \hline \end{array}$

19. $6 \times 1 =$ _____

20. $7 \times 8 =$ _____

21. $6 \times \$6 =$ _____

22. **Reasoning** Complete the pattern. 6, 12, 18, _____, 30, _____

23. Students in a classroom are in groups with
7 students in each group. There are 5 groups
of students. How many students are there
in the classroom?   _____

24. A parking lot has 7 rows of parking spaces.
There are six cars in each row. The charge to
park in this lot is $2 each day. How many cars
are in the parking lot?   _____

25. **Reasoning** How does knowing $3 \times 8 = 24$ help you
find 6×8?

G29 (student p. 2)   MDIS 2.0

Name _____

Multiplying by 8

Use 4s facts to multiply by 8.

1. An 8 × 7 array is _____ rows of _____.

2. Draw a line to separate the 8 × 7 array into two arrays with 4 rows of 7.

3. Since the 8 × 7 array is the same thing as two 4 × 7 arrays, you can find the product of 4 × 7 and then double it.

    4 × 7 = _____

    Double the product: 28
                         +28
                         ‾‾‾‾

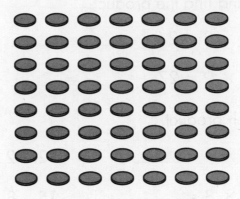

So, 8 × 7 = _____.

You can also use 3s facts and 5s facts to multiply by 8.

4. Draw a line to separate the 8 × 7 array into a 3 × 7 array and a 5 × 7.

    3 × 7 = _____

    5 × 7 = _____

5. Since the 8 × 7 array is the same thing as a 3 × 7 array plus a 5 × 7 array, add the products.

    8 × 7 = 21 + _____

        = _____

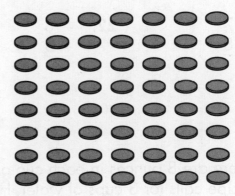

So, 8 × 7 = _____.

6. **Reasoning** Explain two ways to find 8 × 6.

G30 (student p. 1)   MDIS 2.0

Multiplying by 8 (continued)

In Exercises 7–10, use 3s facts, 4s facts and 5s facts to fill in the blanks and find the product.

7. $8 \times 8 = 24 +$ _____ = _____

8. $8 \times 8 = 32 +$ _____ = _____

9. $8 \times 9 = 27 +$ _____ = _____

10. $8 \times 9 = 36 +$ _____ = _____

Find each product.

11. $8 \times 1 =$ _____

12. $2 \times 8 =$ _____

13. $6 \times 8 =$ _____

14. $0 \times 8 =$ _____

15. $8 \times 2 =$ _____

16. $8 \times 4 =$ _____

17. $\begin{array}{r} 1 \\ \times 8 \\ \hline \end{array}$

18. $\begin{array}{r} 8 \\ \times 3 \\ \hline \end{array}$

19. $\begin{array}{r} 8 \\ \times 6 \\ \hline \end{array}$

20. $\begin{array}{r} 9 \\ \times 8 \\ \hline \end{array}$

21. $\begin{array}{r} 7 \\ \times 8 \\ \hline \end{array}$

22. $\begin{array}{r} 8 \\ \times 5 \\ \hline \end{array}$

23. $\begin{array}{r} 8 \\ \times 8 \\ \hline \end{array}$

24. $\begin{array}{r} 4 \\ \times 8 \\ \hline \end{array}$

25. There are 8 ounces in each cup of water. A recipe calls for 3 cups of water. How many ounces of water are needed for the recipe?

_____

26. Each chapter in a book has 8 pages and 3 pictures. There are 6 chapters in the book. How many pages are there in the book?

_____

27. **Reasoning** If $9 \times 8 = 72$, then $8 \times 9 =$ _____.

28. **Reasoning** Find 8×5. Tell how you found it.

Name _____

Multiplying by 10

Answer 1 to 5 to learn how to multiply by 10.

1. Continue skip counting by 10s on the number line below.

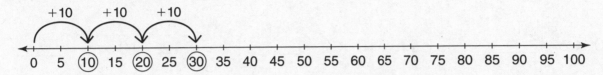

+10   +10   +10

0 5 ⑩ 15 ⑳ 25 ㉚ 35 40 45 50 55 60 65 70 75 80 85 90 95 100

2. Each number a hop lands on is a **multiple** of ten. Circle each multiple of 10 on the number line. Then list them in the blanks below.

_____ _____ _____ _____ _____ _____ _____ _____ _____ _____

3. To find 6 × 10, count by 10s until you have said 6 numbers.

10, 20, _____, _____,

_____, _____

So, 6 × 10 = _____.

4. Do this for each of the 10s facts. Complete the table.

5. **Reasoning** Complete to describe the patterns in the products of the 10s facts.

All the multiplies of 10 end in what number? _____

So, when you multiply a number by 10, you just write the number and a _____.

6. **Reasoning** What is 10 × 7? Explain how you know.

10s Facts

0 × 10 = 0	6 × 10 = _____
1 × 10 = _____	7 × 10 = _____
2 × 10 = _____	8 × 10 = _____
3 × 10 = _____	9 × 10 = _____
4 × 10 = _____	10 × 10 = _____
5 × 10 = _____	

 MDIS 2.0

Multiplying by 10 (continued)

Find each product.

7. $2 \times 10 = $ _____

8. $4 \times 10 = $ _____

9. $6 \times 10 = $ _____

10. $10 \times 6 = $ _____

11. $10 \times 2 = $ _____

12. $10 \times 5 = $ _____

13. $\begin{array}{r} 3 \\ \times\ 10 \\ \hline \end{array}$

14. $\begin{array}{r} 10 \\ \times\ 9 \\ \hline \end{array}$

15. $\begin{array}{r} 8 \\ \times\ 10 \\ \hline \end{array}$

16. $\begin{array}{r} 10 \\ \times\ 8 \\ \hline \end{array}$

17. $\begin{array}{r} 9 \\ \times\ 10 \\ \hline \end{array}$

18. $\begin{array}{r} 5 \\ \times\ 10 \\ \hline \end{array}$

19. $\begin{array}{r} 10 \\ \times\ 3 \\ \hline \end{array}$

20. $\begin{array}{r} 10 \\ \times\ 1 \\ \hline \end{array}$

21. $\begin{array}{r} 1 \\ \times\ 10 \\ \hline \end{array}$

22. $\begin{array}{r} 7 \\ \times\ 10 \\ \hline \end{array}$

23. There are 8 markers in one box. How many markers are in 10 boxes?

_____

24. Reasoning Complete the pattern. 10, 20, _____, _____, 50, _____, 70

25. Reasoning Seven friends get together to play a marble game. Sixty marbles are needed to play this game. Each friend brings ten marbles. Are there enough marbles to play the game?

26. Reasoning Jake said that 10×4 is 100. Is Jake correct? Explain.

MDIS 2.0

Name _____

Multiplying Three Numbers

Does it matter how you multiply $5 \times 2 \times 3$? Answer 1–8 to find out.

To show the factors you are multiplying first, use parentheses as grouping symbols.

1. Group the first two factors together.   (_____ $\times$ _____) $\times$ 3

2. Multiply what is in the parentheses first. $5 \times 2 =$ _____

3. Then, multiply the product of what is in parentheses by the third factor. $10 \times 3 =$ _____

4. So, $(5 \times 2) \times 3 =$ _____ .

5. Start again and group the last two factors together. $5 \times ($_____ $\times$ _____$)$

6. Multiply what is in the parentheses first. $2 \times 3 =$ _____

7. Then, multiply 5 by the product of what is in parentheses. $5 \times 6 =$ _____

8. So, $5 \times (2 \times 3) =$ _____ .

It does not matter how the factors are grouped; the product will be the same.

9. $5 \times (2 \times 3) = (5 \times$ _____$) \times 3$

Find $3 \times 2 \times 4$ two different ways.

10. Do the 3×2 first.

$3 \times 2 =$ _____ $6 \times 4 =$ _____   So, $(3 \times 2) \times 4 =$ _____ .

11. Do the 2×4 first.

$2 \times 4 =$ _____ $3 \times 8 =$ _____   So, $3 \times (2 \times 4) =$ _____ .

G32 (student p. 1)   MDIS 2.0

Multiplying Three Numbers (continued)

Find each product two different ways.

12. $(1 \times 3) \times 6 =$ _____

$1 \times (3 \times 6) =$ _____

13. $(5 \times 2) \times 4 =$ _____

$5 \times (2 \times 4) =$ _____

14. $(2 \times 4) \times 1 =$ _____

$2 \times (4 \times 1) =$ _____

15. $(2 \times 2) \times 5 =$ _____

$2 \times (2 \times 5) =$ _____

Find each product.

16. $2 \times 4 \times 3 =$ _____

17. $7 \times 1 \times 3 =$ _____

18. $3 \times 3 \times 2 =$ _____

19. $3 \times 2 \times 6 =$ _____

20. $(4 \times 2) \times 2 =$ _____

21. $3 \times (0 \times 7) =$ _____

22. $1 \times 7 \times 9 =$ _____

23. $8 \times (2 \times 3) =$ _____

24. $(2 \times 5) \times 6 =$ _____

25. $9 \times 0 \times 3 =$ _____

26. $4 \times 5 \times 1 =$ _____

27. $(3 \times 6) \times 1 =$ _____

28. **Reasoning** When multiplying three numbers, if one of the factors is zero, what will the answer be?

_____

29. A classroom of students is getting ready to take a test. There are 5 rows of desks in the room and 4 students are in each row. Each student is required to have 2 pencils. How many pencils are needed?

_____

MDIS 2.0

Name _____

Meanings for Division

Materials 15 counters and 3 half sheets of paper, per pair

Martina has 15 dolls. She put them into 3 equal groups. Answer
1 to 3 to find how many dolls were in each group.

1. Count out 15 counters. Place the counters on the sheets of paper to form
3 equal groups.

  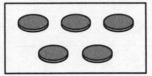

2. Write a number sentence to show division as sharing.

_____ ÷ _____ = _____
     Total   Number of   Number in
                   equal groups   each group

3. How many dolls were in each group? _____

Mrs. Gentry had only 6 tokens. As the students left her room,
she gave each student 2 tokens. Answer 4 to 6 to find how many
students got tokens.

4. Show 6 tokens.

5. Find the number of times 2 can be subtracted from 6 until nothing is left.

$6 - 2 = 4$ 1 time
$4 - 2 = 2$ 2 times
$2 - 2 = 0$ 3 times

6. Write a number sentence to show division as repeated subtraction.

_____ ÷ _____ = _____
     Total   Number subtracted   Number of times 2
                 each time   was subtracted

7. How many students got tokens? _____

   G33 (student p. 1)   MDIS 2.0

Name _____

Meanings for Division (continued)

Draw pictures to solve each problem.

8. Put 20 counters into 5 equal groups. How many counters are in each group?

9. Put 12 counters in a row. How many times can you subtract 4 counters?

_____

10. You put 24 cards into 4 equal piles. How many cards are in each pile?

11. You put 21 chairs into rows of 7. How many rows do you make?

_____

12. You have 30 oranges. If you need 6 oranges to fill a bag, how many bags can you fill?

13. You put 10 marbles into equal groups of 5. How many groups are there?

_____

14. Eight people went to the museum in two cars. The same number of people went in each car. How many people went in each car?

_____

15. **Reasoning** How can you use repeated subtraction to find $30 \div 5$?

G33 (student p. 2)

Writing Division Stories

Materials counters, 18 per student or pair of students

To write a division story for 18 ÷ 3 that is about 18 grapes and
3 sisters, fill in the blanks below.

1. Mrs. _____ put _____ grapes into

   a bowl. Mrs. _____'s daughters,

   _____, _____, and

   _____ shared the grapes equally. How

   many _____ did each sister get?

2. Use counters to show how many grapes there were in all.

3. Divide the 18 counters into 3 equal groups.

 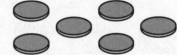

4. How many grapes did each sister get?   _____ grapes

5. Write a division story for 10 ÷ 5 about apples and bags.

   Mr. _____ bought _____ apples. He

   put _____ apples into each bag. How many _____

   did he use?

6. Use counters to show how many apples he bought.

7. Divide the 10 counters into groups with 5 in each group.

8. How many bags did he use?   _____ bags

 MDIS 2.0

Name _____

Writing Division Stories (continued)

Write a division story for each number sentence below. Use the
pictures to help. Then use counters or draw a picture to solve.

9. $15 \div 5 = $ _____

10. $12 \div 3 = $ _____

Write a division story. Then use counters or draw a picture
to solve.

11. $14 \div 2 = $ _____

G34 (student p. 2)   MDIS 2.0

Name _____

Relating Multiplication and Division

Materials 36 color tiles per pair

1. Partner A show an array for 2 × 9, or 2 rows of 9.

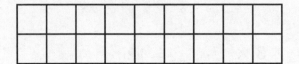

2. Partner B show 18 ÷ 2, by showing a total of 18 tiles in 2 rows.

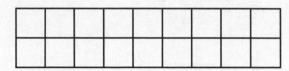

3. What do you notice about the arrays each partner made?

4. Partner A's tiles show:

2 × 9 = _____

5. Partner B's tiles show:

18 ÷ 2 = _____

6. What do you notice about the numbers used in each number sentence?

Multiplication and division are related to each other. A **fact family** shows how they are related.

A fact family has two multiplication and two division number sentences written with the same 3 numbers.

Fact family for 2, 9, and 18

2 × 9 = 18	18 ÷ 2 = 9
9 × 2 = 18	18 ÷ 9 = 2

You can use multiplication to help you divide.

Find 30 ÷ 6.

7. To find 30 ÷ 6, think about the related multiplication problem.

6 times what number equals 30?   6 × _____ = 30

8. Since you know 6 × 5 = 30, then you know 30 ÷ 6 = _____.

G35 (student p. 1) MDIS 2.0

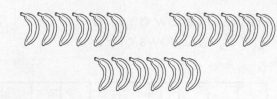

Relating Multiplication and Division (continued)

Use the array to complete each sentence.

9.

$4 \times$ _____ $= 20$

$20 \div 4 =$ _____

10.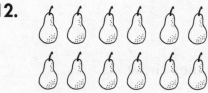

$3 \times$ _____ $= 18$

$18 \div 3 =$ _____

11.

$3 \times$ _____ $= 9$

$9 \div 3 =$ _____

12.

$6 \times$ _____ $= 12$

$12 \div 6 =$ _____

Write a fact family for each product.

13. $3 \times 7 = 21$

_____

_____

_____

14. $2 \times 4 = 8$

_____

_____

_____

15. $3 \times 5 = 15$

_____

_____

_____

16. **Reasoning** Why does the fact family for $3 \times 3 = 9$ only have 2 facts?

G35 (student p. 2)   MDIS 2.0

Dividing by 2 Through 5

Materials Have counters available for students to use.

You can use multiplication facts to help you divide.

Anna Maria has 24 leaves in her collection. She puts 4 leaves on each page in her scrap book. How many pages does she need for all her leaves?

Find $24 \div 4$.

1. To find $24 \div 4$, think about the related multiplication problem.

   4 times what number equals 24? $4 \times$ _____ $= 24$

2. Since you know $4 \times 6 = 24$, then you know $24 \div 4 =$ _____.

3. How many pages does Anna Maria need for all her leaves? _____

Find $45 \div 5$.

4. 5 times what number equals 45? $5 \times$ _____ $= 45$

5. Since you know $5 \times 9 = 45$, then you know $45 \div 5 =$ _____.

A division problem can be written two different ways.

$$30 \div 5 = 6 \qquad\qquad 5\overline{)30}^{\,6}$$

Both problems are read "30 divided by 5 equals 6."

6. Think: $3 \times$ _____ $= 15$ So, $3\overline{)15} =$ _____.

7. Think: $4 \times$ _____ $= 16$ So $16 \div 4 =$ _____.

8. Think: $2 \times$ _____ $= 18$ So $18 \div 2 =$ _____.

Dividing by 2 Through 5 (continued)

Use the multiplication fact to find each quotient.

9. $4 \times$ _____ $= 24$

$24 \div 4 =$ _____

10. $6 \times$ _____ $= 30$

$30 \div 6 =$ _____

11. $2 \times$ _____ $= 12$

$12 \div 2 =$ _____

12. $5 \times$ _____ $= 25$

$25 \div 5 =$ _____

13. $3 \times$ _____ $= 27$

$27 \div 3 =$ _____

14. $4 \times$ _____ $= 28$

$28 \div 4 =$ _____

Find each quotient.

15. $25 \div 5 =$ _____

16. $20 \div 4 =$ _____

17. $12 \div 3 =$ _____

18. $5 \overline{)35}$

19. $4 \overline{)36}$

20. $3 \overline{)21}$

21. Mario has 15 eggs. He wants to share them equally with 3 friends. How many eggs will each friend get?

Think: $3 \times 5 = 15$. So, $15 \div 3 = 15 \div 3 =$ _____ eggs.

22. Todd has 40 whistles. He wants to divide them evenly between his 5 friends. How many whistles will each friend get?

_____

23. **Reasoning** What multiplication fact can you use to find $27 \div 3$? Explain how to find $27 \div 3$.

24. If $4 \times 10 = 40$, then what is $40 \div 4$? _____

MDIS 2.0

Dividing by 6 and 7

Materials Have counters available for students to use.

You can use multiplication facts to help you divide.

Ahmed has 24 bugs to put on 6 boards. He wants the same number of bugs on each board. How many bugs should he put on each board?

Find $24 \div 6$.

1. To find $24 \div 6$, think about the related multiplication problem.

   6 times what number equals 24? $6 \times \underline{\hspace{1cm}} = 24$

2. Since you know $6 \times 4 = 24$, then you know $24 \div 6 = \underline{\hspace{1cm}}$.

3. How many bugs should Ahmed put on each board? _____

Find $21 \div 7$.

4. To find $21 \div 7$, think about the related multiplication problem.

   7 times what number equals 21? $7 \times \underline{\hspace{1cm}} = 21$

5. Since you know $7 \times 3 = 21$, then you know $21 \div 7 = \underline{\hspace{1cm}}$.

6. Think: $6 \times \underline{\hspace{1cm}} = 30$ So, $6\overline{)30} = \underline{\hspace{1cm}}$.

7. Think: $7 \times \underline{\hspace{1cm}} = 49$ So $49 \div 7 = \underline{\hspace{1cm}}$.

8. Think: $6 \times \underline{\hspace{1cm}} = 48$ So $48 \div 6 = \underline{\hspace{1cm}}$.

9. **Reasoning** Explain how to find $63 \div 7$.

MDIS 2.0

Name _____

Dividing by 6 and 7 (continued)

Use the multiplication fact to find each quotient.

10. $6 \times 5 = 30$

$30 \div 6 =$ _____

11. $7 \times 2 = 14$

$14 \div 7 =$ _____

12. $6 \times 1 = 6$

$6 \div 6 =$ _____

13. $7 \times 5 = 35$

$35 \div 7 =$ _____

14. $6 \times$ _____ $= 36$

$36 \div 6 =$ _____

15. $7 \times$ _____ $= 56$

$56 \div 7 =$ _____

16. $6 \times$ _____ $= 24$

$24 \div 6 =$ _____

17. $6 \times 9 = 54$

$54 \div 6 =$ _____

18. $6 \times 7 = 42$

$42 \div 6 =$ _____

Find each quotient.

19. $6\overline{)54}$

20. $7\overline{)42}$

21. $6\overline{)30}$

22. $7\overline{)7}$

23. $6\overline{)42}$

24. $7\overline{)70}$

25. $6\overline{)12}$

26. $7\overline{)14}$

27. $6\overline{)60}$

28. Mrs. Carpenter's class is dividing into groups for group work. There are 28 students in the class and 35 desks. How many students will be in each group if there are 7 groups?

_____

29. **Reasoning** If you know that $6 \times 12 = 72$, then what is $72 \div 6$.

_____

G37 (student p. 2)

Dividing by 8 and 9

Materials Have counters available for students to use.

You can use multiplication facts to help you divide.

At the museum, 32 students are divided into 8 equal groups.
How many students are in each group?

Find 32 ÷ 8.

1. To find 32 ÷ 8, think about the related multiplication problem.

    8 times what number equals 32?   8 × _____ = 32

2. Since you know 8 × 4 = 32, then you know 32 ÷ 8 = _____.

3. How many students are in each group at the museum? _____ students

Find 36 ÷ 9.

4. To find 36 ÷ 9, think about the related multiplication problem.

    9 times what number equals 36?   9 × _____ = 36

5. Since you know 9 × 4 = 36, then you know 36 ÷ 9 = _____.

Find 8)‾8‾0‾

6. To find 8)‾8‾0‾, think about the related multiplication problem.

    8 times what number equals 80?   8 × _____ = 80

7. Since you know 8 × 10 = 80, then you know 8)‾8‾0‾ = _____.

8. **Reasoning** Explain how to find 56 ÷ 8.

Dividing by 8 and 9 (continued)

Use the multiplication fact to find each quotient.

9. $8 \times 2 = 16$

$16 \div 8 =$ _____

10. $9 \times 5 = 45$

$45 \div 9 =$ _____

11. $8 \times 3 = 24$

$24 \div 8 =$ _____

12. $9 \times 6 = 54$

$54 \div 9 =$ _____

13. $8 \times$ _____ $= 32$

$32 \div 8 =$ _____

14. $8 \times$ _____ $= 48$

$48 \div 8 =$ _____

15. $9 \times$ _____ $= 27$

$27 \div 9 =$ _____

16. $9 \times$ _____ $= 90$

$90 \div 9 =$ _____

17. $8 \times$ _____ $= 72$

$72 \div 8 =$ _____

Find each quotient.

18. $9\overline{)63}$

19. $8\overline{)32}$

20. $9\overline{)36}$

21. $8\overline{)64}$

22. $9\overline{)81}$

23. $8\overline{)16}$

24. $9\overline{)45}$

25. $8\overline{)56}$

26. $8\overline{)40}$

27. **Reasoning** If you know that $8 \times 12 = 96$, then what is $96 \div 8$.

_____

28. Nine friends go to lunch and split the $54 ticket evenly. How much does each friend pay?

_____

0 and 1 in Division

Think about related multiplication facts to help you divide.

Find 5 ÷ 1.

1. Think: 1 times what number equals 5? $1 \times$ _____ = 5

2. Since you know $1 \times 5 = 5$, then you know $5 \div 1 =$ _____.

3. If Karina had 5 oranges to put equally in 1 basket,
how many oranges would go in each basket? _____ oranges

Find 9 ÷ 1.

4. $1 \times$ _____ = 9 So, $9 \div 1 =$ _____.

5. What is the result when any number is divided by 1? _____

Find 0 ÷ 7.

6. Think: 7 times what number equals 0? $7 \times$ _____ = 0

7. Since you know $7 \times 0 = 0$, then you know $0 \div 7 =$ _____.

8. If Karina had 0 oranges to put equally in 7 baskets,
how many oranges would go in each basket? _____ oranges

Find 0 ÷ 2.

9. $2 \times$ _____ = 0 So, $0 \div 2 =$ _____.

10. What is the result when zero is divided
by any number (except 0)? _____

Find 5 ÷ 0.

11. **Reasoning** If Karina had 5 oranges to put equally in 0 baskets,
how many oranges would go in each basket? Explain.

You cannot divide a number by 0.

0 and 1 in Division (continued)

Find 4 ÷ 4.

12. Think: 4 times what number equals 4? $4 \times$ _____ $= 4$

13. Since you know $4 \times 1 = 4$, then you know $4 \div 4 =$ _____.

14. If Karina had 4 oranges to put equally in 4 baskets,
how many oranges would go in each basket?   _____ orange

Find 8 ÷ 8.

15. $8 \times$ _____ $= 8$ So, $8 \div 8 =$ _____.

16. What is the result when any number (except 0)
is divided by itself?   _____

Find each quotient.

17. $4 \div 1 =$ _____   **18.** $0 \div 5 =$ _____   **19.** $6 \div 6 =$ _____

20. $3\overline{)0}$ **21.** $9\overline{)9}$ **22.** $5\overline{)5}$

23. $1\overline{)6}$ **24.** $1\overline{)1}$ **25.** $8\overline{)0}$

26. **Reasoning** Use the rule for division by 1 to find $247 \div 1$.
Explain.

27. Larry has 3 friends who would like some cookies but he has
no cookies to give them. How many cookies can Larry give
each friend?

                        MDIS 2.0

Name _____

Mental Math: Multiplication Patterns

Materials place-value blocks: 12 unit cubes, 12 tens rods, and
12 hundreds blocks for each group

There are 300 paint brushes in a box. The art teacher bought
4 boxes of brushes. How many paint brushes did he buy
altogether? Answer 1 to 8.

Use basic facts and place-value blocks to find 4 × 300.

1. What basic fact can you use? _____

2. Show 4 × 3 using unit cubes.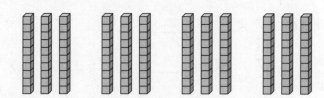

3. What is 4 × 3? _____

4. Show 4 × 30 using tens rods.

5. What is 4 × 30? _____

6. Show 4 × 300 using hundreds blocks.

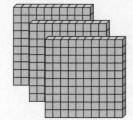 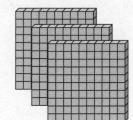 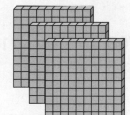 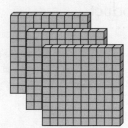

7. What is 4 × 300? _____

8. How many paint brushes did the art teacher buy? _____

9. **Reasoning** How can you use 4 × 3 to find 4 × 300 using zeros
   instead of place-value blocks?

 MDIS 2.0

Name _____

Mental Math: Multiplication Patterns (continued)

Find 5×200.

10. Think: $5 \times 2 =$ _____

11. Think: $5 \times 20 =$ _____

12. Think: $5 \times 200 =$ _____

Use the basic facts and patterns to find each product.

13. $2 \times 3 =$ _____

$2 \times 30 =$ _____

$2 \times 300 =$ _____

14. $3 \times 7 =$ _____

$3 \times 70 =$ _____

$3 \times 700 =$ _____

15. $4 \times 5 =$ _____

$4 \times 50 =$ _____

$4 \times 500 =$ _____

16. $7 \times 6 =$ _____

$7 \times 60 =$ _____

$7 \times 600 =$ _____

17. $5 \times 9 =$ _____

$5 \times 90 =$ _____

$5 \times 900 =$ _____

18. $3 \times 6 =$ _____

$3 \times 60 =$ _____

$3 \times 600 =$ _____

Find each product.

19. 60
        $\times\ 3$

20. 700
         $\times\ 5$

21. 30
         $\times\ 8$

22. 800
         $\times\ 4$

23. Mark, Ryan, and Jenny are each collecting pennies
for a school fundraiser. If each student collects 400
pennies, how many have they collected altogether? _____

24. **Reasoning** How can the basic fact $5 \times 8 = 40$ and zeros help you

find the missing number in the problem $5 \times$ _____$^?$ $= 4,000$?

G40 (student p. 2)

Mental Math: Division Patterns

Materials place-value blocks: 16 ones, 16 tens rods, and 16 hundreds blocks per group

Find 1,600 ÷ 8.

1. Use a basic fact and place-value blocks to find 1,600 ÷ 8.

2. Show 16 unit cubes. Divide them into 8 equal groups.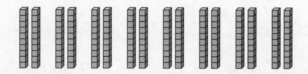

3. How many cubes are in each group? _____

4. What is 16 ÷ 8? _____

5. Show 16 ten rods. Divide them into 8 equal groups.

6. How many ten rods are in each group? _____

7. So, 160 ÷ 8 = 16 tens ÷ 8 = _____ tens = _____

8. What is 160 ÷ 8? _____

9. Show 16 hundred blocks. Divide them into 8 equal groups.

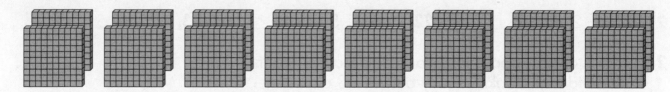

10. How many hundred blocks are in each group? _____

11. So, 1,600 ÷ 8 = 16 hundreds ÷ 8 = _____ hundreds = _____

12. What is 1,600 ÷ 8? _____

13. **Reasoning** How can you use 16 ÷ 8 to find 1,600 ÷ 8 using zeros instead of place-value blocks?

 MDIS 2.0

Name _____

Mental Math: Division Patterns (continued)

14. Find $1,500 \div 5$.

Think: $15 \div 5 =$ _____

Think: $150 \div 5 =$ _____

Think: $1,500 \div 5 =$ _____

Use the basic facts and patterns to find each quotient.

15. $36 \div 6 =$ _____

$360 \div 6 =$ _____

$3,600 \div 6 =$ _____

16. $28 \div 7 =$ _____

$280 \div 7 =$ _____

$2,800 \div 7 =$ _____

17. $16 \div 2 =$ _____

$160 \div 2 =$ _____

$1,600 \div 2 =$ _____

18. $45 \div 9 =$ _____

$450 \div 9 =$ _____

$4,500 \div 9 =$ _____

19. $21 \div 7 =$ _____

$210 \div 7 =$ _____

$2,100 \div 7 =$ _____

20. $64 \div 8 =$ _____

$640 \div 8 =$ _____

$6,400 \div 8 =$ _____

Find each quotient.

21. $60 \div 2 =$ _____

22. $150 \div 3 =$ _____

23. $200 \div 5 =$ _____

24. There are 60 books in a stack. The teacher wants to divide the books equally between 3 classes. There are 20 students in each class. How many books will each class receive?

_____

25. **Reasoning** How are $1,200 \div 2$ and $12 \div 2$ alike and how are they different?

26. How many zeros are in the quotient $7,200 \div 9$? _____

 MDIS 2.0

Name _____

Estimating Products

During Field Day, the students at Sunrise Elementary were placed into 4 activity groups. Each group had 78 students. About how many students were in all 4 groups?

Estimate 4 × 78.

1. What is 78 rounded to the nearest ten? _____

2. What is 4 × 80? _____

3. What is a good estimate for 4 × 78? _____

4. About how many students were in all 4 groups during Field Day? _____ students

5. **Reasoning** How do the place-value blocks below show that 320 is a good estimate for 4 × 78?

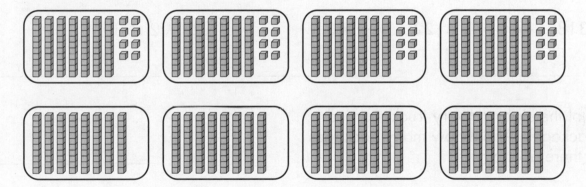

Estimate 6 × 345.

6. What is 345 rounded to the nearest hundred? _____

7. What is 6 × 300? _____

8. What is a good estimate for 6 × 345? _____

 MDIS 2.0

Estimating Products (continued)

Estimate each product.

9. 7 × 38

_____

10. 8 × 34

_____

11. 5 × 91

_____

12. 4 × 57

_____

13. 7 × 47

_____

14. 3 × 72

_____

15. 6 × 52

_____

16. 2 × 75

_____

17. 3 × 87

_____

18. 2 × 623

_____

19. 5 × 177

_____

20. 4 × 532

_____

21. 3 × 318

_____

22. 4 × 863

_____

23. 2 × 804

_____

24. Each of the eight delivery trucks carried
94 packages. About how many packages
were there altogether?   _____

25. There are 43 carrots in each of 7 bags of
carrots. About how many carrots altogether?   _____

26. **Reasoning** What is a good estimate for 6 × 26? Explain
how you estimated.

27. **Reasoning** Mark estimated the product of 4 × 54 to be
about 280. Was his estimation reasonable? Explain your reasoning.

                    MDIS 2.0

Estimating Quotients

The city soccer league has 47 children, between the ages of 8 and 10, signed up to play soccer. The people in charge of the soccer league want to put 9 children on each team. About how many teams should they make?

Estimate 47 ÷ 9 by answering 1 to 4.

1. What number is close to 47 and can be easily divided by 9? _____

2. What is 45 ÷ 9? _____

3. What is a good estimate of 47 ÷ 9? _____

4. About how many soccer teams should the city make? _____

You can use compatible numbers to help you estimate a quotient.

Estimate 543 ÷ 8 by answering 5 to 10.

5. Is 5 ÷ 8 a basic fact? _____

6. Is 54 ÷ 8 a basic fact? _____

7. What is a basic fact that is close to 54 ÷ 8? _____

8. Is 560 close to 543? _____

9. What is 560 ÷ 8? _____

10. What is a good estimate of 543 ÷ 8? _____

Estimate 615 ÷ 2 by answering 11 to 14.

11. Is 6 ÷ 2 a basic fact? _____

12. Is 600 close to 615? _____

13. What is 600 ÷ 2? _____

14. What is a good estimate of 615 ÷ 2? _____

15. **Reasoning** Show how you would estimate 2,398 ÷ 4?

Name _____

Intervention

Lesson **G43**

Estimating Quotients (continued)

Estimate each quotient. Write the numbers you used.

16. $75 \div 4 =$ _____

17. $31 \div 2 =$ _____

18. $824 \div 9 =$ _____

19. $465 \div 9 =$ _____

20. $230 \div 7 =$ _____

21. $630 \div 7 =$ _____

22. $56 \div 3 =$ _____

23. $181 \div 6 =$ _____

24. $414 \div 7 =$ _____

25. $564 \div 6 =$ _____

26. $729 \div 8 =$ _____

27. $311 \div 5 =$ _____

28. $3\overline{)923}$ _____

29. $9\overline{)269}$ _____

30. $5\overline{)345}$ _____

31. $6\overline{)117}$ _____

32. $2\overline{)81}$ _____

33. $6\overline{)552}$ _____

34. The Spencer family drove in their car to their favorite vacation spot. Mrs. Spencer likes to travel at a rate of 55 miles per hour. The Spencers traveled 849 miles in 3 days. Estimate the number of miles driven each day.

_____

35. A manufacturer is packaging paper towels. If 6 rolls complete a package, about how many packages can be made from 327 rolls?

_____

36. **Reasoning** Is 30 a reasonable quotient for $264 \div 9$? Explain your reasoning.

G43 (student p. 2) MDIS 2.0

Multiplication and Arrays

Materials place-value blocks: 9 tens and 40 ones for
each group

To multiply 3 × 38, answer 1 to 7.

1. Show an array of 3 rows with 38 in each row, using
place-value blocks.

2. How many tens in all? _____ tens

3. 9 tens = _____

4. How many ones in all? _____

5. 24 ones = _____

6. Add the tens and the ones together.

9 tens + 24 ones = _____ + _____ = _____

7. What is 3 × 38? _____

To multiply 4 × 27, answer 8 to 11.

8. Show an array of 4 rows with 27 in each row, using
place-value blocks.

9. How many tens in all? _____ tens = _____

10. How many ones in all? _____

11. What is 4 × 27? 4 × 27 = _____ + _____ = _____

 MDIS 2.0

Name _____

Multiplication and Arrays (continued)

Find each product. Draw a picture to help.

12. 3×16

13. 5×21

14. 2×23

15. 3×18

Find each product. Draw a picture to help you multiply with greater numbers.

16. $3 \times 35 =$ _____

17. $6 \times 23 =$ _____

18. $5 \times 18 =$ _____

19. $2 \times 34 =$ _____

20. $6 \times 14 =$ _____

21. $4 \times 28 =$ _____

22. $7 \times 13 =$ _____

23. $5 \times 42 =$ _____

24. **Reasoning** If you draw an array to find
4×35, how many tens will you draw?   _____ tens

How many ones will you draw?   _____ ones

So, $4 \times 35 =$ _____.

G44 (student p. 2)   MDIS 2.0

Name _____

Breaking Apart Numbers to Multiply

Materials place-value blocks: 16 tens and 48 ones per
student or pair

Find 8 × 26 by answering 1 to 6.

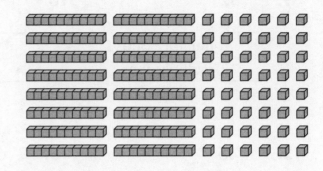

1. Show an array of 8 rows with 26 in
    each row, using place-value blocks.

2. 26 = _____ tens + _____ ones

    = _____ + _____

3. Multiply the ones by 8 and write the product on the left.

    8 × _____ ones = _____ ones

4. Multiply the tens by 8 and write the product on the left.

    8 × _____ tens = _____ tens = _____

5. Add the products together and write the sum below the line,
    on the left.

6. So, 8 × 26 = _____.

$$\begin{array}{r} 26 \\ \times\ 8 \\ \hline \end{array}$$
8 × 6 → _____
8 × 20 → _____

7. Find 3 × 45.

$$\begin{array}{r} 45 \\ \times\ 3 \\ \hline \end{array}$$
3 × 5 → _____
3 × 40 → _____

8. Find 4 × 29. Use place-value blocks or draw pictures to help.

$$\begin{array}{r} 29 \\ \times\ 4 \\ \hline \end{array}$$
4 × 9 → _____
4 × 20 → _____

G45 (student p. 1)   MDIS 2.0

Name _____

Breaking Apart Numbers to Multiply (continued)

Find each product.

9.   32
   × 3
   6 multiply ones
   +90 multiply tens
   96 product

10.   42
   × 5
   10 multiply ones
   +200 multiply tens
   ___ product

11. $64
   × 3

12.   45
   × 2

13.   64
   × 4

14. $23
   × 5

15.   32
   × 6

16.   53
   × 4

17.   47
   × 3

18. $38
   × 2

19.   67
   × 5

20.   74
   × 3

21.   18
   × 7

22.   56
   × 4

23. **Reasoning** Carlo wants to buy 3 model airplanes. If each airplane costs $29, how much money does he need?   _____

24. Salvo called 5 friends and talked 34 minutes with each friend. How many minutes was Salvo on the phone?   _____ minutes

25. **Reasoning** James multiplied 5 × 54 by breaking 54 apart into 5 tens and 4 ones. Then he multiplied 5 × 4 and 5 × 5, and then added 20 + 25. Where did James make his mistake?

G45 (student p. 2)   MDIS 2.0

Multiplying Two-Digit Numbers

Materials place-value blocks: 6 tens and 24 ones per student

Jenny's Market has 4 boxes. Each box holds 16 cans of soup.
Answer 1 to 7 to find the number of cans of soup Jenny's
Market has altogether.

Find 4×16.

1. Show 4 groups of 16 using place-value blocks.

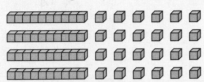

2. Multiply the ones. 4×6 ones = _____ ones

3. Regroup the ones. Trade groups of ten ones for tens.

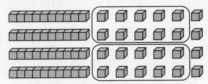

4. $24 = 2$ tens and _____ ones. Record the ones
in the ones column of the Tens and Ones chart.
Record the tens at the top of the tens column
of the chart.

5. Multiply the tens. 4×1 ten = _____ tens

6. Add the regrouped tens to the 4 tens and record
this value in the tens column of the chart.

4 tens $+ 2$ tens = _____ tens

7. So, $4 \times 16 =$ _____. How many cans of soup
does Jenny's Market have altogether?

_____

Tens	Ones
1	6
×	4

G46 (student p. 1)   MDIS 2.0

Name _____

Multiplying Two-Digit Numbers (continued)

Multiply.

8. 17
    × 2

9. 25
    × 3

10. 21
     × 7

11. 34
     × 4

12. 22
     × 6

13. 48
     × 3

14. 37
     × 5

15. 47
     × 4

16. 14
     × 6

17. 18
     × 3

18. 23
     × 4

19. 31
     × 5

20. 27
     × 7

21. 43
     × 4

22. 52
     × 2

23. 65
     × 3

24. 57
     × 5

25. 62
     × 3

26. 75
     × 3

27. 37
     × 8

28. Ron is 26 years old. His grandmother is 3 times
his age. How old is his grandmother?

_____ years

29. A basketball player usually scores 17 points in
each game. How many points would she be
expected to score in 5 games?

_____ points

30. **Reasoning** Write a two-digit number multiplied by a
one-digit number that does not require regrouping.

G46 (student p. 2)

Multiplying Three-Digit Numbers

A parking garage has 6 different levels. There are 128 parking spots on each level. Answer 1 to 13 to find the total number of parking spots.

Find 6 × 128.

1. 128 = _____ hundred + _____ tens + _____ ones

2. Multiply the ones. 6 × 8 ones = _____ ones

3. Do you need to regroup the ones? _____

4. 48 ones = _____ tens + _____ ones

5. Record the ones in the ones column of the chart at the right. Record the regrouped tens at the top of the tens column.

6. Multiply the tens.

   6 × 2 tens = _____ tens

7. Now, add the regrouped tens.

   _____ tens + _____ tens = _____ tens = _____

8. Do you need to regroup the tens? _____

9. 160 = _____ hundred + _____ tens

10. Record the tens in the tens column. Record the regrouped hundreds at the top of the hundreds column.

11. Multiply the hundreds. 6 × 1 hundred = _____ hundreds

12. Now add the regrouped hundreds and record in the hundreds column.

    _____ hundreds + _____ hundred = _____ hundreds = _____

13. So, 6 × 128 = _____.
    How many parking spots are in the garage? _____

Hundreds	Tens	Ones
1	2	8
×		6

 MDIS 2.0

Multiplying Three-Digit Numbers (continued)

Multiply.

14.

Th	H	T	O
	4	5	7
×			3

15.

Th	H	T	O
	5	2	6
×			7

16. 223
× 4

17. 246
× 7

18. 117
× 5

19. 434
× 4

20. 519
× 2

21. 327
× 3

22. 572
× 5

23. 357
× 8

24. 323
× 4

25. 351
× 5

26. 217
× 7

27. 352
× 2

28. A company makes 352 boxes of cereal each day.
How many boxes are made in 7 days? _____ boxes

29. Reasoning Is 243 a reasonable product for 3 × 71?
Use estimation to explain why or why not.

     MDIS 2.0

Multiplying Money

Bryan wants to buy 4 posters. Each poster costs $3.95. Answer 1 to 14 to find how much money Bryan needs.

Find 4 × $3.95.

To find 4 × $3.95, multiply as you would with whole numbers.

1. $3.95 = _____ dollars + _____ dimes + _____ pennies

2. Multiply the pennies. 4 × 5 pennies = _____ pennies

3. Regroup the pennies.

    _____ pennies = _____ dimes and _____ pennies

4. Record the pennies in the pennies column of the chart, even if there are zero. Record the regrouped dimes at the top of the dimes column.

Ten Dollars	Dollars	Dimes	Pennies
☐	☐	☐	☐
	$3	. 9	5
×			4

5. Multiply the dimes.

    4 × 9 dimes = _____ dimes

6. Add the regrouped dimes. _____ dimes + 2 dimes = _____ dimes

7. Regroup the dimes. _____ dimes = _____ dollars and _____ dimes

8. Record the dimes in the dimes column of the chart. Record the regrouped dollars at the top of the dollars column.

9. Multiply the dollars. 4 × 3 dollars = _____ dollars

10. Add the regrouped dollars.

    _____ dollars + _____ dollars = _____ dollars

11. Regroup the dollars.

    _____ dollars = _____ ten dollar and _____ dollars

Multiplying Money (continued)

12. Record the dollars and ten dollars in the chart.

13. Write the answer in dollars and cents by placing the dollar sign and decimal point.

14. How much money will Bryan need for the posters? _____

Find each product.

15. $1.25
× 5

16. $1.10
× 3

17. $8.15
× 7

18. $5.21
× 6

19. $8.39
× 4

20. $2.75
× 6

21. $2.25
× 3

22. $1.21
× 7

23. $2.46
× 7

24. $1.18
× 6

25. $3.62
× 3

26. $4.75
× 3

27. **Reasoning** Ham is on sale for $3.21 per pound and chicken is on sale for $4.35 per pound. How much do 3 pounds of chicken cost? _____

28. **Reasoning** Shanti has $35.00. She wants to buy 4 packs of baseball cards. Each packs costs $8.50. How much do 4 packs of cards cost? If she has enough money, how much change will Shanti get back? If she needs more money, how much more money does she need?

Name _____

Multiplying One-Digit and
Four-Digit Numbers

Each section of a parade float used 1,436 flowers. If the parade float had 4 different sections, how many flowers were used on the entire float?

Find 4 × 1,436 by answering 1 to 19.

1. Multiply the ones. 4 × 6 ones = _____ ones

2. Do you need to regroup the ones? _____

3. Regroup the ones.

_____ ones = _____ tens + _____ ones

4. Record the ones in the
ones column of the chart.
Record the regrouped tens
at the top of the tens column.

Thousands	Hundreds	Tens	Ones
☐	☐	☐	☐
1	4	3	6
×			4

5. Multiply the tens.

4 × 3 tens = _____ tens

6. Add the regrouped tens.

_____ tens + _____ tens = _____ tens

7. Do you need to regroup the tens? _____

8. Regroup the tens. _____ tens = _____ hundred + _____ tens

9. Record the tens in the tens column and record the
regrouped hundreds at the top of the hundreds column.

10. Multiply the hundreds. 4 × 4 hundreds = _____ hundreds

11. Add the regrouped hundreds.

_____ hundreds + _____ hundred = _____ hundreds

12. Do you need to regroup the hundreds? _____

G49 (student p. 1)   MDIS 2.0

Multiplying One-Digit and Four-Digit Numbers (continued)

13. Regroup the hundreds.

_____ hundreds = _____ thousand + _____ hundreds

14. Record the hundreds in the hundreds column. Record the regrouped thousands at the top of the thousands column.

15. Multiply the thousands. 4 × 1 thousand = _____ thousands

16. Add the regrouped thousands.

_____ thousands + _____ thousand = _____ thousands

17. Do you need to regroup? _____

18. Record the thousands in the thousands column.

19. How many flowers were used on the entire float? _____

Find each product.

20.	2,356 × 3	**21.**	5,342 × 4	**22.**	1,081 × 6	**23.**	3,321 × 4
24.	1,431 × 5	**25.**	2,310 × 3	**26.**	8,211 × 2	**27.**	7,201 × 4
28.	1,121 × 4	**29.**	3,002 × 3	**30.**	4,610 × 2	**31.**	5,329 × 5

32. Last year 1,503 people attended a craft show.
This year 3 times as many people attended.
How many people attended the craft show this year? _____ people

33. **Reasoning** Ramon estimated the product of 4,099 × 5 to be around 20,000. Is his estimate reasonable? Explain your reasoning.

Name _____

Dividing with Objects

Materials 7 counters and 3 half sheets of paper for each student or pair

Andrew has 7 model cars to put on 3 shelves. He wants to put the same number of cars on each shelf. How many cars should Andrew put on each shelf? Answer 1 to 8.

Find 7 ÷ 3.

1. Show 7 counters and 3 sheets of paper.

2. Put 1 counter on each piece of paper.

3. Are there enough counters to put another counter on each sheet of paper?   _____

4. Put another counter on each piece of paper.

5. Are there enough counters to put another counter on each sheet of paper?   _____

6. How many counters are on each sheet?   _____

7. How many counters are remaining, or left over?   _____

So, 7 ÷ 3 is 2 remainder 1, or 7 ÷ 3 = 2 R1.

8. How many cars should Andrew put on each shelf? How many cars will be left over?

G50 (student p. 1)   MDIS 2.0

Dividing with Objects (continued)

Use counters or draw a picture to find each quotient and remainder.

9. $8 \div 3 =$ _____

10. $17 \div 3 =$ _____

11. $14 \div 3 =$ _____

12. $11 \div 4 =$ _____

13. $22 \div 4 =$ _____

14. $34 \div 4 =$ _____

15. $13 \div 5 =$ _____

16. $27 \div 5 =$ _____

17. $46 \div 5 =$ _____

18. $14 \div 6 =$ _____

19. $26 \div 6 =$ _____

20. $38 \div 6 =$ _____

21. $17 \div 7 =$ _____

22. $27 \div 7 =$ _____

23. $45 \div 7 =$ _____

24. $18 \div 8 =$ _____

25. $28 \div 8 =$ _____

26. $37 \div 8 =$ _____

27. $14 \div 9 =$ _____

28. $28 \div 9 =$ _____

29. $39 \div 9 =$ _____

30. $12 \div 8 =$ _____

31. $68 \div 7 =$ _____

32. $59 \div 8 =$ _____

33. $9 \div 4 =$ _____

34. $26 \div 5 =$ _____

35. $34 \div 6 =$ _____

36. $14 \div 5 =$ _____

37. $21 \div 6 =$ _____

38. $3 \div 2 =$ _____

39. **Reasoning** Grace is reading a book for school. The book has 26 pages and she is given 3 days to read it. How many pages should she read each day? Will she have to read more pages on some days than on others? Explain.

 MDIS 2.0

Name _____

Interpret the Remainder

Materials counters

Division is an operation that is used to find the number of equal groups or the number of objects that are in each group. Sometimes there is an extra amount. The leftover amount is called the **remainder**.

Can Leroy sort his collection of 14 sports cards into 3 equal piles?

Leroy can't sort 14 sports cards into 3 equal piles. He can put 4 cards in each of the 3 piles, but 2 sports cards are left. The remainder is 2 and can be written as R2; 14 ÷ 3 is 4 R2. Leroy can either give the extra sports cards to a friend or save them until he gets enough to make another pile of 4.

Use counters to solve the following problems.

1. 28 stickers, 5 stickers on a page

How many pages are full? _____

What is the remainder? _____

What does the remainder mean? _____

_____

2. 19 books, 6 books on a shelf

How many shelves are full? _____

What is the remainder? _____

What does the remainder mean? _____

_____

3. 34 marbles, 5 marbles in a group

How many groups are complete? _____

What is the remainder? _____

What does the remainder mean? _____

_____

 MDIS 2.0

Name _____

Interpret the Remainder (continued)

Solve each of the following problems.

4. 62 buttons, 7 buttons on a shirt
    How many shirts can be made? _____
    What is the remainder? _____
    What does the remainder mean? _____

    _____

5. 95 pens, 10 pens in a package
    How many complete packages of pens are there? How many
    pens are extra?

    _____

6. 40 action figures, 6 action figures in a row
    How many complete rows of action figures are there? How many
    action figures are extra?

    _____

7. 74 apples, 9 apples in a bag
    How many bags are full? How many apples are extra?

    _____

8. Robert claims that 57 game tokens can be shared equally among
    himself and 5 friends without having any extra tokens. Is Robert
    correct? Explain.

    _____

    _____

9. Mary is organizing her collection of 37 crayons in groups of 5.
    How many complete groups will she have? Are there any extra
    crayons? What can Mary do with any extra crayons?

    _____

    _____

 MDIS 2.0

Name _____

Using Objects to Divide

Materials place-value blocks: 5 tens and 16 ones for each pair

Jaime has 56 swimming ribbons. He can display 4 ribbons in one frame.
How many frames will he need?
Find 56 ÷ 4 by answering 1 to 11.

1. Use place-value blocks to show the 56 ribbons.

2. Divide the tens evenly into 4 equal groups.

3. Are there any tens leftover? _____

    How many? _____

4. Regroup the leftover ten as ones.

    _____ ten = _____ ones

5. Combine the regrouped ones with the
    other ones.

    _____ ones + 6 ones = _____ ones

6. Divide the 16 ones evenly into the
    4 equal groups.

7. How many ones are in each group?

    _____

8. Are there any ones leftover? _____

9. How many tens and ones are in each group?

    _____ ten and _____ ones

10. So 56 ÷ 4 = _____. How many frames will Jaime
    need to display his swimming ribbons?   _____ frames

11. **Reasoning** How can you check that the quotient is correct?

Using Objects to Divide (continued)

Use place-value blocks or draw a picture to find each quotient.

12. $36 \div 3 =$ _____

13. $42 \div 2 =$ _____

14. $68 \div 4 =$ _____

15. $60 \div 4 =$ _____

16. $75 \div 5 =$ _____

17. $54 \div 3 =$ _____

18. $72 \div 6 =$ _____

19. $57 \div 3 =$ _____

20. $48 \div 3 =$ _____

21. $52 \div 4 =$ _____

22. $76 \div 4 =$ _____

23. $38 \div 2 =$ _____

24. Use place-value blocks or draw a picture to find how many nickels equal the number of pennies in the chart. (Remember: 1 nickel equals 5 pennies.)

25. **Reasoning** Write a division problem that does not require you to regroup the tens. The dividend must be two-digits and greater than 50. The divisor must be one-digit and greater than 5.

Pennies	Nickels
70	
65	
90	
85	

 MDIS 2.0

Name _____

Dividing Two-Digit Numbers

Materials place-value blocks: 6 tens and 15 ones for each pair

Find $65 \div 5$ by answering 1 to 17.

1. Use place-value blocks to show 65.

2. Divide the 6 tens into 5 equal groups.

3. How many tens can go into each group? _____

4. Record the 1 above the 6 in 65, at the right.

5. How many tens were used?

   5×1 ten = _____ tens

6. Record the tens used below the 6 in 65,
   at the right.

7. How many tens are leftover?

   $6 - 5 =$ _____ ten

8. Record the tens left below
   the 5 and the line.

9. Regroup the tens into ones and
   add the other 5 ones.

   _____ ten + 5 ones = _____ ones

10. Bring down the 5 next to the 1, to
    show the 15 regrouped ones.

11. Divide the 15 ones evenly into the
    5 groups. How many ones can go
    in each group?   _____

12. Record the 3 above the 5 in 65.

13. How many ones were used?

    5×3 ones = _____ ones

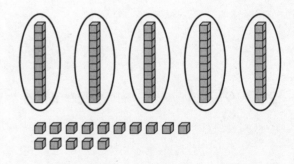

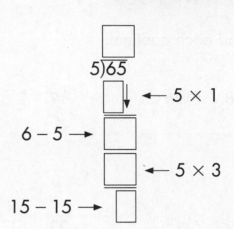

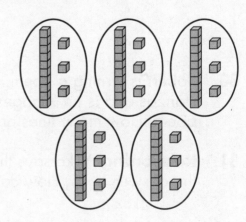

G53 (student p. 1)   MDIS 2.0

Dividing Two-Digit Numbers (continued)

14. Record the ones used below the 15 regrouped ones.

15. How many ones are leftover? 15 − 15 = _____ ones

16. Record the ones left below the 15 and the line.

17. What is 65 ÷ 5? _____

Find each quotient.

18. 8)96 **19.** 2)32 **20.** 3)54 **21.** 5)70

22. 6)84 **23.** 5)75 **24.** 7)77 **25.** 6)78

26. 9)99 **27.** 4)76 **28.** 5)85 **29.** 2)46

30. Robert is writing a poem. The poem is divided into 5
stanzas and is on 2 pages. There are 60 lines in the
poem. How many lines are in each stanza?   _____

31. **Reasoning** Yoko says that when you divide 75 by 5,
the answer is 15. How can you check her answer? Is she correct?

  MDIS 2.0

Name _____

Dividing Three-Digit Numbers

There are 324 baseball players at camp. If the camp counselors put them into 9 equal-sized living groups, how many players are in each group?

Find 324 ÷ 9 by answering 1 to 17.

The place-value blocks at the right show 324.

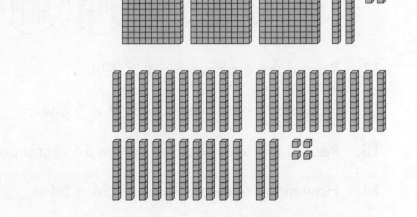

1. Are there enough hundreds in 324 to put one in each of 9 groups?

_____

2. Regroup the hundreds.

3 hundreds + 2 tens = _____ tens

3. How many tens can go into each of 9 groups? _____

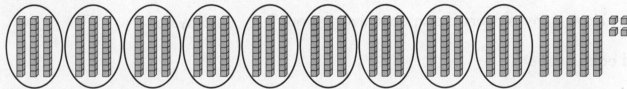
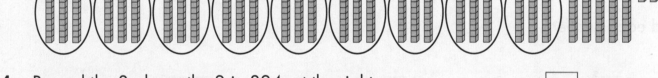

4. Record the 3 above the 2 in 324, at the right.

5. How many tens were used?

9 × 3 tens = _____ tens

6. Record the tens used below the 32 in 324, at the right.

7. How many tens are left over?

32 − 27 = _____ tens

8. Record the tens left below the 27 and the line.

9. Regroup the tens into ones and add the other 4 ones. Bring down the 4 to show the total ones.

5 tens + 4 ones = _____ ones

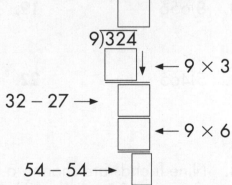

9)324   ← 9 × 3
32 − 27 →   ← 9 × 6
54 − 54 →

G54 (student p. 1)   MDIS 2.0

Dividing Three-Digit Numbers (continued)

10. How many of the 54 ones can go in each of the 9 groups? _____ ones

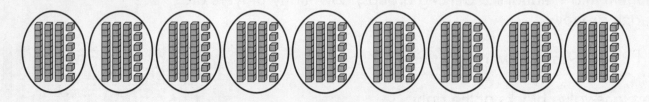

11. Record the 6 above the 4 in 324.

12. How many ones were used? 9×6 ones = _____ ones

13. Record the ones used below the 54 regrouped ones.

14. How many ones are leftover? $54 - 54 =$ _____ ones

15. Record the ones left below the 54 and the line.

16. What is $324 \div 9$? _____

17. How many players are in each living group? _____ players

Find each quotient.

18. $8\overline{)656}$ **19.** $2\overline{)304}$ **20.** $9\overline{)828}$

21. $5\overline{)465}$ **22.** $7\overline{)238}$ **23.** $3\overline{)639}$

24. Nine friends are sharing a box of crackers. The box contains 135 crackers. How many crackers will each friend get if they are divided evenly?

_____

25. **Reasoning** In the division problem $432 \div 5$, should the first step be to divide the hundreds or to regroup the hundreds to tens? Explain your reasoning.

     MDIS 2.0

Name _____

Zeros in the Quotient

Janice has 412 photographs. She wants to put them into 4 albums.
If she puts the same number of photographs in each album,
how many photographs will be in each album?

Find 412 ÷ 4 by answering 1 to 13.

The place-value blocks at the right
show 412.

1. Are there enough hundreds in 412
   to put one in each of 4 groups?   _____

2. How many hundreds can go into
   each of 4 groups?   _____
   Record the 1 in the hundreds place of the quotient, below.

3. How many hundreds were used?

   4 × 1 hundred = _____ hundreds
   Record the hundreds used under the 4 in 412, below.

4. How many hundreds are leftover?

   4 − 4 = _____ hundreds

5. Bring down the 1 ten. How many
   tens can go into each of 4 groups? _____
   Record the 0 in the tens place of the quotient.

6. How many tens were used?

   4 × 0 tens = _____ tens
   Record this 0 below the 1.

7. How many tens are leftover? 1 − 0 = _____
   Record the tens left below the 0 and the line.

8. Regroup the tens into ones and add the other 2 ones.
   Bring down the 2 to show the total ones.

   1 ten + 2 ones = _____ ones

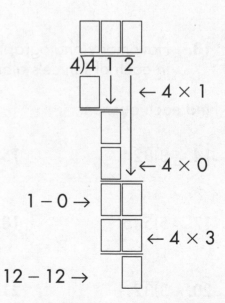

$$4\overline{)4\ 1\ 2}$$

← 4 × 1

← 4 × 0

1 − 0 →

← 4 × 3

12 − 12 →

Name _____

Zeros in the Quotient (continued)

9. How many ones can go into each of 4 groups? _____
Record the 3 in the ones place of the quotient.

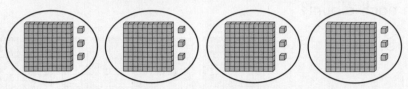

10. How many ones were used? 4×3 ones = _____ ones
Record this 12 below the regrouped 12.

11. How many ones are leftover? $12 - 12 =$ _____
Record the ones left below the 12 and the line.

12. What is $412 \div 4$? _____

13. How many photographs will be
in each of Janice's albums?   _____ photographs

Find each quotient.

14. $8\overline{)824}$ **15.** $2\overline{)611}$ **16.** $9\overline{)9,243}$

17. $5\overline{)545}$ **18.** $7\overline{)2,124}$ **19.** $3\overline{)617}$

20. $3\overline{)32}$ **21.** $5\overline{)541}$ **22.** $7\overline{)285}$

23. **Reasoning** Dante divided 642 by 8 and wrote the quotient as 8
remainder 2. What error did Dante make? What is the correct answer?

                    MDIS 2.0

Dividing Greater Numbers

The Camara family wants to travel the same distance each of 6 days. They need to travel 1,716 miles in all. Answer 1 to 15 to find how far they should travel each day.

Find 1,716 ÷ 6.

1. Are there enough thousands to put one in each of 6 groups? _____

2. Regroup the thousand into hundreds and add the other 7 hundreds.

   1 thousand + 7 hundreds = _____ hundreds

3. How many hundreds can go into each of 6 groups? _____
   Record the 2 in the hundreds place of the quotient, below.

4. How many hundreds were used?

   6 × 2 hundreds = _____ hundreds
   Record the hundreds used below the 17 in 1,716, below.

5. How many hundreds are leftover?

   17 hundreds − 12 hundreds

   = _____ hundreds
   Record the 5 under the 12.

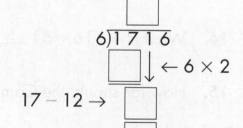

6. Regroup the hundreds into tens and
   add the other 1 ten.

   5 hundreds + 1 ten = _____ tens
   Bring down the 1 ten next to the 5 to show how many tens in all.

7. How many tens can go into each of 6 groups? _____
   Record the 8 in the tens place of the quotient.

8. How many tens were used? 6 × 8 tens = _____ tens
   Record 48 below the 51.

9. How many tens are leftover? _____
   Record the tens left below the 48 and the line.

 MDIS 2.0

Dividing Greater Numbers (continued)

10. Regroup the tens into ones and add
    the other 6 ones. Bring down the 6
    to show the total ones.

    3 tens + 6 ones = _____ ones

```
        28 □
    6)1716
        12
        51
        48↓
         3 □
           □  ← 6 × 6
           □  ← 36 − 36
```

11. How many ones can go into each of
    6 groups? _____
    Record the 6 in the ones place of the quotient.

12. How many ones were used?

    6 × 6 ones = _____ ones
    Record the 36 below the regrouped 36.

13. How many ones are leftover? 36 − 36 = _____
    Record the ones left below the 36 and the line.

14. What is $1,716 \div 6$? _____

15. How far should the Camara family travel each day? _____ miles

Find each quotient.

16. 4)3,560   17. 6)1,836   18. 4)4,112

19. 2)2,246   20. 8)832   21. 7)6,510

22. **Reasoning** How can you use estimation to find out
    if the answer of 286 is reasonable for $1,716 \div 6$?

   MDIS 2.0

Factoring Numbers

Materials color tiles or counters, 24 for each student

The arrays below show all of the factors of 12.

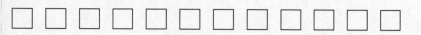

1 × 12

2 × 6   3 × 4   4 × 3   6 × 2

12 × 1

1. What are all the factors of 12?

    _____, _____, _____, _____, _____, _____

2. Create all the possible arrays you can with 17 color tiles.

3. What are the factors of 17? _____, _____

Numbers which have only 2 possible arrays and exactly 2 factors
are prime numbers.

4. Is 17 a prime number? _____

5. Is 12 a prime number? _____

Numbers which have more than 2 possible arrays and more
than 2 factors are composite numbers.

6. Is 17 a composite number? _____

7. Is 12 a composite number? _____

8. What are all the factors of 24? _____

9. Is 24 a prime number or a composite number? _____

Factoring Numbers (continued)

Find all the factors of each number. Tell whether each is prime
or composite.

10. 7

_____

_____

11. 8

_____

_____

12. 21

_____

_____

13. 48

_____

_____

14. 51

_____

_____

15. 9

_____

_____

16. 13

_____

_____

17. 26

_____

_____

18. 40

_____

_____

19. 55

_____

_____

20. 70

_____

_____

21. 83

_____

_____

22. Mr. Lee has 18 desks in his room. He would like them arranged in a
rectangular array. Draw all the different possible arrays and write a
multiplication sentence for each.

23. Reasoning Lee says 53 is a prime number because it is an odd number.
Is Lee's reasoning correct? Give an example to prove your reasoning.

    G57 (student p. 2)   MDIS 2.0

Divisibility by 2, 3, 5, 9, and 10

A number such as 256 is divisible by a number like 2 if 256 ÷ 2 has no remainder. If 256 is a multiple of 2, then 256 is divisible by 2.

Use the divisibility rules and answer 1 to 10 to determine if 256 is divisible by 2, 3, 5, 9, or 10.

Divisibility Rules	
Number	**Rule**
2	The last digit is even: 0, 2, 4, 6, 8.
3	The sum of the digits is divisible by 3.
5	The last digit ends in a 0 or 5.
9	The sum of the digits is divisible by 9.
10	The ones digit is a 0.

1. Is the last digit in 256 an even number? _____

2. Is 256 divisible by 2? _____

3. Is the last digit in 256 a 0 or 5? _____

4. Is 256 divisible by 5? _____

5. Is 256 divisible by 10? _____

6. What is the sum of the digits of 256? $2 + 5 + 6 =$ _____

7. Is the sum of the digits of 256 divisible by 3? _____

8. Is 256 divisible by 3? _____

9. Is the sum of the digits of 256 divisible by 9? _____

10. Is 256 divisible by 9? _____

Use the divisibility rules to determine if 720 is divisible by 2, 5, 9, or 10.

11. Is 720 divisible by 2? _____   12. Is 720 divisible by 5? _____

13. Is 720 divisible by 10? _____   14. Is 720 divisible by 9? _____

 MDIS 2.0

Divisibility by 2, 3, 5, 9, and 10 (continued)

Test each number to see if it is divisible by 2, 3, 5, 9, or 10. List the numbers each is divisible by.

15. 56

_____

16. 78

_____

17. 182

_____

18. 380

_____

19. 105

_____

20. 126

_____

21. 4,311

_____

22. 8,356

_____

23. 2,580

_____

24. 7,265

_____

25. 4,815

_____

26. 630

_____

27. Feliz has 225 baseball trophies. He wants to display his trophies on some shelves with an equal number of trophies on each. He can buy shelves in packages of 5, 9, or 10. Which shelf package should he NOT buy? Explain.

28. **Reasoning** Are all numbers that are divisible by 5 also divisible by 10? Explain your reasoning.

29. **Reasoning** Are all numbers that are divisible by 10 also divisible by 5? Explain your reasoning.

   MDIS 2.0

Divisibility

A number such as 1,875 is divisible by a number like 5 if 1,875 ÷ 5 has no remainder. If 1,875 is a multiple of 5, then 1,875 is divisible by 5.

Use the divisibility rules to determine if 1,875 is divisible by 2, 3, 4, 5, 6, 9, or 10, by answering 1 to 15.

Divisibility Rules	
Number	**Rule**
2	The last digit is even: 0, 2, 4, 6, 8.
3	The sum of the digits is divisible by 3.
4	The last two digits of the number make a number that is divisible by 4.
5	The last digit ends in a 0 or 5.
6	The number is divisible by 2 and 3.
9	The sum of the digits is divisible by 9.
10	The ones digit is a 0.

1. Is the last digit in 1,875 an even number? _____

2. Is 1,875 divisible by 2? _____

3. Is the last digit in 1,875 a 0 or 5? _____

4. Is 1,875 divisible by 5? _____

5. Is 1,875 divisible by 10? _____

6. What is the sum of the digits of 1,875?

   $1 + 8 + 7 + 5 =$ _____

7. Is the sum of the digits divisible by 3? _____

8. Is 1,875 divisible by 3? _____

9. Is the sum of the digits divisible by 9? _____

10. Is 1,875 divisible by 9? _____

11. Is 1,875 divisible by both 2 and 3? _____

 MDIS 2.0

Divisibility (continued)

12. Is 1,875 divisible by 6? _____

13. What number makes up the last two digits of 1,875? _____

14. Is 75 divisible by 4? _____

15. Is 1,875 divisible by 4? _____

Test each number to see if it is divisible by 2, 3, 4, 5, 6, 9, or 10.
List the numbers each is divisible by.

16. 214
_____

17. 313
_____

18. 425
_____

19. 670
_____

20. 2,312
_____

21. 773
_____

22. 470
_____

23. 847
_____

24. 845
_____

25. 400
_____

26. 900
_____

27. 1,002
_____

28. 430
_____

29. 635
_____

30. 3,470
_____

31. 9,630
_____

32. 2,345
_____

33. 5,672
_____

34. 1,236
_____

35. 7,305
_____

36. Camp Many Lakes has 198 campers registered this year.
They are planning many activities and games which must
be completed in groups of equal number of campers. What
different sizes of groups can Camp Many Lakes
divide the campers into? _____

37. **Reasoning** Are all numbers that are divisible by 2 also divisible
by 10? Explain your reasoning.

38. **Reasoning** Are all numbers that are divisible by 10 also divisible
by 2? Explain your reasoning.

 MDIS 2.0

Exponents

Scott is planning to run in a race and asked 2 friends to sponsor him.
The following week, each friend asked 2 more friends to sponsor Scott.
If this continued, how many sponsors did Scott have after seven weeks?

1. Complete the table.

Week	Number of Sponsors (Expanded Form)	Number of Sponsors (Exponential Form)	Number of Sponsors (Standard Form)
1	2	2^1	2
2	2×2	2^2	4
3	$2 \times 2 \times 2$	2^3	8
4	$2 \times 2 \times 2 \times 2$	2^4	
5	$2 \times 2 \times 2 \times 2 \times 2$		
6			
7			

2. How many sponsors will Scott have on the 10th week?

Expanded form: _____

Exponential form: _____   Standard form: _____

3. If Scott started by asking 3 friends to sponsor him and each of those friends asked three friends, how many sponsors would he have on the 4th week?

Expanded form: _____

Exponential form: _____   Standard form: _____

4. Use the table above to complete the following patterns.   16, 8, 4, 2, _____

$2^4, 2^3, 2^2, 2^1,$ _____

$2^0 = 1$. Any number, except zero, to the zero power is 1.

5. What is 5^0? _____

Exponents (continued)

Write each expression in exponential form.

6. $4 \times 4 \times 4$ **7.** $7 \times 7 \times 7 \times 7 \times 7$ **8.** $6 \times 6 \times 6$

_____   _____   _____

9. $10 \times 10 \times 10 \times 10$ **10.** 5×5 **11.** $3 \times 3 \times 3 \times 3$

_____   _____   _____

Write each expression in standard form.

12. 2^7 **13.** 1^7 **14.** 6^3

_____   _____   _____

15. 83^1 **16.** 4^3 **17.** 11^2

_____   _____   _____

18. 2^8 **19.** 10^4 **20.** 7^2

_____   _____   _____

21. 0^5 **22.** 3^3 **23.** 12^0

_____   _____   _____

Write each expression in expanded form.

24. 12^4 **25.** 8^3 **26.** 4^4

_____   _____   _____

27. 32^5 **28.** 3^4 **29.** 200^2

_____   _____   _____

30. **Reasoning** Is 2^5 the same as 5^2? Check by writing both numbers in standard form.

      G60 (student p. 2)   MDIS 2.0

Name _____

Prime Factorization

1. Use the two factor trees shown to factor 240. For the first circle, think of what number times 6 is 24. For the next two circles, factor 10. Continue factoring each number. Do not use the number 1.

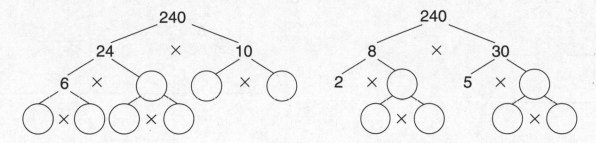

2. What are the numbers at the ends of the branches for each tree?

_____   _____

3. **Reasoning** What do all the numbers at the end of each branch have in common?

4. **Reasoning** What do you notice about the numbers in the two groups?

5. Arrange the numbers from least to greatest and include a multiplication sign between each pair of numbers.   2 × ____ × ____ × ____ × ____ × 5

Your answer to 5 above shows the prime factorization of 240.
If you multiply all the factors back together, you get 240.

6. Write the prime factorization of 240 using exponents.

_____ × 3 × 5

       MDIS 2.0

Name _____

Prime Factorization (continued)

Complete each factor tree. Write the prime factorization with exponents, if you can. Do not use the number 1 as a factor.

7.
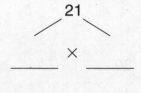

8.
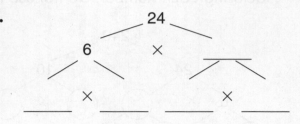

9.
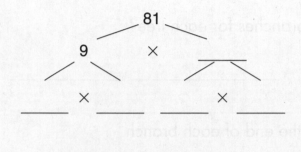

10.
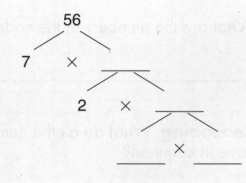

For Exercises 11 to 22, if the number is prime, write <u>prime</u>.
If the number is composite, write the prime factorization of the number.

11. 11   **12.** 18   **13.** 41   **14.** 40

_____   _____   _____   _____

15. 16   **16.** 17   **17.** 80   **18.** 95

_____   _____   _____   _____

19. 35   **20.** 72   **21.** 48   **22.** 55

_____   _____   _____   _____

23. **Reasoning** Holly says that the prime factorization for 44 is 4 × 11. Is she right? Why or why not?

  G61 (student p. 2)   MDIS 2.0

Name _____

Greatest Common Factor

Materials 22 small pieces of paper, 12 in one color and 10 in another
color, per pair

Find the greatest common factor of 48 and 60 by answering 1 to 5.

1. List the factors of 48.

_____

There should be 10 factors. Write the factors of 48, one on each
piece of paper in one color.

2. List the factors of 60.

_____

There should be 12 factors. Write the factors of 60, one on each
piece of paper in another color.

3. Group the factors into three groups: factors that appear only on
one color of paper; factors that appear only on the other color of
paper; and factors that appear on both colors of paper.

Use your groups to fill in the Venn diagram shown. Factors that appear
on both colors of paper go in the shaded area on the Venn diagram.

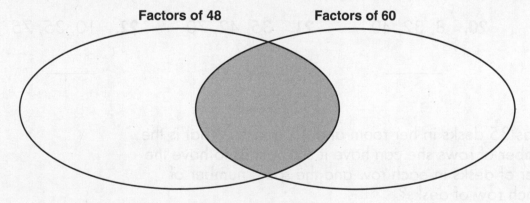

Factors of 48   **Factors of 60**

4. Factors in the shaded area are common
factors. List the common factors.   _____

5. What number is the greatest of these common factors?   _____

This is the greatest common factor (GCF) of 48 and 60.

          MDIS 2.0

Greatest Common Factor (continued)

Find the greatest common factor of 16, 20 and 32 by answering
6 to 10.

6. List the factors of 16. _____

7. List the factors of 20. _____

8. List the factors of 32. _____

9. List the common factors of 16, 20 and 32: _____

10. What is the greatest common factor of 16, 20 and 32? _____

Find the greatest common factor (GCF).

11. 8, 12   **12.** 16, 20   **13.** 15, 25   **14.** 18, 45

_____   _____   _____   _____

15. 35, 81   **16.** 21, 24   **17.** 34, 40   **18.** 7, 31

_____   _____   _____   _____

19. 6, 42   **20.** 8, 32, 40   **21.** 35, 42, 70   **22.** 10, 35, 75

_____   _____   _____   _____

23. A teacher has 35 desks in her room and 45 books. What is the
greatest number of rows she can have if she wishes to have the
same number of desks in each row and the same number of
books for each row of desks?

24. **Reasoning** Hope says the greatest common factor of 12 and 36
is 6. Is she right? Why or why not?

Name _____

Least Common Multiple

A student group is having a large cookout. They wish to buy the same number of hamburgers and hamburger buns. Hamburgers come in packages of 12 and buns come in packages of 8. What is the least amount of each they can buy in order to have the same amount?

Follow 1 to 4 below to answer the question.

1. Complete the table.

Packages	1	2	3	4	5	6
Hamburgers	12	24				
Buns	8	16				

2. What are some common multiples from the table? _____

3. What is the least of these common multiples? _____

   So, the least common multiple (LCM) of 12 and 8 is 24.

4. What is the least amount of hamburgers and buns that the students can buy and have the same amount of each? _____

Find the least common multiple of 6 and 15 by following the steps below.

5. Complete the table.

	2 ×	3 ×	4 ×	5 ×	6 ×	7 ×	8 ×	9 ×	10 ×
6	12	18							
15	30	45							

6. What are the common multiples from the table? _____

7. What are the next three common multiples that are not in the table? _____

8. What is the least common multiple of 6 and 15? _____

                    MDIS 2.0

Least Common Multiple (continued)

Find the least common multiple (LCM).

9. 30, 4

10. 18, 9

11. 12, 36

_____

_____

_____

12. 6, 12

13. 8, 20

14. 3, 14

_____

_____

_____

15. 6, 25

16. 8, 12, 15

17. 3, 4, 5

_____

_____

_____

18. Maria and her brother Carlos both got to be hall monitors today. Maria is hall monitor every 16 school days. Carlos is hall monitor every 20 school days. What is the least number of school days before they will both be hall monitors again?

19. Reasoning Find two numbers whose least common multiple is 12.

20. Reasoning Can you find the greatest common multiple of 6 and 15? Explain.

Mental Math: Multiplying by Multiples of 10

A publishing company ships a particular book in boxes with 6 books each. How many books are in 20 boxes? How many in 2,000 boxes?

Find 20×6 and $2,000 \times 6$ by filling in the blanks.

1. $20 \times 6 = (10 \times 2) \times 6$

$= 10 \times (\underline{\hspace{1cm}} \times 6)$

$= 10 \times \underline{\hspace{1cm}}$

$= \underline{\hspace{1.5cm}}$

2. $2,000 \times 6 = (1,000 \times 2) \times 6$

$= 1,000 \times (\underline{\hspace{1cm}} \times 6)$

$= 1,000 \times \underline{\hspace{1cm}}$

$= \underline{\hspace{1.5cm}}$

3. How many books are in 20 boxes?

$\underline{\hspace{2cm}}$ books

4. How many books are in 2,000 boxes?

$\underline{\hspace{2cm}}$ books

The same publishing company ships a smaller book in boxes with 40 books each. How many books are in 50 boxes? How many are in 500 boxes?

Find 50×40 and 500×40 by filling in the blanks.

5. $50 \times 40 = (5 \times \underline{\hspace{1cm}}) \times$

$(4 \times \underline{\hspace{1cm}})$

$= 5 \times \underline{\hspace{1cm}} \times 10 \times 10$

$= 20 \times \underline{\hspace{1.5cm}}$

$= \underline{\hspace{1.5cm}}$

6. $500 \times 40 = (5 \times \underline{\hspace{1cm}}) \times$

$(4 \times \underline{\hspace{1cm}})$

$= 5 \times \underline{\hspace{1cm}} \times 100 \times 10$

$= 20 \times \underline{\hspace{1.5cm}}$

$= \underline{\hspace{1.5cm}}$

7. How many books are in 50 boxes?

$\underline{\hspace{2cm}}$ books

8. How many books are in 500 boxes?

$\underline{\hspace{2cm}}$ books

MDIS 2.0

Name _____

Mental Math: Multiplying by Multiples of 10 (continued)

Notice the pattern when multiplying multiples of 10.

9. $7 \times 80 =$ _____

   $70 \times 80 =$ _____

   $70 \times 800 =$ _____

10. $4 \times 60 =$ _____

   $40 \times 60 =$ _____

   $40 \times 600 =$ _____

Multiply.

11. $30 \times 40 =$

_____

12. $10 \times 600 =$

_____

13. $70 \times 20 =$

_____

14. $50 \times 400 =$

_____

15. $700 \times 30 =$

_____

16. $40 \times 800 =$

_____

17. $600 \times 30 =$

_____

18. $40 \times 90 =$

_____

19. $90 \times 500 =$

_____

20. $70 \times 500 =$

_____

21. $30 \times 800 =$

_____

22. $200 \times 70 =$

_____

23. $800 \times 80 =$

_____

24. $30 \times 600 =$

_____

25. $40 \times 300 =$

_____

26. A class of 30 students is collecting pennies for a school fundraiser. If each of them collects 400 pennies, how many have they collected all together?

_____ pennies

27. **Reasoning** Raul multiplied 60×500 and got 30,000. Since there are 4 zeros in the answer, he thought his answer was incorrect? Do you agree? Why or why not?

G64 (student p. 2) MDIS 2.0

Name _____

Estimating Products

Mrs. Wilson's class at Hoover Elementary School is collecting canned goods. Their goal is to collect 600 cans. There are 21 students in the class and each student agrees to bring in 33 cans. Answer 1 to 7 to find if the class will meet their goal.

Estimate 21 × 33 and compare the answer to 600.

Round each factor to get numbers you can multiply mentally.

1. What is 21 rounded to the nearest ten?   _____

2. What is 33 rounded to the nearest ten?   _____

3. Multiply the rounded numbers.   20 × 30 = _____

The answer is the same as the number needed to meet the goal.

4. 21 was rounded to 20. Was it rounded up or down?   _____

5. 33 was rounded to 30. Was it rounded up or down?   _____

6. Is 21 × 33 more or less than 21 × 30?   _____

7. Will the goal be reached?   _____

Hoover Elementary School had a goal to collect 12,000 canned goods. There are 18 classes and each class collects 590 cans. Answer 8 to 13 to find if the school will meet their goal.

Estimate 18 × 590 and compare the answer with 12,000.

Round each factor to get numbers you can multiply mentally.

8. What is 18 rounded to the nearest ten?   _____

9. What is 590 rounded to the nearest hundred?   _____

10. Multiply the rounded numbers.   20 × 600 = _____

The answer is the same as the number needed to meet the goal.

Estimating Products (continued)

---

11. 18 was rounded to 20. Was it rounded up or down? _____

590 was rounded to 600. Was it rounded up or down? _____

12. Is 18 × 590 more or less than 20 × 600? _____

13. Will the goal be reached? _____

Round each factor so that you can estimate the product mentally.

14. 71 × 382

_____

_____

15. 27 × 62

_____

16. 45 × 317

_____

17. 58 × 176

_____

_____

18. 831 × 24

_____

19. 16 × 768

_____

20. 87 × 67

_____

_____

21. 373 × 95

_____

22. 57 × 722

_____

23. Debra spends 42 minutes each day driving to
work. About how many minutes does she spend
driving to work each month? _____

24. **Reasoning** If 64 × 82 is estimated to be 60 × 80,
would the estimate be an overestimate or an underestimate?
Explain.

G65 (student p. 2) MDIS 2.0

Using Arrays to Multiply Two-Digit Factors

Materials crayons or markers

Find 12 × 26 by answering 1 to 4.

The array shows how to find each partial product.

1. Color the part of the array which shows 10 × 20 and write the product in the array and in the computation at the right.

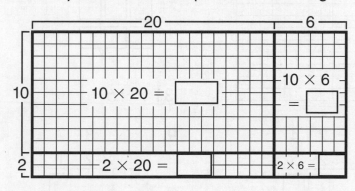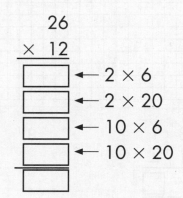

2. Use a different color for each of the other parts of the array. Color each and write the product in the array and in the computation above.

3. Each product you found is part of the product 12 × 26, so each is a partial product. Add the partial products.

4. What is 12 × 26? _____

5. Use the grid to find the partial products and the product 15 × 22.

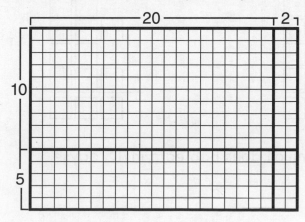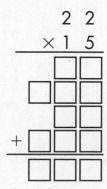

22 × 15 = _____

Name _____

Using Arrays to Multiply Two-Digit Factors (continued)

Use an array to help complete the calculations.

6. 16×31

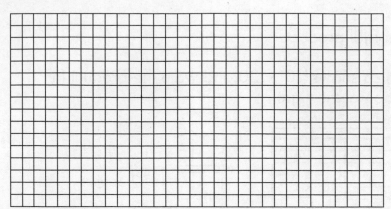

$$31 \times 16 = \underline{\qquad}$$

7.
$$
\begin{array}{r}
3\ 1 \\
\times 1\ 4 \\
\hline
\end{array}
$$

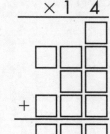

8.
$$
\begin{array}{r}
2\ 4 \\
\times 2\ 5 \\
\hline
\end{array}
$$

9.
$$
\begin{array}{r}
3\ 2 \\
\times 2\ 1 \\
\hline
\end{array}
$$

10.
$$
\begin{array}{r}
1\ 9 \\
\times 1\ 8 \\
\hline
\end{array}
$$

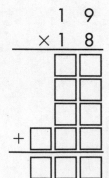

11.
$$
\begin{array}{r}
2\ 6 \\
\times 1\ 7 \\
\hline
\end{array}
$$

12.
$$
\begin{array}{r}
3\ 4 \\
\times 2\ 6 \\
\hline
\end{array}
$$

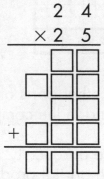

13. Bob earns $25 per day at his job. How much does Bob earn in 15 days?

_____

14. **Reasoning** What four simpler products can you use to find 32×27?

G66 (student p. 2)   MDIS 2.0

Name _____

Multiplying Two-Digit Numbers by Multiples of 10

A yearly membership to a museum costs $30. What is the total cost for 24 memberships, one for each student in Mr. Clark's class?

Find 24 × 30 by answering 1 to 10.

1. What is 24 × 0? _____

2. Put a zero in the ones place of the product at the right.

3. Multiply the 4 ones in 24 by the 3 tens in 30.

   What is 4 × 3 tens? _____ tens

$$\begin{array}{r} \square \\ 24 \\ \times\ 30 \\ \hline \square \end{array}$$

4. Regroup.

   12 tens = _____ hundred + _____ tens

5. Write the tens in the tens place and the hundred above the 24, in the computation above.

6. Multiply the 2 tens in 24 by the 3 tens in 30.

   What is 2 tens × 3 tens? _____ hundreds

7. Add the regrouped hundreds.

   6 hundreds + 1 hundred = _____ hundreds

8. Write the hundreds in the hundreds place of the product.

9. What is 24 × 30? _____

10. How much do 24 memberships cost? _____

Find 43 × 50 by answering 11 to 17.

11. What is 43 × 0? _____

    Put a zero in the ones place of the product at the right.

12. What is 3 × 5 tens? _____ tens

$$\begin{array}{r} 43 \\ \times\ 50 \\ \hline \square \end{array}$$

   MDIS 2.0

Multiplying Two-Digit Numbers by Multiples of 10 (continued)

---

13. Regroup. 15 tens = _____ hundred + _____ tens
Write the tens in the tens place of the product at the
right and the hundred above the 43.

$$\begin{array}{r} \square \\ 43 \\ \times\ 50 \\ \hline \square 0 \end{array}$$

14. What is 4 tens × 5 tens? _____ hundreds

15. Add the regrouped hundreds.

20 hundreds + 1 hundred = _____ hundreds

16. Regroup. 21 hundreds = _____ thousands + _____ hundred
Write the hundreds in the hundreds place of the product
above and the thousands in the thousands place.

17. What is 43 × 50? _____

Multiply.

18.   21
        × 10

19.   35
        × 30

20.   27
        × 30

21.   34
        × 40

22.   47
        × 20

23.   23
        × 30

24.   64
        × 10

25.   19
        × 40

26.   54
        × 30

27.   72
        × 20

28.   48
        × 40

29.   28
        × 50

30. Mr. Zacharias works 40 hours a week.
How many hours does he work in 36 weeks?   _____ hours

31. **Reasoning** When multiplying any number by a multiple of
10, what is always the last digit of the product? Explain.

G67 (student p. 2)   MDIS 2.0

Multiplying by Two-Digit Numbers

On a cross-country trip, the Katz family drove an average of 58 miles each hour. How far did they drive in 26 hours?

Find 26 × 58 by answering 1 to 12.

1. What is 6 × 8? _____

2. Regroup the ones.

48 ones = _____ tens +

_____ ones

Record the ones in the ones place of the first partial product in the chart at the right. Record the tens above the 58.

Thousands	Hundreds	Tens	Ones
☐	☐	☐	☐
		5	8
×		2	6

3. What is 6 × 5 tens? _____ tens

4. Add the regrouped tens.

30 tens + 4 tens = _____ tens

5. Regroup the tens. 34 tens = _____ hundreds + _____ tens
Record the tens in the tens place of the first partial product in the chart above. Record the hundreds in the hundreds place.

6. What is 2 tens × 8? _____ tens

7. Regroup the tens. 16 tens = _____ hundred + _____ tens
Record a zero as a place holder in the ones place of the second partial product in the chart above. Record the tens in the tens place of the second partial product. Record the hundred above the 58.

8. What is 2 tens × 5 tens? _____ hundreds

9. Add the regrouped hundreds.

10 hundreds + 1 hundred = _____ hundreds

 MDIS 2.0

Multiplying by Two-Digit Numbers (continued)

10. Regroup the hundreds.

11 hundreds = _____ thousand + _____ hundred
Record the hundred in the hundreds place of the second partial product in the chart. Record the thousand in the thousands place of the second partial product in the chart.

11. Add the partial products. What is 26 × 58? _____

12. How far did the Katz family drive in 26 hours? _____ miles

Multiply.

13.   27
        × 15

14.   25
        × 13

15.   21
        × 27

16.   34
        × 24

17.   37
        × 33

18.   81
        × 46

19.   62
        × 44

20.   32
        × 65

21.   61
        × 53

22.   84
        × 42

23.   72
        × 77

24.   84
        × 34

25.   17
        × 17

26.   21
        × 14

27.   32
        × 22

28.   27
        × 35

29. Jason's dad's car can go 27 miles on each gallon of gasoline. When the tank is full, the car holds 21 gallons of gasoline. If the car is going 55 miles per hour, how far can it go on one full tank of gasoline?   _____

30. **Reasoning** How much greater is the product of 24 × 23 than the product of 24 × 21? Explain.

         MDIS 2.0

Name _____

Multiplying Greater Numbers

An airline company owns a plane that holds 267 passengers. How many passengers can the plane transport in 34 trips?

Find 34 × 267 by answering 1 to 17.

1. What is 4 × 7? _____

2. Regroup the ones.

28 ones = _____ tens + _____ ones

Use the chart below. Record the ones in the ones place of the first partial product. Record the tens above the 267.

3. What is 4 × 6 tens? _____ tens

4. Add the regrouped tens.

24 tens + 2 tens = _____ tens

5. Regroup the tens.

26 tens = _____ hundreds +

_____ tens

Record the tens in the tens place of the first partial product in the chart. Record the hundreds above the 267.

Thousands	Hundreds	Tens	Ones
☐	☐	☐	☐
	2	6	7
×		3	4

6. What is 4 × 2 hundreds? _____ hundreds

7. Add the regrouped hundreds.

8 tens + 2 hundreds = _____ hundreds

8. Regroup the hundreds.

10 hundreds = _____ thousand + _____ hundreds

Record the hundreds in the hundreds place of the first partial product above. Record the thousand in the thousands place.

9. What is 3 tens × 7? _____ tens

10. Regroup the tens.

21 tens = _____ hundreds + _____ ten

 MDIS 2.0

Multiplying Greater Numbers (continued)

Record a zero as a place holder in the second partial product in the chart at the right. Record the 1 ten in the tens place of the second partial product. Record the 2 hundreds above the 267.

Thousands	Hundreds	Tens	Ones
	2	2	
	2	6	7
×		3	4
1	0	6	8

11. What is 3 tens × 6 tens?

_____ hundreds

12. Add the regrouped hundreds.

18 hundreds + 2 hundreds = _____ hundreds

13. Regroup the hundreds.

20 hundreds = _____ thousands + _____ hundreds
Record the hundreds in the hundreds place of the second partial product. Record the thousands above the 267.

14. What is 3 tens × 2 hundreds _____ thousands

15. Add the regrouped thousands.

6 thousands + 2 thousands = _____ thousands
Record the thousands in the thousands place of the second partial product in the chart.

16. Add the partial products. What is 34 × 267? _____

17. How many passengers can the plane transport? _____ passengers

Multiply.

18. 227
      × 40

19. 425
      × 13

20. 721
      × 28

21. 534
      × 24

22. Reasoning The school cafeteria prepares breakfast for 115 students each morning. In purchasing food for the week, they will need 2 apples and 35 ounces of juice for each student. How much juice will the cafeteria need for the week? _____

MDIS 2.0

Name _____

Mental Math: Using Properties

1. Use the Distributive Property to complete the number sentence and make it true.

   $23 \times (15 + 12) = (23 \times 15) + (23 \times \underline{\hspace{1cm}})$

The Distributive Property can be used to break apart numbers and make it easier to multiply.

2. Use the Distributive Property to find 4×17 by filling in the blanks.

   $4 \times 17 = 4 \times (10 + \underline{\hspace{1cm}})$

   $= (4 \times \underline{\hspace{1cm}}) + (4 \times \underline{\hspace{1cm}})$

   $= \underline{\hspace{1cm}} + 28 = \underline{\hspace{1cm}}$

3. Use the Commutative Property of Multiplication to complete the number sentence and make it true.

   $19 \times 12 = \underline{\hspace{1cm}} \times 19$

4. Use the Associative Property of Multiplication to complete the number sentence and make it true.

   $(38 \times 4) \times 25 = 38 \times (\underline{\hspace{1cm}} \times 25)$

The Commutative and Associative Properties can be used to make computations easier when there are compatible numbers in the factors.

5. Use the Commutative and Associative Properties to find $4 \times (287 \times 25)$ by filling in the blanks.

   $4 \times (287 \times 25) = 4 \times (\underline{\hspace{1cm}} \times 287)$ Which property? _____

   $= (\underline{\hspace{1cm}} \times 25) \times 287$ Which property? _____

   $= \underline{\hspace{1cm}} \times 287$

   $= \underline{\hspace{1cm}}$

6. Use the Identity Property of Multiplication to complete the number sentence and make it true.

   $573 \times 1 = \underline{\hspace{1cm}}$

7. Use the Identity Property of Multiplication to find $793 \times (238 - 237)$ by filling in the blanks.

   $793 \times (238 - 237) = 793 \times \underline{\hspace{1cm}} = \underline{\hspace{1cm}}$

G70 (student p. 1)   MDIS 2.0

Mental Math: Using Properties (continued)

8. Use the Zero Property of Multiplication to complete the number sentence and make it true.

$489 \times 0 =$ _____

9. Use the Zero Property of Multiplication. $793 \times 0 \times 83 =$ _____

Fill in the blanks to show how to use mental math to find the product.
Name the property or properties used.

10. $5 \times (83 \times 2) = 5 \times ($ _____ $\times 83)$ Which property? _____

$\qquad\qquad\quad = (5 \times$ _____ $) \times 83$ Which property? _____

$\qquad\qquad\quad =$ _____ $\times 83$

$\qquad\qquad\quad =$ _____

11. $35 \times 128 \times 0 =$ _____ Which property? _____

12. $12 \times 1 \times 4 = 12 \times 4$ Which property? _____

$\qquad\qquad\quad =$ _____

13. $3 \times 45 = (3 \times 40) + (3 \times$ _____ $)$ Which property? _____

$\qquad\quad =$ _____ $+$ _____

$\qquad\quad =$ _____

14. $(70 \times 4) \times 25 = 70 \times ($ _____ $\times 25)$ Which property? _____

$\qquad\qquad\qquad = 70 \times$ _____

$\qquad\qquad\qquad =$ _____

15. **Reasoning** A bookcase has 4 shelves. Each shelf has 5 hard-cover books and 23 paperback books. How many books are on the shelves? Explain how to find the total number of books mentally.

 MDIS 2.0

Dividing by Multiples of 10

Use the multiplication sentences to find each quotient. Look
for a pattern.

1. $4 \times 20 =$ _____ $80 \div 20 =$ _____

   $40 \times 20 =$ _____ $800 \div 20 =$ _____

   $400 \times 20 =$ _____ $8{,}000 \div 20 =$ _____

2. What basic division fact is used in each quotient above?

   _____ $\div$ _____ $=$ _____

Use basic facts and a pattern to find $2{,}400 \div 80$. Answer 3 to 5.

3. What basic division fact can be used to find $2{,}400 \div 80$?

   _____ $\div$ _____ $=$ _____

   In $24 \div 8 = 3$, 24 is the dividend, 8 is the divisor, and 3 is the quotient.

4. Look for a pattern.

Number Sentence	Zeros in the Dividend	Zeros in the Divisor	Zeros in the Quotient
$240 \div 80 =$ _____	1	1	0
$240 \div 8 =$ _____			
$2{,}400 \div 8 =$ _____			
$2{,}400 \div 80 =$ _____			

Complete.
Zeros in the dividend − Zeros in the divisor = _____ in the quotient

5. **Reasoning** Use the pattern to explain why $2{,}400 \div 80$ has one zero.

                   MDIS 2.0

Dividing by Multiples of 10 (continued)

Divide. Use mental math.

6. 300 ÷ 30 = _____   **7.** 60 ÷ 20 = _____   **8.** 200 ÷ 40 = _____

9. 240 ÷ 60 = _____   **10.** 490 ÷ 70 = _____   **11.** 450 ÷ 90 = _____

12. 100 ÷ 50 = _____   **13.** 2,700 ÷ 90 = _____   **14.** 1,800 ÷ 60 = _____

15. 3,500 ÷ 70 = _____   **16.** 1,500 ÷ 30 = _____   **17.** 800 ÷ 40 = _____

18. 640 ÷ 80 = _____   **19.** 3,600 ÷ 60 = _____   **20.** 140 ÷ 70 = _____

21. 1,200 ÷ 20 = _____   **22.** 8,100 ÷ 90 = _____   **23.** 560 ÷ 80 = _____

24. 600 ÷ 30 = _____   **25.** 400 ÷ 20 = _____   **26.** 2,400 ÷ 60 = _____

27. 1,200 ÷ 40 = _____   **28.** 2,500 ÷ 50 = _____   **29.** 2,100 ÷ 70 = _____

30. 4,500 ÷ 90 = _____   **31.** 480 ÷ 80 = _____   **32.** 450 ÷ 50 = _____

33. Dan has a coin collection. His sister Michaela has just started collecting. Michaela has 20 coins, and Dan has 400 coins. About how many times larger is Dan's collection?

34. Hector must store computer CDs in cartons that hold 40 CDs each. How many cartons will he need to store 2,000 CDs?

_____   _____

35. **Reasoning** Write another division problem with the same answer as 2,700 ÷ 90.

G71 (student p. 2)   MDIS 2.0

Estimating Quotients with Two-Digit Divisors

A charity needs to mail 209 boxes. The workers can mail 28 boxes each day. About how many days do they need to mail all the boxes?

Estimate the quotient of 209 ÷ 28 by answering 1 to 7.

1. What is 28 rounded to the nearest ten?   _____

2. To find compatible numbers for 209 and 30, list some of the multiples of 3.

   3, 6, _____, _____, _____, _____, _____, _____

3. Which multiple of 3 is closest to the first digit or two of 209?   _____

4. What is 209 rounded to the nearest compatible number?   _____

5. What is 210 ÷ 30?   _____

6. What is a good estimate for 209 ÷ 28?   _____

7. About how many days do the workers need to mail all
   the boxes?   _____ days

Estimate the quotient of 4,156 ÷ 72 by answering 8 to 10.

8. What is 72 rounded to the nearest ten?   _____

9. What is 4,156 rounded to the nearest compatible number?   _____

10. What is a good estimate for 4,156 ÷ 72?   _____

   _____ ÷ _____ = _____

Estimate the quotient of 8,273 ÷ 43 by answering 11 to 13.

11. What is 43 rounded to the nearest ten?   _____

12. What is 8,273 rounded to the nearest compatible number?   _____

13. What is a good estimate for 8,273 ÷ 47?   _____

   _____ ÷ _____ = _____

       MDIS 2.0

Name _____

Estimating Quotients with Two-Digit Divisors (continued)

Estimate each quotient. Write the compatible numbers you used.

14. 465 ÷ 89 =

_____

_____

15. 2,304 ÷ 74 =

_____

_____

16. 637 ÷ 82 =

_____

_____

17. 3,561 ÷ 37 =

_____

_____

18. 181 ÷ 61 =

_____

_____

19. 4,149 ÷ 73 =

_____

_____

20. 564 ÷ 62 =

_____

_____

21. 7,198 ÷ 82 =

_____

_____

22. 3,118 ÷ 57 =

_____

_____

23. 1,590 ÷ 42 =

_____

_____

24. 1,235 ÷ 19 =

_____

_____

25. 7,118 ÷ 77 =

_____

_____

26. 32)‾902‾

_____

_____

27. 62)‾1,130‾

_____

_____

28. 28)‾2,112‾

_____

_____

29. The school band is raising money to go on a trip. The 68 members hope to raise $6,400. The trip will be 4 days in length. Estimate the amount that each member should raise. _____

G72 (student p. 2) MDIS 2.0

Name _____

Dividing by Two-Digit Divisors

A carpenter cut a board that is 144 inches long. He cut pieces 32 inches long. How many pieces did he get and how much of the board was left?

Find $144 \div 32$ by answering 1 to 11.

1. First, estimate to find the approximate number of pieces.

$150 \div 30 =$ _____

2. Write the estimate in the ones place of the quotient, on the right.

$$32\overline{)1\ \ 4\ \ 4}$$ with 5 above, and three boxes below

3. Multiply. $32 \times 5 =$ _____

4. Compare the product to the dividend. Write > or <.

$160 \bigcirc 144$

Since 160 is too large, 5 was too large. Try 4.

5. Multiply. $32 \times 4 =$ _____

6. Compare the product to the dividend. Write > or <.

$128 < 144$

Since 128 is less than 144, 4 is not too large. Write 4 in the ones place of the quotient on the right. Write 128 below 144.

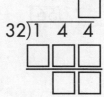

$$32\overline{)1\ \ 4\ \ 4}$$

7. Subtract. $144 - 128 =$ _____

8. Compare the remainder to the divisor. Write > or <.

$16 \bigcirc 32$

Since the remainder is less than the divisor, the division is finished.

9. What is $144 \div 32$? _____ R _____

10. How many 32-inch pieces did the carpenter cut? _____ pieces

11. How much of the board was left? _____ inches

G73 (student p. 1)   MDIS 2.0

Name _____

Dividing by Two-Digit Divisors (continued)

Divide.

12. 32)‾202‾

13. 94)‾260‾

14. 45)‾345‾

15. 62)‾137‾

16. 28)‾212‾

17. 58)‾552‾

18. 82)‾657‾

19. 32)‾131‾

20. 93)‾824‾

21. 89)‾465‾

22. 74)‾204‾

23. 78)‾637‾

24. 77)‾561‾

25. 61)‾181‾

26. 73)‾419‾

27. 63)‾564‾

28. 82)‾718‾

29. 57)‾318‾

30. A vegetable stand sells 192 cucumbers and 224 squash during the month of July. About how many cucumbers did they sell each day? _____

31. **Reasoning** To start dividing 126 by 23, Miranda used the estimate 120 ÷ 20 = 6. How could she tell 6 is too high?

G73 (student p. 2) MDIS 2.0

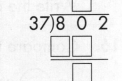

One- and Two-Digit Quotients

Trinity wants to buy a computer which costs $802. With her part-time job, she can save $37 a week. How many weeks does she need to save to have enough money to buy the computer?

Find 802 ÷ 37 by answering 1 to 11.

1. Begin by estimating the quotient.

800 ÷ 40 = _____

Since the estimate has two digits, begin by dividing the tens.

2. Write the first digit of the estimate in the tens place of the quotient.

3. What is 37 × 2 tens? _____ tens
Write the product below the 80.

4. What is 80 tens − 74 tens? _____ tens
Write the difference below the 74 and the line.

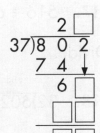

5. Regroup. 6 tens and 2 ones = _____ ones
Bring down the ones to show the total ones.

6. How many groups of 37 are there in 62? _____
Write this number in the ones place of the quotient.

7. What is 37 × 1? _____ Write the product below the 62.

8. What is 62 − 37? _____
Write the difference below the 37 and the line.

9. Compare the remainder to the divisor. Write > or <.

25 ◯ 37

Since the remainder is less than the divisor, the division is finished.

10. 802 ÷ 37 = _____ R _____

11. **Reasoning** How many weeks does Trinity need to save to have enough money to buy the computer? Explain.

G74 (student p. 1) MDIS 2.0

One- and Two-Digit Quotients (continued)

Find 516 ÷ 63 by answering 12 to 17.

12. Begin by estimating the quotient: 480 ÷ 60 = _____

Since the estimate has one digit, begin by dividing the ones.

13. Write the estimate in the ones place of the quotient.

14. What is 63 × 8? _____
Write the product below the 516.

15. What is 516 − 504? _____
Write the difference below the 504 and the line.

$$63\overline{)516}$$

16. Compare the remainder to the divisor. Write > or <.

12 ◯ 63

Since the remainder is less than the divisor, the division is finished.

17. 516 ÷ 63 = _____ R _____

Divide.

18. $32\overline{)602}$ **19.** $94\overline{)960}$ **20.** $25\overline{)545}$

21. $43\overline{)285}$ **22.** $28\overline{)147}$ **23.** $61\overline{)485}$

24. $35\overline{)993}$ **25.** $19\overline{)213}$ **26.** $31\overline{)558}$

27. The local museum's records indicate that 874 people participated in the guided tours in June. There were 38 guided tours in the month of June and each tour had the same number of people. How many people were on each tour?

28. Reasoning Is 25 R32 a reasonable answer for the problem 607 ÷ 23? Why or why not?

   G74 (student p. 2)   MDIS 2.0

Dividing Greater Numbers

A charity collected 5,782 cans of food. They put 28 cans in each box.
How many boxes were full and how many cans were left over?

Find 5,782 ÷ 28 by answering 1 to 16.

1. Begin by estimating the quotient. 6,000 ÷ 30 = _____

Since the estimate has three digits, begin by dividing the hundreds.

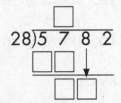

2. Write the first digit of the estimate in the hundreds
place of the quotient.

3. What is 28 × 2 hundreds? _____ hundreds
Write the product below 5,782.

4. What is 57 hundreds − 56 hundreds? _____ hundred
Write the difference below the 56 and the line.

5. Regroup. 1 hundred + 8 tens = _____ tens
Bring down the tens to show the total tens.

6. How many groups of 28 are there in 18? _____
Write the 0 in the tens place of the quotient below.

7. Multiply 28 × 0 tens and write the product below 18,
in the computation at the right.

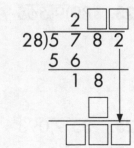

8. Subtract 18 − 0 and write the difference below the 0
and the line.

9. Regroup. 18 tens + 2 ones = _____ ones
Bring down the ones to show the total ones.

10. How many groups of 28 are there in 182? _____
Write the 6 in the ones place of the quotient.

11. What is 28 × 6? _____
Write the product below 182.

12. What is 182 − 168? _____
Write the difference below the 168 and the line.

 MDIS 2.0

Name _____

Dividing Greater Numbers (continued)

_____

13. Compare the remainder to the divisor. Write > or <.

14 $\bigcirc$ 28

Since the remainder is less than the divisor, the division is finished.

14. 5,782 ÷ 28 _____ R _____

15. How many of the charity's boxes are full? _____ boxes

16. How many cans are left over? _____ cans

Divide.

17. 32)9,602

18. 94)1,960

19. 25)5,345

20. 22)6,257

21. 32)5,731

22. 43)8,024

23. 89)9,565

24. 58)6,237

25. 33)4,219

26. 35)9,093

27. 19)2,213

28. 31)4,558

29. A book distributor orders 5,175 books on anthropology that it will distribute to 23 bookstores. The book is listed at $26. How many books will each store receive?

30. **Reasoning** Kwan says that 2,162 ÷ 12 equals 180. Is she correct? Why or why not?

 MDIS 2.0

Name _____

Using Mental Math to Multiply

Jeremy needs to order one uniform for each player in the Millwood baseball league. There are 6 teams in the league, and each team has 19 players. How many uniforms should Jeremy order?

Use this information to answer 1 to 7.

1. How many teams are in the league? _____

   How many players are on each team? _____

2. What are you asked to find? _____

3. What is one way you can use mental math to find the answer?

4. What number is close to 19 and easy to multiply? _____

   Did you add or subtract to find the new number? _____

   How many did you add or subtract? _____

5. What multiplication sentence will you write using the new number?
   6 × _____ = _____

6. How will you adjust the answer?

   What is the solution? _____

7. When you adjusted, how did you know whether to add or subtract?

G76 (student p. 1)   MDIS 2.0

Name _____

Using Mental Math to Multiply (continued)

In 8 through 13, use compensation to find each product.

8. 5×38

Substitute: $5 \times$ _____ $= 200$

Adjust: _____ $- 10 =$ _____

9. 3×42

Substitute: $3 \times$ _____ $= 120$

Adjust: _____ $+ 6 =$ _____

10. 59×4

Substitute: _____ $\times 4 =$ _____

Adjust: _____ $-$ _____ $=$ _____

11. 3×94

Substitute: $3 \times$ _____ $=$ _____

Adjust: _____ $+$ _____ $=$ _____

12. 4×32

Substitute: $4 \times$ _____ $=$ _____

Adjust: _____ $+$ _____ $=$ _____

13. 6×41

Substitute: $6 \times$ _____ $=$ _____

Adjust: _____ $+$ _____ $=$ _____

For Exercises 14 through 20, find each product mentally.

14. $5 \times 33 =$ _____

15. $4 \times 18 =$ _____

16. $8 \times 43 =$ _____

17. $31 \times 7 =$ _____

18. $39 \times 4 =$ _____

19. $53 \times 3 =$ _____

20. $6 \times 27 =$ _____

 MDIS 2.0

Name _____

Adding and Subtracting on a Number Line

At the beginning of June, 62 children arrived at Camp Firefly. A week later, 17 more children arrived. At the end of June, 25 children went home. How many children were at Camp Firefly at the end of June? Find $62 + 17 - 25$.

Use this information to answer 1 to 6.

1. What are you asked to find? How many children arrived at the camp at the beginning of June?

   _____

2. How can you use a number line to find the answer? How do you show addition? How do you show subtraction?

3. Which number is added? _____

   Why is it added? _____

4. Which number is subtracted? _____

   Why is it subtracted? _____

5. Use the number line to solve the problem.

   $62 + 17 - 25 =$ _____

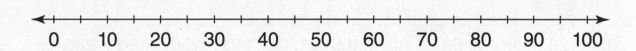

6. How did you know where the second and third arrows should begin?

G77 (student p. 1)   MDIS 2.0

Adding and Subtracting on a Number Line (continued)

In 7 through 11, use the number line to solve the problem.

7. 45 + 28 = _____

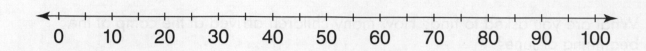

8. 22 + 73 = _____

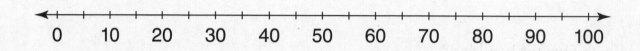

9. 98 − 77 = _____

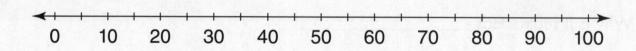

10. 167 − 55 + 30 = _____

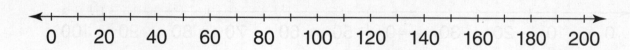

11. 95 + 90 − 65 = _____

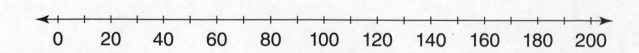

G77 (student p. 2)   MDIS 2.0

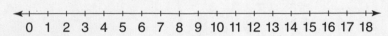

Skip Counting on the Number Line

Caroline is setting up tables for a party. She sets up 4 tables. If she puts 4 chairs at each table, how many chairs will there be in all?

Use this information to answer 1 to 9.

1. How many tables is Caroline setting up for the party?

    There are _____ tables.

2. How many chairs does Caroline put at each table?

    She will put _____ chairs at each table.

3. What are you asked to find?

4. How many people will be able to sit at 1 table? _____

Draw 1 jump on the number line to show the number of chairs at 1 table.

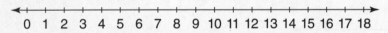

0 1 2 3 4 5 6 7 8 9 10 11 12 13 14 15 16 17 18

5. How can you use skip counting to find the number of chairs at 2 tables?

    _____, _____

Use the number line to show the number of chairs at 2 tables.

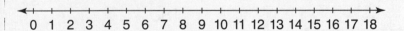

0 1 2 3 4 5 6 7 8 9 10 11 12 13 14 15 16 17 18

6. Explain in words how you can use a number line to find the number of chairs at 4 tables.

7. Use a number line to solve the problem.

0 1 2 3 4 5 6 7 8 9 10 11 12 13 14 15 16 17 18

There will be _____ chairs in all.

 MDIS 2.0

Name _____

Skip Counting on the Number Line (continued)

_____

8. How can you use skip counting to find the total number of chairs?

_____, _____, _____, _____

9. What multiplication sentence does the number line show?

_____ × _____ = _____

In 10 and 11, find each solution on the number line.

10. Trevor reads 3 books a week. How many books can he read in 5 weeks? Draw jumps on the number line to show how many books he can read.

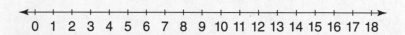

Trevor can read _____ books in 5 weeks.

11. Ms. Light's students worked on a science project in groups of 4. How many students were in 3 groups? Draw jumps on the number line to show the number of students.

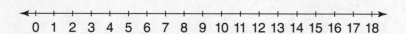

There were _____ students in 3 groups.

In 12 and 13, show the multiplication fact on the number line. Write the product.

12. $8 \times 2 =$ _____

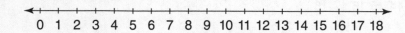

13. $6 \times 3 =$ _____

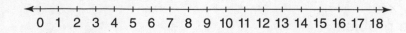

G78 (student p. 2)   MDIS 2.0